Understanding Management Research

Understanding Management Research

An Introduction to Epistemology

Phil Johnson and Joanne Duberley

SAGE Publications
London • Thousand Oaks • New Delhi

SAGE Publications Ltd
6 Bonhill Street
London EC2A 4PU

SAGE Publications Inc.
2455 Teller Road
Thousand Oaks, California 91320

SAGE Publications India Pvt Ltd
32, M-Block Market
Greater Kailash – I
New Delhi 110 048

British Library Cataloguing in Publication data

A catalogue record for this book is available
from the British Library

ISBN 0 7619 5294 9
ISBN 0 7619 5295 0 (pbk)

Library of Congress catalog card number 00 132732

Typeset by Mayhew Typesetting, Rhayader, Powys
Printed in Great Britain by The Cromwell Press Ltd,
Trowbridge, Wiltshire

Contents

Preface

This book is an introduction to a key issue in management research that usually goes unnoticed – epistemology and its variability. Our thesis is that management research can never be isolated from epistemological commitments whose diversity leads to different possible ways of approaching and engaging with any substantive area. While we attempt to give a general overview of the epistemologies which have had a significant impact upon the aims, processes and content of management research, we have tried not to sacrifice depth for comprehensiveness. Instead we have been selective regarding the perspectives covered, their philosophical exemplars and their management advocates so as to introduce a series of complex ideas and rationales to the reader. Hence we have covered what we feel to be important not just in terms of influence but also in terms of variability. So throughout we have tried to explain the points of connection and departure between rival epistemologies.

Inevitably, writing a book like this will upset some readers. This might be because of what we have or have not covered – but more likely it will be with how we have classified particular scholars' contributions as positivist, conventionalist, postmodernist and so on. Throughout we try to be clear about our underlying criteria for classification. Here, however, we would also like to emphasize our view that many writers vary their own epistemological position in different pieces of work. So the classificatory outcome in this book might thus seem rather unfair – a particular author might only appear under one particular epistemological heading whereas much of their other work is elsewhere. By way of apology, the point for us is that we are selectively using scholars' work as illustrative examples and we do not mean to squeeze any particular author exclusively into a particular category.

We would like to thank Marianne Lagrange for her initial support and enthusiasm for the idea of this book and the subsequent help and encouragement of Rosemary Nixon and her colleagues at Sage. The ideas presented in this book have been discussed with many people over the years – sometimes only inferentially, sometimes controversially but always in a manner that has been stimulating. We would like to thank our friends and colleagues at Sheffield Hallam University, Sheffield University and elsewhere, as well as our students past and present, who have consciously or inadvertently contributed to our understanding of epistemology and its impacts upon management research. We would particularly like to acknowledge Tony Berry, Neil Burns, Murray Clark, John Darwin, John Desmond, Keith Duberley, Anne Fearfull, Bob Grafton-Small, John Gill, David Golding, Yvonne Hill, John Kawalek, Janet Kirkham, Steve Linstead, Mary Mallon, Stuart Manson, Hugh Willmott and Joe Nason. We would also like to thank Cathy Cassell, Laurie Cohen, John McAuley, Gill Musson and Ken Smith who were kind enough to read earlier drafts and give helpful and incisive feedback. Last, but by no means least, thanks to Carole for her support and Andy for his provision of entertaining diversions as well as his support over so many months.

1
Introduction – The Importance of Epistemology in Management Research

Organizational scholars can resist philosophy as long as they assume the ends of institutions and the current definitions of those ends by participants or scholars.

(Zald, 1996: 257)

The main objective of this book is to provoke debate and reflection upon the different ways in which we engage with management and organization when undertaking research. Our argument is that how we come to ask particular questions, how we assess the relevance and value of different research methodologies so that we can investigate those questions, how we evaluate the outputs of research, all express and vary according to our underlying epistemological commitments. Even though they often remain unrecognized by the individual, such epistemological commitments are a key feature of our pre-understandings which influence how we make things intelligible. Therefore this book tries to offer the reader an overview of the principal epistemological debates in social science and how these lead to, and are expressed in, different ways of conceiving and undertaking management and organizational research. Obviously, in a book of this size it is impossible to do justice to the full range of issues raised by this objective. Instead we hope that it will provide a concise and accessible introduction which will stimulate the reader's interest in epistemological issues and their implications for thinking about management and organization.

One reason why we feel that these objectives are important derives from our experience that students in the UK are increasingly expected to demonstrate a reflexive understanding of their own epistemological commitments as they engage with management and organizations in undertaking empirical research for theses and dissertations. Previously, researchers in management studies have been criticised for being uncritical and ill informed in their adoption of particular positions with regard to research (see, for example, Whitley, 1984a). This is beginning to change and some of these issues are covered in a disparate set of journals (e.g.

Organization Studies; *Academy of Management Review*; *Organization*; *Accounting, Organizations and Society*; and *Human Relations*, to name only a few). Their style and language-in-use, however, are often daunting and inaccessible to those yet to be admitted into the conventions of philosophical discourse.

Nevertheless many students and researchers are still expected to read and comprehend a burgeoning literature which increasingly deploys epistemological concepts and language. For instance, in order to understand the current debate in the literature between modernists, critical modernists and postmodernists (whether this is about corporate strategy, human resources management or accountancy etc.) a high level of prior epistemological understanding is essential. Hence a key rationale for this book is to give readers an accessible grounding in epistemology that helps them to comprehend these ongoing debates and to engage with their own pre-understandings when trying to make sense of management and organization.

An underlying assumption of the book is that both within and outside our work organizations our behaviour is internally motivated, and internally justified, by what we believe about 'the world'. At the same time, even though we might not be immediately conscious of it, everyone has a view about what demarcates justified from unjustified belief. Indeed our claims about being rational or irrational or about what is true as opposed to what is false are tacitly grounded in such implicit differentiations. Perhaps these ways of thinking are so embedded in our language and culture that if we were to reflect upon them they would appear to be a matter of common sense and therefore natural and irresistible. Nevertheless our debates and conjectures about *what* is true presuppose prior agreement (a pre-understanding that is shared) about *how* we determine whether or not something is true. Similarly, any epistemological analysis of the grounds of certain knowledge or the scientificity of truth claims involves ontological assumptions about the nature of the world (Bhaskar, 1975). This signifies that in our everyday lives we are all epistemologists – or at least we routinely take certain epistemological conventions to be so self-evident we rarely feel the need consciously to express, discuss or question them. Indeed it may be the case that to notice and then consciously to reflect upon such conventions are the first steps in making the commonsensical and self-evident, precarious and problematic.

Although scientists and philosophers have debated epistemological questions since the time of Plato and Aristotle, the term 'epistemology' remains somewhat esoteric for most people and usually it obfuscates more than it reveals. However once we break down the word into its constituent parts it seems much less daunting. The word derives from two Greek words: '*episteme*' which means 'knowledge' or 'science'; and '*logos*' which means 'knowledge', 'information', 'theory' or 'account'. This aetiology demonstrates how epistemology is usually understood as being concerned with knowledge about knowledge. In other words, epistemology is the study of the criteria by which we can know what does and does not constitute warranted, or scientific, knowledge. Therefore it would seem that epistemology assumes some vantage point, one step removed from the actual practice of science itself. At first sight this promises to provide some foundation for scientific knowledge: a methodological and theoretical beginning located in normative standards that enable the evaluation of knowledge by specifying what is permissible and hence the discrimination of warranted belief from the unwarranted, the rational from the irrational, the scientific from pseudoscience.

According to Richard Rorty, a North American philosopher, this notion that epistemology is the discipline that enables the judgement of all other disciplines arose in seventeenth-century Europe. It expresses the desire 'to find "foundations" to which one might cling, frameworks beyond which one must not stray, objects which impose themselves, representations which cannot be gainsaid' (1979: 315). Accordingly, by seeking to explain ourselves as knowers, by telling us how we ought to arrive at our beliefs, epistemology is pivotal to science since 'proper' scientific theorizing can only occur after the development of epistemological theory. It follows that a key question must be: how can we develop an epistemological theory – a science of science?

One answer to the above question is suggested by Quine (1969) where he argues that epistemology should abandon any philosophical questions and become a branch of experimental psychology which analyses human cognitive processes through empirical research. The aim would be to produce a science of science where the laws of cognition tell us why and how we hold the theories that we do. At first sight this programme seems an eminently sensible solution – to paraphrase Quine, a science of science which is science – but one which, incidentally, may make this book rather pointless. However two interrelated problems arise here.

First, since epistemology determines the criteria by which justified knowledge is possible, it must not itself take for granted the results of particular forms of empirical inquiry such as experimental psychology. Secondly, we cannot presuppose that there exists some analytical space that may be occupied by experimental psychologists that is somehow free from the very philosophical assumptions that influence how we engage in justifiable 'knowing'. Experimental psychology is itself based upon a plethora of philosophical assumptions regarding the possibility of knowledge in experimental psychology which are themselves contestable. So it would appear that Quine's rejection of philosophical questions merely creates an unsustainable philosophical vacuum that is promptly filled by default by some new, but unrecognized, set of philosophical commitments.

Here the paradox, as shown in Figure 1.1 below, is that epistemology confronts a fundamental problem of circularity, from which it cannot escape, in that any theory of knowledge (i.e. any epistemology) presupposes knowledge of the conditions in which knowledge takes place. In

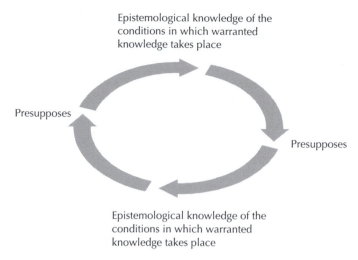

Epistemological knowledge of the
conditions in which warranted
knowledge takes place

Presupposes

Presupposes

Epistemological knowledge of the
conditions in which warranted
knowledge takes place

Figure 1.1   The circularity of epistemology

effect, this prevents any grounding of epistemology in what purports to be scientific knowledge – psychological or otherwise – because one cannot use science in order to ground the legitimacy of science.

Hence the seventeenth-century promise of epistemology to provide secure foundations for scientific knowledge seems a forlorn hope precisely because of circularity. For instance Otto Neurath has described this problem of circularity in terms of a nautical metaphor:

> we are like sailors who on the open sea must reconstruct their ship but are never able to start afresh from the bottom . . . They make use of some drifting timber of the old structure, to modify the skeleton and the hull of their vessel. But they cannot put into dock in order to start from scratch. During their work they stay on the old structure and deal with heavy gales and thundering waves. (1944: 47)

For Neurath the problem of circularity means that we cannot dump philosophy by detaching ourselves from our epistemological commitments so as to assess those commitments objectively – indeed we would depend upon them in order to undertake that task. It follows that there are no secure or incontestable foundations from which we can begin any consideration of our knowledge of knowledge – rather what we have are competing philosophical assumptions about knowledge that lead us to engage with management and organizations in particular ways. Therefore the reader who hopes that this book will provide them with irreducible epistemic standards to guide and improve their research will be disappointed. Perhaps the most we can hope for in considering epistemology is to become more consciously reflexive. This involves an attempt at self-comprehension through beginning to notice and then criticize our own pre-understandings in a more systematic fashion while trying to assess their impact upon how we engage with the social and natural worlds. Such self-comprehension not only

entails identifying our epistemological pre-understandings and their philosophical derivation, it also requires us to challenge them by noticing and
exploring alternative possible commitments.

The point is that everyone adheres to some theory about what constitutes warranted knowledge – a set of epistemological commitments
which provide us with criteria for distinguishing between reliable and
unreliable knowledge. If we didn't have such theories, no matter how
tacit, we would never be able to make what we construe as legitimate
claims about what we think we know or think we have experienced.
Mundane claims such as 'I saw it with my own eyes' or 'The facts speak
for themselves' presuppose that such appeals refer to evidence which is
epistemologically legitimate. Such commitments provide us with criteria
which we use to assess which kinds of description and explanation of our
social or natural worlds are appropriate. Moreover, as we have just shown,
closely allied to those commitments are also notions about what might
warrant the status of being 'scientific'. Indeed epistemological commitments also provide tacit answers to questions about:

1 What are the origins, nature and limits of scientific knowledge?
2 What constitutes scientific practice?
3 What are the processes through which scientific knowledge advances
   or is such progress a forlorn hope?

So, for instance, because of their education and training scientists are
commonly thought to be, in principle, objective observers of the world.
Their expertise and rigorous deployment of accepted procedures and
protocols allow scientists to collect empirical evidence about the social and
natural worlds. The apprehended form and content of either world is
usually understood to be separate from, or independent of, the methodological means by which scientists engage with it. In other words the data
collected, rather than the processes of observation, dictate the findings and
theories of science. Mistakes can and do happen: individual scientists may
misunderstand the significance of their data, they may make methodological errors and indeed they might be wilfully biased or even corrupt.
Nevertheless it is commonly assumed that errors and biases can be
corrected through improvements in the training, recruitment and selection
of scientists as well as by the surveillance of scientific findings by a wider
community of scientists. The key epistemological assumption is that the
stock of knowledge advances as scientists actually learn more about the
world as well as through the exposure of the fraudulent and the eradication
of mistakes through critical processes akin to quality control undertaken by
peers. Hence science is progressive; moreover its outputs can be trusted
because its ultimate arbiter is to be found in the objective observational
processes encoded into its methodology and self-regulation which make it
a superior means of knowledge acquisition.

The above account of science expresses what Robert K. Merton (1938–
70) called the 'ethos of science'. In his analysis of seventeenth-century

England Merton argues (*ibid.*: 136–8) that Puritan values that emphasized utility, rationality, empiricism and worldly asceticism contributed significantly to the rise of modern science in England and its subsequent diaspora. In support of this notion he considered that the over-representation of Puritans amongst the founding membership of the Royal Society proffers evidence of the link between Puritanism and the modern scientific community. For Merton these values became embedded in the ethos of science which, now severed from the religious commitments of its founders, enables the production and arbitration of knowledge claims with an objectivity that 'precludes particularism'.

In 1938 Merton's account of what he had observed as the scientific ethos was to a degree aimed at defending science from what he saw as Nazism's anti-intellectual contempt for science which at the time had tied some of the German sciences to an ideology steeped in racism and the occult. Merton summarized this scientific ethos (*ibid.*: 259) as being composed of four sets of 'institutional imperatives': 'universalism', the principle that scientific truth is dependent upon pre-established impersonal criteria which ensure intellectual honesty; 'communism', the principle that scientific truth is the product of social collaboration; 'organized scepticism'; and 'disinterestedness' where the activities of scientists are subject to rigorous impersonal policing against fraudulent contributions. Thus Merton seems to argue that while modern scientific methodology and epistemology are in many respects an historical evolution of particular religious values, these values are functional to the advancement of science – they aid the search for objectivity and truth. So just as Merton accords science some socio-cultural status by giving credence to the view that the religious values propagated by the reformation ushered in a new science, he also proceeds to accord science an extra-socio-cultural status by in effect arguing that those values enabled science to develop to a level that transcended social influences because of the epistemological protection they afford.

The notion that science is a mode of inquiry that transcends social influences so that it can be free from ideological contamination accords with Weber's demand for a value-free social science (1949). Here Weber made a categorical distinction between empirical facts and value dispositions: the former derive from a cognitively accessible reality, whereas the latter derive from cultural dispositions. For Weber science dealt with facts; it does not and cannot resolve matters of value – a commitment that is adhered to by many contemporary scholars of management and organization. An effect of this stance is to render scientific activities as sociologically unproblematic and functional to the advancement of warranted knowledge.

Of course, as we shall show in this book, such a view of science as value-free is itself grounded in a particular epistemological tradition which when subject to critical examination becomes highly contentious. Moreover that it is only a particular tradition implies the existence of heterodox alternatives which may be just as significant if less familiar and common-sensical. Indeed criticizing the expression of Merton's and Weber's views in management and organization as an establishment myth is an increasingly popular pastime, albeit now more commonly associated with the political Left rather than the Right. Often, but by no means exclusively, such attacks will tacitly accord with Bloor's view that knowledge

> is whatever men take to be knowledge. It consists of those beliefs which men (sic) confidently hold to and live by . . . what is collectively endorsed, leaving the individual and idiosyncratic to count as mere belief. (1976: 2–3)

Here Bloor is taking the position that knowledge and science are the arbitrary outputs of social processes from which no one is exempted – there are no objective ways of discriminating the warranted from the unwarranted – all we have are just different culturally derived ways of knowing the world which vary in their substance and to the extent that they have been accorded social legitimation. From this perspective Merton's ethos of science should not be seen as defining clear social obligations to which scientists conform. Rather they may be understood as 'flexible vocabularies employed by participants in their attempts to negotiate suitable meanings for their own and others' acts in various social contexts' (Mulkay, 1979: 72) – vocabularies which are bounded by the social and technical cultures shared by the scientists' particular problem-centred community. While the unorthodox might not be allowed a public forum since their assertions are outside the accepted repertoire, the precise meaning of the orthodoxy has to be re-established through symbolic negotiation, particularly when new domains or problems emerge (*ibid.*: 78–95).

Of course it would be interesting, if also rather mischievous, to speculate upon what Bloor or Mulkay would make of Merton's target, Nazi science and its repercussions, since it would seem that its epistemic status would be equivalent to any other body of knowledge which had been collectively endorsed: just another culturally derived process which presumably cannot therefore be criticized because all the critic would be doing is imposing their own culturally embedded beliefs?

However the point to which we wish to limit ourselves here is merely that our epistemological commitments influence the processes through which we develop what we take to be warranted knowledge of the world. Such deeply held taken-for-granted assumptions about how we come 'to know' influence what we experience as being true or false, what we mean by true or false, and indeed whether we think that true and false are viable constructs. As we shall show, this is even the case where, as is increasingly popular in management and organizational research, Merton's ethos is rejected in favour of a view of science as a relative outcome of intuition, paradigm, metaphor, discourse, social convention or fashion. Even to say that there can be no reliable knowledge (in Merton's sense) beyond some ethnocentric collective endorsement, and hence cast doubt upon the relevance of epistemology as a philosophical endeavour, is paradoxically grounded in the 'hidden hand' of epistemological reasoning as to why no such asocial, objective, value-free knowledge is ever possible.

So in any discipline, profession, occupation or everyday activity where knowledge claims are routinely made, epistemology contributes by clarifying the conditions and limits of what is construed as justified knowledge – whether or not the people involved recognize this as so. No one can stand outside epistemological processes, whether they be researchers or managers. Indeed many writers have reminded us that managers routinely undertake research as they try to make sense of organizational events and phenomena or discern and evaluate possible courses of action (for example, Mintzberg, 1973; Schon, 1983). It follows that every management strategy, every policy and intervention, implicitly or explicitly, articulates an epistemological position that authorizes the knowledge claims that justify its substantive content. The mere act of describing something as 'evidence' is to evaluate it epistemologically and accord it some kind of epistemic status. So if we take seriously the argument that a key skill that any manager should possess is the ability to reflect critically upon the modes of engagement they deploy in making sense of their experience, then the importance of epistemology to practitioners is only too evident because studying epistemology exposes to critical interrogation the often unnoticed taken-for-granted assumptions and values which influence how versions of reality are socially constructed – which then influence action.

In this book we are not so much directly concerned with everyday management practices as with how we engage with 'management and organization' as social phenomena. This is because how we construct our understandings of the nature of the various management disciplines, of management practice and of management research in many respects depends upon our ideas concerning epistemology. Until recently these assumptions were usually left tacit or implicit and were rarely clearly presented or subjected to sustained reflection and evaluation through their juxtaposition, or confrontation, with possible alternatives. It is to this relatively new reflexive spirit (see Willmott, 1995) that this book seeks to appeal, contribute and encourage by attempting to clarify the different relationships we can have with our subject of interest – management and organization.

While it is evident that this new spirit has gained some popularity and influence, it is also evident that the prevailing received view of management and organizational research engenders the deployment of what are assumed to be the methodologies reputedly so successful in the natural sciences. This involves the endorsement of significant epistemological commitments around which a silence only too often reigns so that they are 'forgotten' and any reflexivity is 'skillfully avoided' (Chia, 1996b: 7–8). Presumably, if pressed, this silence would be justified by the mainstream by the claim that their commitments are so innocent and commonsensical they are not worth discussing. But to make unexamined epistemological assumptions and remain unaware of their origins has to be poor practice, particularly when even a cursory examination of the philosophy of science would suggest that not only is epistemological commitment unavoidable, but also that any epistemological commitment is highly contentious. In the epistemological literature we will find that there is considerable, and it would seem irresolvable, disagreement over epistemology and the standards by which we may discriminate warranted knowledge. Therefore rather than providing an incontestable scheme of epistemological rules to govern research, the study of epistemology provides one with a range of different approaches to management and organizational research. The implication is that when engaging in any management research or practice people need to reflect upon the nature of the philosophical assumptions which they inevitably make since there is no aphilosophical space available. An aim of this book is to facilitate such reflexivity – obviously the extent to which we meet this aim is a matter for the reader's own critical judgement.

Organization of the book

The book begins by introducing the variety of approaches classified as positivist. The development of positivism during the Enlightenment and its attack upon prior metaphysical epistemologies are outlined and the key epistemological assumptions and debates within positivism are examined. Following on from this Chapter 3 then addresses positivist management research. Positivism is split into two chapters to do justice to the amount of material to be covered and this perhaps reflects its dominant status in the field for many years. Although, as the chapter discusses, this dominance is not necessarily the result of a well-thought-out stance towards research, rather it is often the result of an attempt to copy the natural sciences or sometimes an unthinking (some might say naïve) empiricism. Chapter 4 moves on to address conventionalism, focusing on the work of Kuhn, Wittgenstein and others. Particular attention is given to the paradigm incommensurability debate and the use of metaphorical understandings of organizations in management research. Moving on to postmodernism, Chapter 5 addresses those theorists who thrive on relativism. For post-modernists truth is no longer 'out there', rather there are a multitude of truths each of which vies for attention but none of which has more validity than any other. Clearly this suggests a radically different approach towards management research and the postmodernists' focus on deconstruction, which has led some to characterize their work as parasitical, is examined. This chapter finishes with a detailed discussion of some of the problems of relativism and the contradictions inherent in much postmodernist writing. Critical theory, which is examined in Chapter 6, focuses in particular on the work of Habermas and discusses the ways in which Habermas attempts to avoid the spectre of relativism in order that some basis for critique (and change) is maintained. The last of our substantive chapters focuses on critical realism. Here we examine the works of writers such as Bhaskar who have attempted to go beyond the divide between objectivism and relativism. Our final chapter attempts to bring the discussion from preceding chapters together by focusing on the notion of reflexivity in research. As we have already commented, we feel that it is essential for researchers to be aware of their pre-understandings. Reflexivity, however, exists at a number of levels and, following the work of Holland (1999) and others, we try to 'unpack' those levels and examine the implications for the different epistemological stances.

Each of these chapters in many ways can stand on its own and perhaps readers will choose which approach they feel is closest to their view of the world and look only at that. However, a word of caution – throughout the book we define key terms as they arise: hence many of the later chapters use terminology which is explained in earlier chapters. Also, whilst we would in no way wish to dictate how the book should be read, we would like to think that it would be useful to compare the different approaches and that this may lead to a more informed and reflexive approach towards management research. In that sense this book is intended merely as a starting point and we recognize that each chapter can provide only a brief overview which, in trying to identify the underpinning assumptions of each approach, focuses on where writers converge, at the expense of a detailed discussion of the divergences. We are also well aware that some may resent the inclusion of particular authors under a particular heading. For example some postmodernists are now critical theorists or may resent the use of labels of any kind. This is always a problem and we have tried to take account of what writers have said about their own epistemological and ontological stance before assigning their work to any particular grouping – although clearly the edges between these groups are blurred and there may be overlap between some of them.

Finally, we have found that writing this book caused us to examine in much greater depths our own assumptions about undertaking management research. In that sense it has been a very worthwhile exercise. It will be even more worthwhile if it also sparks some interest in epistemological issues in others.

2
Positivist Epistemology – The Search for Foundations?

'Now, what I want is, Facts. Teach these boys and girls nothing but Facts. Facts alone are wanted in life. Plant nothing else, and root out everything else . . . stick to Facts, Sir! . . . In this life we want nothing but Facts' . . . Thomas Gradgrind . . . A man of realities. A man of fact and calculations.

(Charles Dickens, *Hard Times* (1854: 1–2))

Over 20 years ago Karl Popper claimed responsibility for the death of what he called logical positivism (1976: 88) – a demise he thought he had stimulated by his earlier work, *The Logic of Scientific Discovery* (1959). So it might seem curious to begin a book on management and epistemology by considering a philosophical position which, as far as any philosophy can die, is thought by some to be dead, or at least abandoned. Indeed some readers might perceive this to be a curiosity exacerbated by the title of this chapter. However, as we shall illustrate, the situation is far more complex than that implied by Popper's bold claim. Indeed other commentators (for example, Halfpenny, 1982) have argued that although some of its simpler forms may have been discredited, adapted or abandoned, positivism's assumptions remain pervasive and continue to provide the general rationale that underpins most theory and research in the social sciences. In this chapter and the following one we shall show that this positivist underpinning is particularly the case in the management and organizational research. Moreover it is ironic that the most pervasive adaptation of positivism has been Popper's own reformulation which seems to have only substituted logical positivism's principle that it was possible to verify and prove theories with the principle that it was only possible to falsify them.

It is important to begin our analysis of the philosophical dimensions of management research with positivist epistemology for several interrelated reasons. First, many aspects of positivism remain so embedded in Western cultures that they are virtually an aspect of our common sense. For instance the availability and application of Mr Gradgrind's 'Facts' to arbitrate reality are part of our taken-for-granted ways of judging truthfulness in our everyday lives, as well as in legal disputes and in science. In a sense we are therefore beginning with the most familiar epistemological orientation – at least in the English-speaking Occident. Secondly, positivism in a variety of guises remains the dominant epistemological orientation of the management disciplines despite it having recently been under increasing attack from a variety of rival orientations. However this dominance is usually camouflaged since hardly anyone openly applies a positivist label to their own work – despite the odd notable exception (for example, Donaldson, 1995; 1996). Indeed the term 'positivist' is more commonly used as an epithet for someone else's work. Thirdly, the recent attacks upon positivism and the debates they have spawned cannot be fully understood without a clear idea of what positivist epistemology is, since by and large their trajectories begin with their distinctive critiques of what they portray as positivist orthodoxy which can entail a tendency to build positivistic straw persons to suit the critic's purposes. As Lincoln and Guba observe, 'the particular form of definition offered by any commentator depends heavily on the counterpoints he or she wishes to make' (1985: 24). Therefore the epistemological alternatives to positivism define themselves through reference to, criticism of and controversy with, what they take to be positivism's assumptions. Indeed, as we will show, some ostensible anti-positivists do not live up to their self-perceptions. So while positivism is an obvious place to start, we need to be cautious about how we do this.

With this complexity in mind the aim of this chapter is to establish the key dimensions of positivist epistemology. We feel that positivism is so important it is worth devoting a whole chapter to its content before considering its deployment in management and organizational research in the next chapter. So here we shall introduce the reader to what we think are key epistemological concepts and debates which not only have to be grasped in order to understand positivism and it various emanations but also are critical for understanding the rationale of the alternatives to positivism which will be explored in subsequent chapters. We shall begin these tasks by tracing positivism's roots in rationalism, empiricism and the Enlightenment.

Rationalism, empiricism and the Enlightenment

Although its origins may be traced back to archaic times and Plato's quest for absolute truth through objectivity, positivism is primarily a post-Enlightenment philosophy of science. The Enlightenment (see Box 2.1) is a term used to characterize the anti-authoritarian cultural changes that occurred in eighteenth-century western Europe which were most spectacularly expressed by political upheavals, such as the French Revolution, which attempted to replace the remaining vestiges of feudalism by more egalitarian social orders.

Box 2.1

According to Isaiah Berlin, the key characteristics of the Enlightenment were: 'the conviction that the world . . . was a single whole, subject to a single set of laws, in principle discoverable by the intelligence of man; that the laws which governed inanimate nature were in principle the same as those which governed plants, animals and sentient beings; that man was capable of improvement; that there existed certain objectively recognizable human goals which all men . . . sought after, namely, happiness, knowledge, justice, liberty, and . . . virtue; that these goals were common to all men as such, were not unattainable, nor incompatible, and that human misery, vice and folly were mainly due to ignorance either of what these goals consisted in or of the means of attaining them – ignorance due in turn to insufficient knowledge of the laws of nature . . . Consequently the discovery of general laws that govern human behaviour, their clear and logical integration into scientific systems – of psychology, sociology, economics, political science and the like (though they did not use these names) – and the determination of their proper place in the great corpus of knowledge that covered all discoverable facts, would, by replacing the chaotic amalgam of guess work, tradition, superstition, prejudice, dogma, fantasy and "interested error" that hitherto did service as human knowledge and wisdom . . . create a new, sane, rational, happy, just and self perpetuating human society'. (Berlin, quoted in Gray, 1995: 136–7)

According to Immanuel Kant, the motto of the Enlightenment was 'dare to know' which voiced an optimism with respect to the possibility that human reason would triumph over ignorance and superstition. Its victory would ensure progress through allowing the application of human reason to the control of human affairs. Here reason may be characterized as when a person

> who in perceiving the world takes in 'bits' of information from his or her surroundings, and then processes them in some fashion, in order to emerge with the 'picture' of the world he or she has; who then acts on the basis of this picture to fulfill his or her goals, through a 'calculus' of means and ends. (Taylor, 1993: 319)

Obviously central to this endeavour are the epistemic processes through which we construct our 'pictures' of the world and which we take to be valid. Very broadly speaking, philosophers at this time thought that our pictures, or more precisely our knowledge, of the world could arise from two sources – thinking or observing. Epistemologically the rationalists gave priority to the former in that they claimed that the true foundations of knowledge are available to the contemplative mind. In contrast, the empiricists gave priority to observation in that they presumed that knowledge could only be established by accessing the world through our senses. As we shall demonstrate below, an outcome of the Enlightenment was the radicalization of earlier epistemologies like those of rationalists such as René Descartes and those of empiricists such as John Locke and Francis Bacon.

In his works *Discourse on Method* (1637) and *Meditations on Philosophy* (1641) Descartes presented the rationalist view that valid knowledge could be accumulated through the individual's sceptical contemplation of an external reality. In this he posited a world consisting of two kinds of entity: an external 'extended' God-given world and human thought. In Descartes' philosophy these entities are construed as separate and independent of one another. This differentiation is known as a Cartesian dualism: a bifurcation of nature into mind and matter (i.e. extension); into observer and observed; into knower and known; into subject and object.

In his exposition of the Cartesian method Descartes argued that sensory experience can be deceptive and we can never be sure if we are being misled. But he also thought that God would not have created people in such a way that their senses and reason would always systematically deceive them. For Descartes it followed that there must exist an external world which was cognitively accessible to human thought. But our sensory grasp of this world may be misleading, hence the necessity for systematic scepticism about the deliverables of our senses. For Descartes scepticism entailed subjecting the objects of sensory experience to doubt in order to see if any of them were beyond doubt. An example of this method is illustrated by Box 2.2.

Box 2.2

> Descartes' scepticism made him question whether he, Descartes, actually existed. The only thing he could not doubt was that he was able to doubt since even if he doubted that he could doubt he was still doubting. He therefore realized that because doubting was a form of reasoning and thinking he had to be certain that he was a thinking being and thus existed. As he saw it, *'Cogito ergo sum'* – 'I think therefore I am'.

Descartes argued that only something which survives systematic scepticism has rational justification. This process of reasoning had to be the basis of valid knowledge since Descartes assumed that it allowed one to differentiate true, or rational, knowledge from false, or irrational, knowledge. Ultimately Descartes maintained that rational knowledge depended upon our ideas resembling objects in the external world. He thought that God would not allow us to be continuously misled since such a deception would be incompatible with God's goodness. Indeed he thought that it was our capacity for reasoning that could eventually allow humans to gain mastery over the natural world. The articulation of this possibility and the differentiation of knowledge through the sceptical reasoning of the mind were highly influential upon later positivist thought. Perhaps the most influential of Descartes' ideas were the epistemological notions that our minds and the objects of external reality are independent of one another (this is known as a Cartesian dualism between knower and known) and that truth lies in the mind coming into agreement with reality: to know the truth was to correctly represent in one's mind what existed outside the mind. Nevertheless an equally significant influence upon the development of positivism derived from empiricism.

John Locke is widely regarded as the founder of modern empiricism. In his *Essay Concerning Human Understanding* (1690) Locke attempted to remove the connections between science and religion by considering from where ideas derive and if people can rely upon what their senses indicate. He saw that religious faith entailed the acceptance of propositions on the basis of the theological authority that articulated them. In effect, by proposing the empiricist maxim that the only criterion for determining valid knowledge is by subjecting it to the test of sense-experience, he defended science from what he considered to be the dogmatic pronouncements of theocrats.

But for Locke knowledge did not arise automatically from our sensation of the objects of experience which exist independently of our knowing them. The mind, albeit a blank slate or *tabula rasa* at birth, is not a passive receiver of sense-data. Rather, through reflection (reasoning, believing and doubting) the mind processes sense-data. Sense-data enter our minds as simple, discrete units of experience. Complex ideas arise out of the manipulation of these sense-data through the operation of reflection. Locke argued that our senses can objectively reproduce what he called 'primary qualities' (e.g. size, weight, motion and quantity) which were inherent in the objects of experience themselves. Other sensations created what he called 'secondary qualities' (e.g. smell, taste and warmth) which varied according to the individual's subjective predilections. Knowledge arises through our reflection upon our sensations in which we internally perceive and give order to what we see, hear, feel and smell etc. and thereby create complex ideas out of simple sensations. For Locke valid knowledge is traceable back to simple sensations and 'primary qualities' while knowledge which is not traceable in this manner has to be rejected. In sum, central to empiricism is the view that human beliefs about the external world only become valid knowledge when they have survived the test of experience. Such epistemological commitments aided human emancipation by wiping the slate clean through sanctioning a rejection of received ideas embedded in the authority of tradition. Through sensation and reflection anchored in gathering objective sense-data, Locke's empiricism assumed that scientists could start from scratch and could inductively generate universal laws (see Box 2.3).

Box 2.3

> Induction is a reasoning process through which theory is generated out of specific instances of observation and experience. So inductive reasoning entails making general inferences about a phenomenon through the observation of particular instances of the phenomenon. For example, if we observe in N examples of phenomenon X that all have so far possessed property p, 'thus' all future examples of phenomenon X will have property p. Obviously the problem is how we justify the inductive inference implied by 'thus'. For empiricists the question is whether or not the 'thus' inference is only justifiable by tracing it back to empirical experience and observation. After all, for empiricists, like Locke, the sole criterion for valid knowledge is experience, but how could experience ever justify the 'thus' inference – the extrapolation to all future unexperienced instances of phenomenon X? Yet the claim to be able inductively to generate universally applicable laws implies that the 'thus' inference is possible. This conundrum was to haunt inductive empiricists until the twentieth century.

Locke's view that universal laws could be generated out of observation follows the earlier work of Francis Bacon. In his *Novum Organum* (1620) Bacon launched an attack upon the then dominant Aristotelian philosophy. The latter saw knowledge (*episteme*) as an end in itself divorced from the beliefs (*doxa*) suitable only for the conduct of practical everyday affairs. For Bacon this endowed a passivity on the part of people with regard to nature's vagaries. Bacon's mission was to recover 'man's dominion' over nature which he had lost in the 'Fall'. He aimed to replace Aristotelian submissiveness with a science which could, through the discovery of physical regularities, enable people to assert practical control over nature. Central to this task was Bacon's provision of a systematic description of induction. Here scientists begin by making and recording observations of as yet unexplained phenomena. As this body of shared sense-data accumulates, general patterns emerge which enable scientists to formulate general theoretical statements which causally link the observed phenomena to each other. In this scientists try to verify the emergent theory by finding more supportive evidence. If they succeed in so verifying the theory they have discovered a universal scientific law that adds to the available stock of scientific knowledge and which allows human beings then to manipulate and exercise control over nature.

Drawing upon Descartes, Locke and Bacon, the later Enlightenment philosophers embraced empiricism and used it to launch attacks upon religion and theocratic knowledge based upon what they construed as anathema – metaphysical speculation and revelation. The empiricist tradition aimed to make truth-claims about reality objectively assessable. A key step in attaining this aim was to purge metaphysics from the domain of science. Metaphysics (literally 'beyond physics') entailed the speculative analysis of issues which lay beyond the empirically discernible world and therefore could not be settled by observation or experience. So, for instance, although they came to different conclusions, François Voltaire and Denis Diderot in France as well as David Hume and Adam Smith in Scotland all advocated the empiricist view that valid knowledge should be based upon sensory experience and used this to attack what they perceived to be theological dogmatism. However this is not to suggest that all Enlightenment philosophers shared the atheism of Diderot or the agnosticism of Hume. Many, such as Voltaire, were deists who believed that since the creation the universe had continued to function without divine intervention. They thought that God was revealed through the laws of nature – it was irrational ecclesiastical dogma, which served to obscure these laws, which needed to be dismissed rather than the notion of a supreme being itself. Thus deists naturalized religion in that it became a matter of reason, not faith.

Considerable controversy still exists about the role of metaphysics in science and the relationship of science to metaphysical beliefs such as religious dogma (see Box 2.4). However metaphysical controversy is not limited to religious beliefs. As will be illustrated in later chapters, the possibility of eradicating metaphysics from science is disputed by most non-positivist epistemologies. Here a shared theme is that metaphysics lays the groundwork for interpretation and understanding in any tradition (including, for instance, empiricism) no matter what its public aspirations may be. How we engage with the world is thus seen to be based in part upon the background expectations and assumptions that we have about the world that are inevitably metaphysical and thus whether or not they are warranted is not empirically testable. For instance such metaphysical assumptions cover issues such as: how the world originated; what its purpose is; how society is constructed; where society is heading; what the aims of science are; and, ironically, whether or not a Cartesian dualism is possible in the first place. So while empiricism (and later positivism) may have claimed to purge metaphysics from science it would seem that this was a forlorn hope since any epistemology, including empiricism, inevitably rests upon metaphysical assumptions.

In contrast to the deists, Hume's agnosticism is expressed in his scepticism which stimulated his doubts about the possibility of induction. In his key work *A Treatise of Human Nature* (1739–40) Hume advocated Locke's empiricism but combined it with a thoroughgoing scepticism which cast doubt upon both the notion of causality and the possibility of Bacon's inductive programme for science. In this he argued that there are two different types of perception – impressions and ideas. The former are our immediate sensations of external reality; the latter are recollections of past impressions stored in the mind. However during the process of recollection the mind could construct false ideas severed from the collections of impressions that initially stimulated them. Therefore Hume opposed all ideas which could not be traced back to corresponding sense impressions. The implications for Hume were only too clear:

> If we take in our hand any volume, of divinity or . . . metaphysics, for instance, let us ask, Does it contain any abstract reasoning concerning quantity or number? No. Does it contain any experimental reasoning concerning matter of fact and existence? No. Commit it then to the flames; for it can contain nothing but sophistry and illusion. (Hume, 1748–1975: sec. vii, pt iii)

This empiricism led Hume to put forward a particularly important view of causation. He argued that just because we have always seen the event B follow the occurrence of the event A, it does not necessarily mean that the occurrence of event A causes event B to happen. Hume thought that the expectation that A causes B could not lie in the events themselves since the notion of cause is basically unobservable and cannot be validated by experience. In Hume's terms we have no 'impression' of any force by means of which A produces B. Rather the causal associations we anticipate lie in our customs or 'force of habit' – ideas which we have developed from our perceived repetition of the relevant experience (see Box 2.5).

Thus Hume did not explicitly deny causality; rather he reconstructed it as a *de facto* constant conjunction, or regular succession, of ideas in which one type of event is invariably followed by another type. Science, for Hume, entailed the passive sensing of atomistic events and the recording of their constant conjunctions. Nevertheless he was guarded about the possibility of induction. For instance only the first three conditions in Box

Box 2.4

> From the Editor: Whenever we feature an article concerning scientific evidence of evolution, I can be certain of two things: the story will represent the latest physical evidence presented by leading scientists in the study of early life – and my office will be deluged with letters from readers who reject evolutionary theory. Most of the critics object as a matter of scriptural principle; others say they have scientific evidence that calls evolution into question. This month's story about the origins of life will only add to that debate.
>
> Faith and science have at least one thing in common: both are lifelong searches for truth. But while faith is an unshakable belief in the unseen, science is the study of testable, observable phenomena. The two coexist, and may at times complement each other. But neither should be asked to validate or invalidate the other. Scientists have no more business questioning the existence of God than theologians had telling Galileo the Earth was at the center of the universe.
>
> National Geographic's respect for faith, the core beliefs that stir billions of people around the world, is reflected in recent articles . . . Science is in a perpetual state of becoming. Yesterday's observations give rise to today's theories, which will be tested through painstaking research. Just as any good scientist must be ready to abandon a bad idea, he or she must stand by the results of unbiased empirical evidence and experimentation. The current studies of how life arose, most scientists believe, stand up to that scrutiny.
>
> (*National Geographic*, March 1998: 1)

Box 2.5

> For Hume we perceive causality when four conditions pertain between the occurrence of two events: first, a constant conjunction, where the manifestation of each event is continuously associated one with another; secondly, an antecedence, where the events occur sequentially in the respect that what is taken to be the cause chronologically precedes what is taken to be the effect; thirdly, a contiguity, where both events are spatially in the same location; fourthly, a necessity, where there has to be no alternative possible cause of the observed effects. An example often used to illustrate Hume's view of causality as constant conjunction is that of striking a match, causing it to light. Here, to believe that striking a match (A) causes it to light (B) is an outcome of repeated observation that A is followed by B and where we observe B, A has already happened. There is no need to identify any underlying causal, or generative, mechanisms such as the chemical constitution of the match head as a means of explaining its inflammation. Cause is thus understood as the habitual expectation that striking the match is invariably followed by its inflammation – when one event constantly follows another a causal relationship is said to exist. However to know that event A definitely causes event B would demand that we know that nothing other than A could have caused, or will cause, B to happen. To know this we would need to fulfil the fourth of Hume's conditions – to observe match inflammation in all possible circumstances. Since such an endeavour would be impossible it is never possible to come to a definite conclusion about any proposed causal relationship.

2.5 are possible in the sense that they may be empirically observed. But these three are necessary but not sufficient conditions. Sufficiency can only be supplied by the fourth condition – observing B in all possible circumstances – which is impossible to achieve. Alternatively the absence of any of the first three conditions would allow us to rule out the existence of causality – a point which is taken up by later falsificationists, such as Popper, and which is embedded in many of the statistical techniques used today to test hypotheses.

Thus Hume's empiricism led him to question the possibility of grounding scientific laws in an inductive accumulation of observations. He saw that no finite number of observations can ever justify a universal conclusion. In other words, he argued that we cannot generalize with any certainty from events which we have experienced to those which we have not yet experienced and which remain unknowable. Remarkably, the scepticism central to Hume's empiricist critique of induction was virtually ignored until Popper's work some 150 years after Hume's death. Nevertheless key aspects of Hume's empiricism and Descartes' rationalism can be identified in the work of Auguste Comte (1853) who not only coined the term 'positivism' but also played a significant role in shaping the emerging social sciences in the latter half of the nineteenth century – a legacy, albeit reformulated, which is still influential today.

Comtean positivism

When Comte coined the term 'positivism' he was expressing the Enlightenment desire to rid science of what he saw to be dogma. Thus Comte (1853) identified three chronological stages in the development of knowledge: the theological or fictitious; the metaphysical or abstract; and the scientific or positive. In the first stage phenomena are explained as the product of the acts of supernatural agencies – for example God. In the second stage people attribute phenomena to a single abstract force, invisible power or underlying entity – for example nature. The third stage is characterized by the examination of the 'positively given' – that which is directly available through sensory perception. At this stage Comte saw that 'the human mind' rejected all religion and metaphysics as a distraction from sense-data and

> confines itself to the discovery, through reason and observation combined, of the actual laws that govern the succession and similarity of phenomena. The explanation of the facts, now reduced to its real terms, consists in the establishment of a link between various phenomena and a few general facts, which diminish in number with the progress of science. (quoted in Andreski, 1974: 20)

It is evident that Comte, in proposing that the basis for scientific knowledge was only that which was 'positively given', had drawn upon and transformed the empiricist and rationalist traditions of Descartes, Locke and Hume (see Box 2.6). In most respects the doubt and scepticism of those forebears was dropped so that Comte could equate the empirical world with a domain of objective facts which were cognitively accessible through the rationality encoded into a scientific methodology derived from physics. Of course, by doing so, Comte enshrined an uncritical attitude towards one's own experience while proposing a unity of the sciences grounded in a deterministic view of social phenomena. He thought that, just like natural phenomena, the social domain was subject to general laws that operated independently of individual will and consciousness. So for Comte both social and natural science were limited to, and united by, the value-free observation, description, explanation and prediction of an external world. The shared aim of the sciences was inductively to generate statements of universal laws which stated the necessary and invariant causal relationships between social or natural phenomena. Due to its empirical base positive social science was unlike earlier forms of knowledge in that it was useful and certain. Its discovery of laws in a causal and therefore predictive form enabled human intervention so as to alter (causative) social conditions and thereby bring about desired end-states (effects). Comte saw that only such a positive social science could have access to factual and certain knowledge which could then be applied to the administration and reform of society's institutions.

Comte's work influenced John Stuart Mill in England who defended empiricism as an inductive method which proceeded from observation

Box 2.6   Data

The term 'data' is often formally used in research to refer to accumulated empirical experience against which theory is tested – Mr Gradgrind's 'Facts'. Probably Comte would have approved of the literal translation of the Latin derivation of this term: *dare* – to give; *data* – things given. In contrast the scepticism of Hume could, for instance, tell researchers that the 'facts' are not 'given' – they do not 'speak for themselves'; rather data are always interpreted and organized through our scientific activities. The question here is whether these interpretative processes only refer to the *implications* of incontestable (i.e. given) facts for our theories or whether those interpretative processes also extend to the *constitution* of the facts in themselves.

through to the generation of causal laws pertaining to the relationships between independently existing and observable facts. Like Comte, Mill urged social scientists to adopt the methods that had been apparently so successful in the natural sciences. For Mill scientific inquiry was largely, but not exclusively, a matter of inductive inference and generalization from the results of empirical observation and experiment. As such scientific knowledge advances through, and is justified by, the discovery of causal relationships between phenomena.

In his work *A System of Logic* (1874) Mill developed a set of methods which he thought scientists used to discover causal relationships which were in turn generalizeable into scientific laws. Mill's methods (see Box 2.7) underpin experimental logic and in many respects the development of experimental methodology has added greater control over the circumstances and phenomena being studied, thereby enabling greater precision and greater confidence in the generalizability of the predictions which are inductively generated. Mill declared that the fundamental principle of induction was that 'nature is uniform'. By this he meant that once causal relations had been discovered through the application of his 'methods' those findings could be extrapolated to future instances. This principle of Mill attempts to justify the 'thus' inference illustrated in Box 2.3. Of course this principle is questionable and cannot itself be established or justified by either induction or empiricism. Nevertheless Mill is a good exemplar of an inductivist position which reached its apotheosis in a distinctive twentieth-century brand of positivism known usually as 'logical positivism' and less commonly as 'logical empiricism'.

Logical positivism

In many respects the development of positivism was highly influenced by its socio-historical contexts. Its rationalist and empiricist traditions are traceable to before the Enlightenment whose radicalizing effects reached

Box 2.7   Mill's inductive methods

1   *The Method of Agreement* – where two or more instances of a phenomenon have only one circumstance in common, that circumstance is the cause or effect of the phenomenon:

Instance	Circumstances	Phenomenon
1	@bcd	X
2	@efg	X

2   *The Method of Difference* – if an instance in which the phenomenon occurs is compared to an instance in which it doesn't and it is evident that each instance is the same save for one circumstantial element that only occurs in the former instance, then that unique circumstantial element is part of the cause or effect of the phenomenon:

Instance	Circumstances	Phenomenon
1	@bcd	X
2	bcd	–

3   *The Method of Concomitant Variations* – if some part of the set of circumstances varies as the phenomenon varies, this part of the set of circumstances is causally related to the phenomenon:

Instance	Circumstances	Phenomenon
1	abcd	x
2	Abcd	X
3	A̲bcd	X̲

4   *The Method of Residues* – remove from the phenomenon what prior inductive inference indicates to be the effects of certain circumstances. The residue of the phenomenon is the effect of the remaining circumstances:

Instance	Circumstances	Phenomenon
1	ab(c)	xy(z)
2	a(b)	x(y)
3	a	x

their clearest expression in the work of Comte. While lauding Hume as one of their founding philosophical fathers, logical positivists were also a product of their times. For instance, logical positivism is most closely associated with a group of socialist and liberal intellectuals based in Vienna during the 1920s and 1930s. They included Rudolf Carnap, Otto Neurath, Alfred Ayer, Friedrich Waismann, Herbert Feigl and the group's founder, Moritz Schlick. Dubbed the 'Vienna Circle', their epistemology was inspired by developments in physics (relativity theory and quantum mechanics) and was in part a response to the rise of fascism in western Europe. As Callinicos observes, the Vienna Circle was engaged in a defence of Enlightenment reason against 'the various forms of irration-alism that were only too visible a feature of postwar Vienna' (1989: 46). In this the Circle's members saw that the true concern of philosophy was to protect science from metaphysics by analysing and clarifying the concepts to be used in the language of science: the task was to analyse knowledge claims so as to make the propositions clear and unambiguous. In this context Scriven describes the Vienna Circle as

> a band of cutthroats that went after the fat burghers of Continental metaphysics who had become intolerably inbred and pompously verbose . . . It performed a tracheotomy which made it possible for philosophy to breath again. (1969: 195)

This desire to eliminate metaphysics and the Circle's sustained opposition to fascism and support for democratic ideals were at considerable personal risk and one member, Moritz Schlick, was murdered by a Nazi student. Despite being eventually driven out by the rise of Hitler and the Nazi *Anschluss* the Circle's ideas continued to be developed after World War II by its dispersed members and fellow travellers. Indeed it remained a dominant epistemological force in English-speaking countries well into the 1960s.

Although the logical positivists had numerous internal disagreements, and despite the risk of over-simplification, it is still possible to distil four interrelated webs of epistemological commitments:

1 Logical positivists believed that observation of the empirical world – through our senses – provides the only foundation for knowledge. Their version of empiricism entails the claim that such observation can be neutral, value-free and objective.

Logical positivism assumes that there is a neutral point at which an observer can stand back and observe the external world objectively. This is called a subject-object dualism where the observations that are regis-tered about an external social and natural world (i.e. the object) by a passive knower (i.e. the subject) are separate and independent of the processes of observation (i.e. a dualism). Thus Locke's empiricism is combined with a somewhat unsceptical version of Descartes' rationalism to produce a neutral observational language. Here truth is to be found in the observer's passive registration of Comte's sensory 'positively given' – the facts that constitute social and natural reality.

For instance in his early work Wittgenstein (1922) argues that language gains its meaning from its direct correspondence with the objects of an external reality. In this 'picture theory' of language, a sentence can only be meaningful in two ways: either by picturing a fact; or by analysis breaking it down into more basic sentences which picture facts. The relationship between language and external reality is called 'picturing' because words stand for objects just as points on the surface of a picture represent physical space. So as to justify this 'representational' view of language, Wittgenstein claimed that the character of external reality and the language used to describe it must match, otherwise our propositions about the world would be meaningless (a position which he later repudiated). Logical positivists construed Wittgenstein's picture theory of language as legitimizing empiricism by justifying the assumption that experience constructs language, and not *vice versa*. This in turn sustains the possibility of a neutral observational language.

The assumption of the possibility of a neutral observational language is crucial to a logical positivist research programme as it enables the correspondence theory of truth which is central to all versions of positivism. As Hindess points out:

> it makes possible a very precise conception of the testing of theory against observation. The testing of theory against irreducible statements of observation is equivalent to a direct comparison between theory and the real. If they fail to *correspond* then the theory is false and therefore may be rejected. (1977: 18) (our emphasis)

Not only can science thereby be a value-free activity in that it deals only with facts; its outcomes are also value-free. For the logical positivist, science must only concern itself with the generation of factual knowledge and since values cannot be derived from empirical facts, nor *vice versa* (Ayer, 1971: 46–8) it follows that science cannot produce evaluative conclusions. Hence moral or other evaluative sentences, because they are not confirmable through empirical observation, are considered to be cognitively meaningless.

2 Since primary importance is placed upon what is taken to be observable reality, the postulation of non-observable mechanisms (e.g. the subjective or the unconscious) is rejected as metaphysical speculation and beyond the realm of 'science'. It follows that all theoretical statements must be capable of, and subject to, empirical testing. Hence empirical verification is the key to scientific research.

Logical positivists' antipathy towards metaphysics is expressed in their commitment to empiricism. In the main they followed Bertrand Russell's view that

> Nothing can be known to exist except by the help of experience . . . if we wish to prove that something of which we have no direct experience exists, we must have among our premises the existence of one or more things of which we have direct experience. Our belief that the Emperor of China exists, for example, rests upon testimony, and testimony consists in the last analysis of sense-data seen or heard. (1912: 74–5)

This commitment is illustrated by Reichenbach's argument that speculative metaphysical philosophy erroneously conceived knowledge as transcending the observable whereas scientific philosophy regarded 'knowledge as an instrument of prediction and for which sense observation is the only criterion of non empty truths' (1963: 252). So here logical positivists have argued that any statement about the world is only meaningful if it can be shown to be true or false through observation. This is known as the 'verifiability principle of meaning' – that something is only meaningful if it is empirically verifiable through sense-experience or observation. Ayer states this principle succinctly:

> The criterion which we use to test the genuineness of apparent statements of fact is the criterion of verifiability. We say that a sentence is factually significant to any given person, if, and only if, he knows how to verify the proposition it purports to express – that is, if he knows what observations would lead him, under certain conditions, to accept the proposition as being true, or reject it as being false. (1971: 48)

Thus, for Ayer, the cognitive meaning of a statement *is* its method of verification. An easy target for this principle was religion. For instance Ayer (*ibid.*) argued that religious statements such as 'God exists' are metaphysical and therefore they are not amenable to verification through observation. It follows that since such a statement lacks a method of verification it may be dispensed with as meaningless. Such statements are neither true nor false – rather they are nonsensical statements because it isn't possible to specify how they might be verified through empirical observation.

However this exclusion of the ostensibly metaphysical from the realm of science has implications for how we understand the legitimate domain of the social sciences since it may be used to justify what we shall call 'scientific naturalism'. The latter arises out of the view that since the postulation of non-observable mechanisms and entities constitutes metaphysical speculation, it is necessary to specifically exclude from warranted science the realm of human subjectivity in explaining human action (for example, Abel, 1958). This is because such 'inner' subjective causes of behaviour are unobservable and as explanations of behaviour are therefore unverifiable. As Lessnoff comments:

> it was once normal to suppose that the fall of a tree over a path might be a malicious act on the tree's part . . . [this is an explanation] . . . of physical phenomena in terms of a mind, attributed either to physical objects themselves, or to an invisible power that controls them. Empiricists draw the moral that the social sciences, can and should cease to use mental concepts in explanation, replacing them by genuinely scientific explanations. (1974: 95–6)

At best the 'intuitive or empathic grasp of consciousness' is regarded only as a possible source of hypotheses about human conduct and not as a focus for social science in its own right (Giddens, 1976: 19). This exclusion removes human subjectivity as a possible characteristic that justifies the differentiation of the social world from the natural world. It in effect supports, and is in turn supported by, the belief in a continuity between the natural and social sciences. In essence their different subject matters – behaviour of human beings and physical objects – may be analysed and explained in the same way. This continuity allows the view that methods apparently so successful in the natural sciences are readily transferable to research in the social sciences – the third characteristic of logical positivism.

3   The natural sciences, particularly physics, provide the model for all the sciences including the social sciences.

This claim is often known as 'scientism' or 'methodological monism'. It means that there are no methodological differences between the natural and social sciences. This methodological unity is usually expressed through the deployment of experimental logic in social science where human behaviour is conceptualized as measurable and automatic responses to external causative stimuli. The latter may be either administered by an experimenter or operationalized through the use of metrics such as those, for instance, encoded into a questionnaire *pro forma*. This perceived unity of method and the exclusion of the subjective from the legitimate domain of the social sciences reinforces and is in turn supported by a non-sceptical version of Hume's 'constant conjunction' which is seen as a legitimate means of explaining cause and effect. In other words, where one event follows another in a regular and predictable manner – where the first three of Hume's conditions hold (see Box 2.5) – a causal relationship may be said to exist.

Following Hume, the actual causal mechanism itself is essentially unobservable – no attempt need, nor indeed should, be made to identify it. As Shotter (1975) argues, an outcome of this epistemology in the social sciences is a determinism which treats human beings as if they were analogous to unthinking inanimate entities, such as an atom, at the mercy of external causative stimuli. This is because the unobservable causal mechanism, excluded by the Humean approach in the social sciences, relates to actors' interpretative or subjective understandings of their situation. The result is that the unity of natural and social science is preserved at the expense of human subjectivity – and at the expense of other processes deemed unobservable such as Freud's unconscious. Their deterministic neglect of human subjectivity has led to the emergence of major critiques of positivism and its influence on research methodology. However, as we shall argue, such an 'interpretative' critique of positivism does not necessarily entail a break with all of positivism's other commitments – as some of these ostensible critics assume. In many respects it is more a debate about what is observable which, while having implications for the plausibility of methodological monism and the unity of science, often preserves positivist commitments to a correspondence theory of truth couched in a putative neutral observational language.

4   Logical positivists see that the task of science is to enable the prediction and control of social and natural events. As such it produces instrumentally useful knowledge.

Logical positivists conserve a recurrent theme traceable back to Bacon, Descartes, Locke, Comte and Mill. This emphasizes the need for science to provide knowledge and theory for the control of the social and natural worlds through the discovery of laws which allow the prediction, manipulation and control of social and natural phenomena (see Tiles, 1987). For instance Hempel (1965), although he rejected induction as the model for science, thought that the purpose of science was the formulation of universal covering laws. Such laws explain the behaviour of phenomena in different conditions and the use of experimental logic enables the specification conditions which limit their applicability. An example would be that water boils at 100 degrees Centigrade, at sea level. Once these laws and their ranges are known they can be applied to exert control over social and natural phenomena through the manipulation of causal variables. By adding to our stock of knowledge and by improving our ability to exert control, logical positivists optimistically assume that the development of scientific knowledge will be to our advantage – it assures 'progress' and therefore we should trust science's reason. Here a further justification for scientism/methodological monism emerges: for logical positivists it was self-evident that the natural sciences had provided instrumentally useful knowledge – for social science to reproduce that contribution to human welfare they must copy the methodology whose deployment they presumed had enabled the apparent successes of the natural sciences.

In sum, logical positivism is constituted by a web of mutually supportive epistemological commitments which are traceable back to the development of rationalism and empiricism before and during the Enlightenment. However some internal contradictions did exist – a key one being created by their simultaneous commitment to induction and empiricism. It was this contradiction that provided the springboard for the next development – positivism's deductive reformulation by Karl Popper.

Karl Popper and the 'demise' of logical positivism

We now turn to Karl Popper's famous critique of logical positivism and attempt to evaluate his own claim that he stimulated its demise. By implication we will therefore evaluate the appropriateness of the association of Popper's work with 'postpositivism' which is made by some commentators (for example, Guba and Lincoln, 1994: 106–7). This is of critical importance because Popper's work has been very influential in the social sciences generally and in the management disciplines in particular. Basically Popper attacks the inductive basis of logical positivism which he thought to be dogmatic as it sought to apply and confirm laws 'even to the point of neglecting refutations' (1967: 50). Moreover, for Popper, logical positivism was bound to run into trouble because it excluded as 'sheer gibberish . . . metaphysical ideas [which] are often the forerunners of scientific ones' (1976: 80). Here he argues that scientific activity had often emerged out of metaphysical speculation. For instance, an idea which at one time is based upon superstitious or religious and hence untestable metaphysical conceptions may become testable and therefore, for Popper, scientific.

The key outcome of Popper's thesis in his work *The Logic of Scientific Discovery* (1959) was the replacement of logical positivism's inductive and verificationist principles with those of deduction and falsification – the hypothetico-deductive method. The shocking conclusion of this work showed how the notion that the sciences provide bodies of established fact was fundamentally mistaken – since it was impossible. As he claimed:

> The empirical basis of science has nothing 'absolute' about it. Science does not rest upon solid bedrock. The bold structure of its theories rise, as it were above a swamp. It is like a building erected on piles. The piles are driven down from above into the swamp but not down to any natural or 'given' base; and if we stop driving the piles deeper, it is not because we have reached firm ground. We simply stop when we are satisfied that the piles are firm enough to carry the structure at least for the time being. (1959: 111)

The above claim is an outcome of Popper's revitalization of Hume's scepticism regarding the possibility of induction and the problems associated with establishing an empirical basis for induction and verificationism. It emphasizes that the results of scientific activity can never be certain – science can never produce definitive accounts of the way the world is. Hence the principles of the hypothetico-deductive method express what Popper called a 'critical attitude' which he later defined as the willingness to change laws and theories 'to test them; to refute them; to falsify them, if possible' (1967: 50). In this sense Popper's epistemology resurrected systematic scepticism by exploiting the empirical asymmetry between verification (i.e. proof) and falsification (i.e. disproof). To put it bluntly, science can in principle falsify any knowledge by confronting it with empirical data but it can never prove a knowledge claim.

As we have seen, the logic of induction entails the movement from the empirical observation of data by means of experiments to the inference of theories and general laws verified by the causal relations exhibited by that data. Hume's problem of induction arose because the inductive verification of a theory is inevitably based upon a finite number of observations; even if every observation that is made confirms the assertions put forward by the theory, logically we can never be certain whether some future observations might demonstrate instances in which the theory does not hold. The unreliability of inductive inference is vividly illustrated by Bertrand Russell's story, presented in Box 2.8.

From his evaluation of induction Russell concluded that we can never be really sure that science is true – but it is more likely to be true than anything else that was available. Similarly, Popper's scepticism led him to reject the absolute certainty of Descartes' rationalism and yet preserve the view that knowledge of an external reality is possible – albeit that it is uncertain, fallible and can never be proven. Theories can only be tentative conjectures about the world which are ultimately unverifiable by empirical

Box 2.8

One day a chicken was hatched. By chance, it stumbled upon corn and water. It was a happy chick. The next day it happened again and again the next. Being an intelligent chicken, it considered the possibility that supplies might stop and wondered whether it would be necessary to take precautions. It decided to investigate the world to see whether, given a large number of cases and a wide variety of conditions, there were grounds to suppose that the pattern of events so far witnessed would continue in the future. The benefit would be that no precaution against non-supply of corn and water need be taken. After months of careful observations and noting that differences in weather, configurations of the stars, beings encountered, mood and many other things did not stop the supplies, the chicken concluded that the world truly was a wonderful place. The very next day, everything changed. It was 24 December. (Bertrand Russell, *Human Knowledge, Its Scope and Limits* (1948))

evidence. For Popper the point is 'that there is no rule of inductive inference – inference leading to theories or universal laws – ever proposed which can be taken seriously' (1976: 146–7).

Popper thought that the actual selection, development and promotion of specific theories were intimately tied to the traditions and history of the host discipline. In many respects he considered that where theories come from is irrelevant. Their discovery is an unanalysable metaphysical process which entails 'an irrational element or a creative intuition' (1959: 32) – imaginative leaps which are the forerunners of scientific activity. However theory can be falsified by empirical tests – just as Christmas Eve did for the optimistic world view of the inductive chicken! It is the process whereby predictive and thereby testable hypotheses are deduced from theoretical conjectures and subjected to confrontation with a cognitively accessible world which is, according to Popper, the distinctive attribute of a critically rational science. So for Popper science is a sequence of conjectures and refutations, revised conjectures and additional refutations which deductively proceed from the universal to the particular through the elaboration of predictive hypotheses. Thereby Popper rejects what he considers to be verificationist dogma and avoids Hume's problem of induction by proposing the maxim of falsificationism: that a scientific theory must be capable of empirical testing which involves rigorous attempts at falsifying a theory.

According to Popper, methodological rules must be designed in such a way 'that they do not protect any statement in science against falsification' (1959: 54). Popper therefore thought that any statement which was protected from refutation was metaphysical and therefore was non-scientific or 'pseudo science'. In contrast, a scientific theory has to state the empirical conditions in which it will deem itself as having failed. Here scientists have to deduce from their theories hypothetical statements which make empirical predictions as to what should be expected if the theory holds. If, after the collection of empirical evidence, it is apparent that the predictions do not occur then the theory is refuted. In effect, science advances through the detection and elimination of error (Popper, 1967: 25) as falsified theories fall away leaving a core of theory which has not been, as yet, disproved.

So by trial and error science learns which theories it can use for the time being and which it should discard. As such science can only ever be incomplete and provisional. In the case of the social sciences it can, at most, only ever justify human intervention in the form of a 'piecemeal social engineering'. Popper defines social engineering as 'the planning and construction of institutions with the aim, perhaps, of arresting or of controlling or quickening social developments' (1961: 44–5). This involves the use of 'technological predictions' which through experimental testing would enable human intervention so as purposively to manipulate social processes, thereby solving the 'practical questions of the day' (*ibid.*: 58–9). However such social engineering should be 'piecemeal' since 'piecemeal tinkering . . . combined with critical analysis is the main way to achieve practical results in the social as well as the natural sciences' (*ibid.*: 58).

At first sight Popper seems to be arguing that falsification is a relatively unproblematic process since only one contradictory observation is required to refute a theory. However in practice Popper recognizes that scientists do not automatically reject theories in such circumstances – and this is appropriate since 'a few stray basic statements contradicting a theory will hardly induce us to reject it as falsified' (1959: 86). However Popper is unspecific as to what counts as a decisive falsification – rather he infers that a theory is only discarded when it has been falsified and there is a new unfalsified theory available to replace it (see Figure 2.1).

In essence Popper's falsificationism leads to an epistemological Darwinism in which the 'fitness' of a theory to survive a test is an indicator of its acceptability and the 'strong' theories, in effect, drive out the 'weak'. Although he concedes that through the deductive production of predictive hypotheses a scientist is always operating from a theoretical perspective (e.g. 1959: 107; 1967: 47) he doesn't suggest that the subsequent testing process is anything but a neutral and independent process. Rather Popper preserves a Cartesian dualism through an inverted form of the correspondence theory of truth which depends upon testing a theory to see whether it does *not* fit the facts of a cognitively accessible external social or natural world. Thus he shares with the logical positivists the epistemological commitment that empirical data are the final arbiter of the veracity of theory – albeit in terms of empirical refutation through contradiction of hypothetical predictions.

Here it is evident that Popper's notion of falsity or non-correspondence can only be conceptualized through reference to what is taken to be true or corresponding. In this Popper proposes that the truth of a theory, in terms of its correspondence with the facts, is a regulative ideal in which

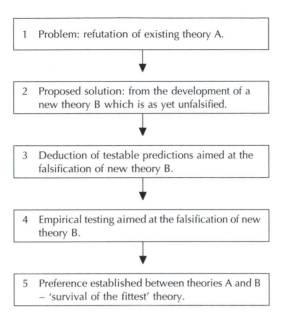

1 Problem: refutation of existing theory A.

2 Proposed solution: from the development of a new theory B which is as yet unfalsified.

3 Deduction of testable predictions aimed at the falsification of new theory B.

4 Empirical testing aimed at the falsification of new theory B.

5 Preference established between theories A and B – 'survival of the fittest' theory.

Figure 2.1 Popper's epistemological Darwinism

science through conjecture and refutation gets closer and closer to the truth. However we can never know if science has achieved such correspondence since no amount of empirical testing can ever provide such certainty. In other words, truth in the correspondence sense exists but we have no criteria for knowing when we have achieved it. In reflecting upon the contribution made by *The Logic of Scientific Discovery* Popper observed that

> we can never justify a theory. But we can sometimes 'justify' . . . our preference
> for a theory, considering the state of the critical debate; for a theory may stand
> up to criticism better than its competitors . . . This itself I linked with the ideal
> of a better and better approximation to truth, or of increasing truthlikeness or
> verisimilitude. According to this view, finding theories which are better
> approximations to truth is what the scientist aims at . . . This involves the
> growth of the content of our theories, the growth of our knowledge of the
> world. (1976: 149–50)

Popper (1962: 216–18) argues that scientists are not unbiased, neutral individuals; on the contrary, they can be highly prejudiced defenders of (especially their own) particular theories. However he also claims that the 'critical attitude' built into the norms of the scientific method militate against individual prejudice as it sanctions the freedom to propose and criticize theory and, most importantly, demands that theory be expressed in a testable form. In principle this allows disputes to be resolved, and prejudice eradicated, through recourse to the impersonal arbitration of replicable 'public experience'. This implies the availability of a neutral observational language as well as invoking Merton's (1938–70) scientific ethos (see Chapter 1).

It follows that, despite his ambiguous denials, Popper's falsificationism still depends upon the possibility of a neutral observational language which allows an appeal to an independent point of reference constituted by the facts of an external social or natural world (see: Giddens, 1976: 140–1; Mulkay, 1979: 54). In other words, Popper's position amounts to a non-inductive form of empiricism where experience is the judge of truth through indicating whether a theory does not fit the facts. As Lessnoff concludes:

> for Popper social reality is an objective fact, a description of it is true if and only if it corresponds to the reality, and scientific consensus, at any moment, may in principle be true or false (though, given human fallibility, it is unlikely to be completely true). (1974: 165)

Meanwhile, although Popper conceded that the subject matter of the social sciences differs from that of the natural sciences this is only with regard to an aspect of causality. In the social sciences causality is always contingent whereas in the natural sciences it is invariable. Indeed he was concerned to preserve the methodological unity of natural and social sciences – this he attempted by dismissing any criticism of the application of natural science methodology to the social sciences by arguing that such criticisms were based upon 'some very common misunderstandings of the methods of physics' (1961: 2). However what is unclear is whether Popper's elaboration of the hypothetico-deductive method is a description of, or a prescription for, scientific practice. If it is a description this obviously raises questions as to whether it is accurate and to whether scientific practices actually follow his critically rational scientific ethos – a point which we will take up when in Chapter 4 we will consider the work of Kuhn. On the other hand, if it is a prescription, what are the implications for currently accepted theory whose basis is not embedded in the deployment of his critical attitude?

In sum, Popper's epistemology can be seen as a significant critique of some aspects of logical positivism. Indeed he effectively demolishes verificationism by pointing to the contradictions between empiricism and induction. However this is a critique which does not abandon central features of a logical positivist legacy nor does it imply the elaboration of a postpositivist position. If anything, Popper's work maintains and revitalizes certain key logical positivist commitments: the possibility of a theory-neutral observational language; a modified correspondence theory of truth; a sceptical anti-metaphysics; the methodological unity of the sciences; and the utility of science for enabling human intervention into the social and natural worlds. If one accepts that such commitments are manifest in his work, then Popper's own claim to be logical positivism's assassin can be refuted.

While it might be harsh to dismiss Popper as 'just a tiny puff of hot air in the positivist teacup' (Feyerabend, 1987: 282) it is also evident that any proclamation of the demise of positivism based upon Popper's thesis is premature. Moreover it is also evident that elements of positivist epistemology also influence those who have overtly challenged what they take to be positivism. Here we are primarily referring to a fairly disparate group who are united by their attacks upon logical positivism's methodological monism and who try to re-establish human subjectivity as a legitimate domain for scientific work. Below we will consider the main thrust of these arguments and evaluate the extent to which they entail a fundamental break with, or a reformulation of, positivist epistemology.

The re-emergence of subjectivity and a break with positivism?

As we have shown above, a key element of positivism is the exclusion of the metaphysical from what is taken to be warranted knowledge. This is a key theme which can be traced from the pre-Enlightenment philosophers through to the logical positivists of the twentieth century. While this theme originated in demands to liberate science from the constraints of theological dogmatism, it was interpreted by logical positivists as excluding from the domain of legitimate scientific activity the intangible, and the subjective or abstract, precisely because they were assumed to be empirically unobservable.

Here it is important to note that positivism's rejection of the metaphysical immediately runs into trouble because it is self-contradictory. It rejects as meaningless the abstract, metaphysical knowledge of subject–object relationships on which any epistemology, including positivism's own, is ultimately grounded. As Hindess points out (1977: 135), positivism thereby contradicts itself since it excludes from its conceptualization of warranted knowledge its own grounds for warranted knowledge. Due to circularity that is inevitable in any epistemology (see Chapter 1) it would appear that since positivism cannot account for itself on its own terms, it becomes indefensible in its own terms and is in danger of slipping into the very dogmatism its epistemology was originally aimed at destroying.

It follows that positivism is on shaky grounds where it dismisses the metaphysical as nonsense since it simultaneously relies upon metaphysical knowledge to establish a neutral observational language. However attacks upon positivism over the issue of metaphysics tend to ignore this internal contradiction and instead have mainly focused upon the possibility of science in an area it includes in the category 'metaphysical' – namely the role of human subjectivity in explaining human behaviour. A key theme of such supposed 'anti-positivism' is an attempt at (re-)establishing human subjectivity as a legitimate domain for social scientific endeavour and thereby (re-)establishing a discontinuity between the natural and social sciences. This is illustrated by Laing (1967) who points out the error of blindly following the approach of the natural sciences in the study of the social world:

> the error fundamentally is the failure to realise that there is an ontological discontinuity between human beings and it-beings . . . Persons are distinguished from things in that persons experience the world, whereas things behave in the world. (Laing, *ibid.*: 53)

Here Laing draws attention to how human action has an internal logic of its own which must be understood in order to make it intelligible. The rightful aim of social science is to understand this internal logic – a process called '*verstehen*' (see Box 2.9).

Box 2.9

Verstehen: the interpretative *understanding* of the meaning a set of actions has to an actor through some form of contact with how they experience their experience.
Erklaren: the *explanation* of behaviour by providing a deterministic account of the external causal variables which brought about the behaviour in question through the observation of the empirically discernible features and antecedent conditions of that behaviour.

Because the subject matters of the natural sciences do not have subjective capacities, the natural scientist can quite legitimately impose an *a priori* external logic upon its behaviour in order to explain it – a process called '*erklaren*'. But the social world cannot be understood by excluding the subjective basis of action. It follows that social science research must entail analyses of human action generated inductively from an *a posteriori* understanding of the interpretations deployed (i.e. cultures) by the actors who are being studied.

These anti-positivist claims have a very practical significance for researchers since they demand an inductive approach to gathering data about the constellations of norms beliefs and values (i.e. cultures) that influence actors' sense-making activities and thereby legitimate and explain the particular courses of social action they adopt. For instance, Hammersley and Atkinson (1995) argue that ethnographic fieldwork shares these inductive commitments. As such, ethnographers' explanations of observed behaviour usually remain at the level of *a posteriori* 'thick description' (Denzin, 1978; Geertz, 1973) of actors' interpretative procedures which goes beyond the 'reporting of an act (thin description) but describes the intentions, motives, meanings, contexts, situations, and circumstances of action' (Denzin, *ibid.*: 39). In this, theorization is limited to the inductive generation of a descriptive conceptual framework of, or grounded in (see Glaser and Strauss, 1967), actors' interpretative procedures.

However acceptance of the significance and scientific legitimacy of human subjectivity in explaining human action does not necessarily entail the rejection of other logical positivist commitments. Despite their evident differences, the interpretative anti-positivism outlined above shares what we previously described as a fundamental tenet of positivism – the grounding of warranted knowledge in observation. Although each disputes what may be scientifically observable, they share the tacit assumption that there exists a neutral observational language in which the researcher is construed as a neutral conduit of sense-data who can objectively elucidate and present the 'facts' of a cognitively accessible empirical world and/or the dimensions of actors' subjectivity. As Knights has observed, interpretative approaches 'who claim a distance from positivistic beliefs' are often 'representational' in that they 'rest on a privileging of the consciousness of the researcher who is deemed capable of discovering the "truth" about the world' (1992: 515). In other words, the observers' registered observations are epistemologically privileged as they are construed as being independent of the processes of the observer observing. Therefore it is claimed that 'truth' is to be found in the observers' passive sensory registration of the facts that constitute external reality through the application of a neutral observational language. Thus the veracity of accounts may be adjudicated through reference to their *correspondence* with the facts of a cognitively accessible external social world.

The picture of science which emerges – of getting access to some form of reality and being able to (re)present that data neutrally – is little different from traditional modes of positivism as it shares what Rorty has called a 'mirror metaphor'. For Rorty (1979: 46) a correspondence theory of truth inevitably relies upon the received wisdom that the facts of an external objective social reality can be 'mirrored' in the 'glassy essence' of the observer. This mirror metaphor construes the relationship between the researcher and their area of interest in terms of an epistemic dualism – that by deploying the appropriate methodological rigour it is possible to acquire knowledge that is independent of the observer and is uncontaminated by the act of observation or knowing. In positivism this would be construed as a subject–object dualism – a differentiation of the knower-researcher from the known-observed. In a supposedly anti-positivist interpretative approach this same dualism would be combined with a subject-subject dualism – a differentiation of the knower-researcher from their descriptions of what other knowers know. Both dualisms entail the assumption that there is a mirror inside the mind of the researcher that can be methodologically polished so as to allow their mind's eye to gaze upon accurate reflections of an external, independent, social world.

Such issues are especially problematic for interpretivists' reputedly anti-positivist commitment to accessing members' interpreted worlds so as to reveal their subjectivities. For Hammersley (1992) it creates a contradiction between an objectivist impulse that emphasizes how such interpretative accounts should correspond with members' subjectivity and an interpretative impulse that suggests that people socially construct versions of reality – culturally derived epistemic processes to which researchers are not immune. Acceptance of a lack of immunity justifies the view that the interpretivist claim to be able to 'bracket' assumptions (for example, Sharrock and Anderson, 1986) and 'become the phenomenon' (for example, Mehan and Wood, 1975) are merely rhetorical devices that create the impression of objectivity. In other words, 'the notion of interpretation . . . is used in the research process, but not "turned back" onto the researchers/theorists themselves' (Chia, 1996a: 132). This impression management avoids the issue of how social scientists' accounts of members' socially constructed worlds are not the product of 'the immaculate perception' (Van Maanen, 1988) but are themselves socially constructed interpretations – a point which we shall take up in Chapter 4 where we consider conventionalist epistemology.

Indeed, as Habermas points out in his analysis of positivism, the subliminal positivist basis of this ostensibly interpretative work may well have performed the 'prohibitive function' of protecting any ensuing discourse from 'epistemological self-reflection' (1972: 67). Its positivist vestiges serve to silence epistemological debate and protect them from epistemological reflexivity. Just like logical positivism, this supposed anti-positivism expresses an epistemological objectivism, the key difference being with regard to the role of actors' interpretative processes, not the researchers'. The interpretations of the former are understood as being cognitively accessible while the latter's impacts are ignored by the tacit deployment of epistemic dualism(s). So, far from wistfully celebrating positivism's wake, many of the publicly avowed anti-positivists may have merely sublimated their own positivist commitments, given positivism a new interpretative identity and thereby reinvigorated it.

Conclusions

In this chapter we have reviewed the historical development of the main tenets of positivist epistemology. We have also outlined two key attacks upon logical positivism – that of Karl Popper and that of the ostensibly anti-positivist interpretative approach. Perhaps each provides a cautionary tale which illustrates the difficulty of eschewing all the epistemological commitments of positivism – even when you think you are attacking it (see Table 2.1). It is evident that logical positivism may be modified by falsificationism, or by an interpretative attack upon methodological monism through a disputation of what is usually taken to be unobservable by the positivist mainstream. Nevertheless, the commitment to a neutral observational language and a correspondence theory of truth have remained remarkably unscathed by these attacks. If one agrees that these empiricist commitments are the epistemological glue that sustains logical

Table 2.1   Three positivist approaches compared

	Logical positivism	Popperian	Interpretative
Epistemic commitments			
Neutral observational language	Yes	Yes	Yes
Correspondence theory of truth	Yes	Yes	Yes
Inductive verification of theory	Yes	No	Yes
Deductive falsification of theory	No	Yes	No
Practical utility of theory	Yes	Yes	Yes
Unity of natural and social science methodology	Yes	Yes	No

positivism and both its Popperian and interpretative critics, then positivism still remains a significant influence in the social and natural sciences. Indeed, conceived in this way, most reported and published research in the social sciences remains rooted in positivist epistemological commitments. In the case of the management disciplines this hegemony is all the more evident – as we shall illustrate in Chapter 3. However it is also important to realize that it is precisely this epistemological glue that binds the different versions of positivism which has been the focus of attack by conventionalists, postmodernists, critical theorists and critical realists – the subjects of Chapters 4, 5, 6 and 7 respectively.

Further reading

For an engaging and most thorough introduction to philosophy which, except for the logical positivists and Popper, covers many of the key epistemological contributions, the reader should turn to Jostein Gaarder's *Sophie's World* (1995). Bertrand Russell's *History of Western Philosophy* (1946) similarly provides a clear exposition of the main currents in epistemology up to its time of writing along with a cogent analysis of their social and economic contexts. Alternatively Bryan Magee's *The Great Philosophers* (1987) is an accessible introduction to philosophy. The most rigorous and accessible account of logical positivism is still Peter Halfpenny's *Positivism and Sociology* (1982). While Popper has helpfully summarized his thesis in his autobiography *Unended Quest* (1976), the main thrust of his critique of logical positivism may be found in *The Logic of Scientific Discovery* (1959). A useful overview of Popper's work is Bryan Magee's *Popper* (1985).

3
Positivism – The Management Mainstream?

> though the mode of thought expressed by the terms positive and positivism is widely spread, the words themselves are, as usual, better known through the enemies of that mode of thinking than through its friends.
>
> (John Stuart Mill, 1865 (quoted in Kilduff and Mehra, 1997: 453))

In the last chapter we illustrated the development of positivist epistemology and its main tenets. Our task now is to examine how those principles have been put into practice in the field of management research. Interestingly, if one searches management journals the word 'positivism' is used infrequently, and when it is used it is often by those wishing to disparage, reject or distance themselves from that philosophical mode. This is not because management researchers are strangers to positivist approaches. Just because researchers are not calling themselves 'positivist' does not mean that they are not adopting positivist assumptions (Kolakowski, 1972). On the contrary, a quick scan of the majority of management journals, particularly those from the USA, provides clear examples of positivist assumptions. However, it also becomes evident that many of those adopting a positivist approach do so without discussing their rationale – reflecting, perhaps, that the dominance of this perspective is such that it is ingrained into common-sense assumptions about how to do research. Rather more surprisingly, as we will show, even some of those who claim to reject positivism have not necessarily eschewed all elements of a positivist approach.

Whilst we argue that positivism has achieved some dominance, it is important to remember that management is not in any sense a unified field (Tinker and Lowe, 1982; Whitley, 1984a). The practice of management is eclectic and pragmatic, with managers drawing on knowledge from a variety of different fields ranging from sociology and anthropology to statistics and mathematics (Easterby Smith et al., 1992). Mirroring this, the study of management has been approached from a variety of different disciplines, each having their own traditions and approaches. The use of an increasingly standardized, positivist approach towards conducting management research has been suggested as one way of overcoming this fragmentation (Pfeffer, 1995).

Table 3.1 Central tenets of positivism in management research

Aim of research	
Generation of causal laws	The aim of research should be to identify causal explanations and fundamental laws that explain regularities in human social behaviour.
Research approach	
Unity of natural and social science method	The method of the natural sciences is the only rational source of knowledge and should therefore be adopted in the social sciences. This implies preoccupations with: • internal validity; • external validity; • reliability; • operationalization.
Relationship of researcher with researched	
Independence theory and neutral observational language	The observer is independent of what is being observed. Therefore the observer can stand back and observe the world objectively.
Value freedom	The choice of what is to be studied, and how to study it, can be determined by objective criteria rather than by human beliefs and interests.
Correspondence theory of truth	Theory can be tested against irreducible statements of observation – the 'facts' of the situation. Research is concerned with producing accounts that correspond to an independent reality.

It is also evident, however, that whilst in certain sub-disciplines philosophical and epistemological issues have come more into the spotlight, particularly with the development of critical and postmodernist approaches towards management studies, in many others we rarely see philosophers cited or explicit links to philosophical issues noted (Zald, 1996). Thus there remains a distance from philosophical analysis, even though researchers often use terms that have a strong philosophical tradition, for example 'rationality' and 'utility'. Hence, rather than a well-thought-out positivist stance, management research is criticized for adopting a 'naïve and unreflecting empiricism which expects to explain everyday phenomena in such a way that underlying productive mechanisms can be identified' (Whitley, 1984b: 387) and where commonsense accounts are taken as unproblematic.

As we have shown in the previous chapter, there are a number of different approaches towards positivism, indeed Halfpenny (1982) identified 12 such perspectives. Following on from the previous chapter, we have represented positivism as a set of assumptions concerning the aims of research, the appropriate research methods and the relationship between the researcher and the researched (see Table 3.1).

In this chapter we will focus on each of these three core issues in order to understand the implications of positivism for management research. First we will examine the aims of research from this perspective and consider the debate in management research over the need for relevance. We will then address the implications of positivism for doing management research, focusing on the methods which are utilized and the rationales for using them. We then move on to assess the underlying assumptions concerning the role of the actors in the research process. We will explore the ways in which the researchers and the researched (managers and other organizational actors) are construed in a positivist approach towards management. One of our aims in this chapter is to challenge the assumption that a positivist approach equates with the use of quantitative methods and that therefore those adopting qualitative methods are necessarily anti-positivist. Hence we will argue that the relationship between epistemology and method should not be reduced to a simplistic 'quantitative versus qualitative' debate (Bryman, 1993; Hammersley, 1992; Hartley, 1994) and we will explore the ways in which positivism can be seen to imbue both quantitative and qualitative methods in the social sciences in general and management research in particular.

The aims of positivist research

From a positivistic perspective the aim of research in the field of management is to generate laws which govern the ways in which organizations operate. The generation of these causal relationships or laws will enable management to become more scientific and managers to become better able to predict and control their environments. The focus is on the observable and the approach to the analysis of organizations assumes that their reality is objectively given, functionally necessary and politically neutral (Willmott, 1992; 1997). Determinism prevails, with human behaviour often reduced to the product of external forces of the environment. Thus, social interactions are to be studied in the same way as physical elements – as a network of causal relations linking aspects of behaviour to context and stimuli in the external environment thus conditioning people to behave in a certain way. This is perhaps seen most clearly in the work of Lex Donaldson who, when discussing management strategy, argues that

> a fully positivist approach would not presume to call the approach strategic management but would rather call it corporate development. It would seek to ascertain the laws that cover corporate development, that is the laws that explain changes in corporate size, diversification, geographic extensiveness, innovation and so on. Attention would be paid to material factors as explanatory variables . . . The search would be for parsimonious models utilising as few variables as possible with the variables being of an objective kind. Subjective variables, including strategies would be included to fill in unexplained variance.
> (1997: 87)

Thus from this perspective individuals' sense-making processes are either ignored, as they are unobservable and therefore cannot be validly researched, or they are considered as mediating variables when there is a need to explain why a particular causal relationship did not bring about the expected result.

As we discussed in the previous chapter, positivism can be differentiated from empiricism, however, in its concern to test theory against empirical observation. Hence, while research from this perspective is concerned with observational statements, this is not the totality of its concern as there is also an attempt

> to connect observations with theoretical statements constructed in rational non-observational concepts in an isomorphism of theory and observation. This isomorphism is achieved in terms of laws and theories which have been interpreted by abstractive connection to empirical events for at least some of their relevant scope. (Clegg and Dunkerley, 1980: 261).

As we discussed in the previous chapter, empiricism, on the other hand, is concerned with empirical generalizations or causal connections through the observation of empirical association. This raises a very important point, though, as it has been argued that management research has tended towards empiricism and that theory has played a marginal role in much management research (Clegg and Dunkerley, 1980; Whitley, 1984b).

The concern to develop causal propositions supported by data and logic (Davis, 1985) underpins an emphasis on experimental and cross-sectional survey research designs. From this perspective, empirical research is of utmost importance. Theories are accepted or rejected on the basis of their correspondence with the facts seen in the objective world. Hence we see attempts to study particular phenomena rigorously in order to be sure that we are getting to the truth against which we can then develop propositions and test out hypotheses. This attempt to get to the truth involves the development of sophisticated, replicable data collection techniques and careful attention to sampling to ensure that we can develop generalizable propositions that give insight or have predictive powers (Pugh, 1983).

A number of management research textbooks (for example, Bryman, 1992; Easterby Smith et al., 1992) focus on the Aston Studies as an exemplar of positivistic research (although Clegg and Dunkerley (1980) suggest that it is more of an example of empiricism). This was a programme of research which identified the basic dimensions of organizational structure and examined which factors were important in influencing the structure and functioning of organizations (see Pugh and Hickson, 1976; Pugh and Hinings, 1976).

In a later work, Pugh calls himself an 'unreconstructed positivist' (1983) when he discusses the five assumptions underpinning the general research strategy of the Aston Studies:

1 The need for comparative studies to distinguish problems specific to particular organizations from those common to all organizations.
2 Meaningful comparisons require common standards for measurement.
3 The nature of an organization will be influenced by its objectives and environments so these must be taken into account.
4 Study of the work behaviour of individuals or groups should be related to the study of the characteristics of organizations in which the behaviour occurs.
5 Studies of organizational processes of stability and change should be undertaken in relation to a framework of significant variables and relationships established through comparative study. (Pugh, 1983: 50)

Thus central to the Aston approach, and the contingency approach towards organizations in general, was a desire to standardize measurement in order that organizations could be compared along objective lines and to identify what aspects of an organization's context caused or influenced aspects of its structure.

From this section then we can begin to see some of the central features of positivist management research which will be returned to later in the chapter. One interesting issue for researchers, however, is the question of relevance. As we will discuss below, the positivist search for tight causal links tested under experimental conditions has been questioned by a number of management researchers in terms of how well the findings can be translated into management practice. This concern is not necessarily new in the social sciences; for example over 40 years ago Blau (1955) argued that the quantification which is required to support generalizations has often produced an artificial atomism of the social structures under investigation. However it is clearly an issue for those management researchers who believe in a close link between theory and practice.

The relevance of positivistic management research to management practice

I don't want to be interesting I want to be good.

(Van der Roche, quoted in Kilduff and Mehra, 1997)

A major criticism of positivist management research is that there has been a neglect of the need for relevance (Bharadwaj, 1998; Schon, 1995; Van Maanen, 1995a). Schon uses the metaphor of the high ground and the swamp. He suggests that much management research sits on the high ground where manageable problems lend themselves to solution through the use of research-based theory and technique. In the swampy lowlands (which he suggests equates with management practice) problems are messy and confusing and incapable of technical solution. He argues that the problems of the high ground, on the other hand, are unimportant to society and individuals (1995). Van Maanen goes a step further, commenting that 'our generalisations often display a mind numbing banality and an inexplicable readiness to reduce the field to a set of unexamined, turgid, hypothetical thrusts' (1995a: 139). Similarly, Di Maggio discusses the problem concerning views of theory in management involving the search for covering laws which he argues relies on a view of scientific progress as a kind of 'r^2 sweepstakes' (1995). This relies on an image of a world in which variables explain one another – all parts of the perspective that Abbott (1988) has derided as ordinary linear reality. The end point of this approach, according to Di Maggio, can be seen in the work of a small group of economists who admit they don't care if their assumptions are implausible so long as their r^2s are high! The extent to which this view ignores the work of certain fields which have been very useful to management is shown in Box 3.1.

Box 3.1 Relevant positivistic management research

A valid criticism?

Hogan and Sinclair dispute the criticism that positivist management research lacks relevance, commenting that:

> Industrial psychologists have, as organizational consultants, advocated a general method that involves identifying the requirements of a job (i.e. description), identification of a set of characteristics that enable an individual to meet those requirements (i.e. explanation) and development of methods of selection to identify individuals with desired amounts of those characteristics (i.e. prediction). These methods are rational, theoretically derived, and depend on replicable and generalizable empirical validation to determine whether or not they work. If poor choices are made, poor results are obtained. Although these methods are imperfect, organizations that utilize the basic process hire people with less adverse impact than they did 30 years ago – while simultaneously advancing understanding of the theoretical domain of job performance. This process is not simply the effective utilization of prediction technology; the technology is founded on certain theoretical notions concerning the nature of human performance. (1996: 439)

Notwithstanding the work of writers like Hogan and Sinclair (1996), a common critique of positivistic management research is that, in searching to identify causal relationships, the focus has become narrower and narrower, to the extent that propositions being tested do not reflect the complex situations in which managers actually find themselves. While trying to generate theories which enable prediction and control, the result can be propositions which apply in such a narrow band of circumstances that they bear little relation to everyday managerial work. The problem here is that in order to have validity, any theory of management has to take account of the context in which management is practised. Hence we have seen a move towards more interpretative methods of inquiry.

Research methodology

> we are conditioned by our scientific training to associate progress with
> far greater rigour, greater precision, disintegrative analysis, more empiri-
> cal documentation of a phenomenon and the progressive exorcism of
> value laden questions in favour of a purer pursuit of 'truth' that is a
> closer and closer fitting of our theories to the one objective reality we
> presume exists.

> (Mitroff and Pondy, 1978: 145–6)

Positivist approaches towards management research are generally associated with quantitative methods. Whilst there is an increased acceptance of
qualitative methods, the popularity of quantitative approaches in management research should not be underestimated. Blau and Scott (1963)
represent the views of many more recent academics when they argued that
in order for knowledge of organizational phenomena to be expanded,
researchers should collect quantitative data from large-scale studies rather
than individual cases. The prevalence of this view was supported by Daft
(1980) who found that between 1959 and 1980 there was an almost
two-fold increase in the number of quantitative papers accepted by
Administrative Science Quarterly. The continued dominance of quantitative
approaches in different aspects of management research has also been
commented upon by a number of authors (see, for example, Brownell and
Trotman, 1988; Eilon, 1980; Hirschman, 1986), with writers such as
Meyer bemoaning its dominance, commenting that 'we live in orgies of
counting . . . Actors come in secure categories of varying specificity but all
standardised: persons, workers, assemblers, labour per hour' (1986: 347).
Similarly Brown (1993: 28) discusses how the low and disreputable status
of marketing has provided an incentive for academics in this area to prove
marketing research 'more scientific than science'. However while these
authors are arguing for a more interpretative approach, others are arguing
that what is actually needed is a more sophisticated approach towards
rigorous quantitative research (Marsh, 1979; Pfeffer, 1995).

Therefore while on one hand it is suggested that there has been an
emphasis on approaches perceived to be more scientific, others complain
that there is too wide a diversity of approach towards research methodology. For example, Pfeffer claims that organizational science has suffered
from insufficient paradigm development as a result of theoretical and
methodological diversity. He suggests that in order for this to occur there
is a need for consensus (over method) and technical certainty. Holding up
economics as an exemplar, Pfeffer (1995: 614) argues that in order to
progress, management research needs to develop consensus through the
enforcement of theoretical and methodological conformity.

Pfeffer's call for conformity has been responded to by Jon Van Maanen
who sees this step as retrograde, and a vehement debate has ensued

between the two (see Pfeffer, 1993; Pfeffer, 1995; Van Maanen, 1995b). This illustrates vividly the very different perspectives on management research. An interesting point here relates to the subtlety of the language used in research and how this underpins particular ways of working. For example Van Maanen, in his critique of Pfeffer, insists on using his first name, talking about 'Jeff's approach'. While this may seem trivial, it does seem to make the critique far more personal and also highlights how traditional academic conventions have developed which remove the researcher as a person from the presentation of our research.

While debate rages between these two established academics, it appears that positivism (or at least elements of it) retains its dominant status. Central to this is an assumption that the methods of the natural sciences offer the way forward in understanding the workings of organizations.

Unity of social science and natural science method

We display more than a little physics envy when we reach for covering laws, causes, operational definitions, testable hypotheses and so forth.

(Van Maanen, 1995b: 134)

The desire to replicate the methods of the natural sciences in the social sciences leads to a focus upon the observable, following the assumption that all constructs used to explain the world ought to be tied directly and rather tightly to what can be observed (Slife and Williams, 1995). Hence the human beings under study in the social sciences are viewed in a similar way to animals or inanimate objects that may be the focus of natural science study. Objectivity is generally equated with quantification (Downey and Ireland, 1979). Hence the focus of research from a positivist perspective is upon that which can easily be measured and, as discussed earlier, subjective aspects of a phenomenon are either ignored or considered to be mediating variables which explain any unexpected variance. In this section we will examine the link between epistemology and method. We begin with a consideration of experimental research design and surveys as these are most commonly cited as positivistic and illustrate most closely the link between social and natural science methods.

The impact of the methods of the natural sciences upon the social sciences can be seen most clearly in the idealization of the experimental method in some areas of management research. Experimental methods provide the clearest possibility of establishing cause–effect relationships. The main aim of experimental designs is to maximize what Campbell calls internal validity (1957). See Box 3.2 for a definition, although, as will be discussed later, this is often at the expense of external validity.

Box 3.2 **Evaluating research**

> Internal validity: Whether or not what has been identified as the cause actually produces the effect.
>
> External validity: The extent to which the research findings can be extrapolated beyond the immediate research sample.
>
> Reliability: The consistency of results obtained in research. Whether another researcher could replicate the original research or the same researcher could replicate the original research at a different time.

Classical experimental design involves the formation of an experimental and a control group. Subjects are generally randomly assigned to each[1] and the assumption is made that all extraneous variables are thus randomized throughout the two groups. Conditions for the experimenter group are then manipulated by the experimenter in order to assess their effect in comparison with members of the control group. The combination of random assignment and the use of a control group means that experiments have a high internal validity. However the control that is afforded by laboratory experiments is purchased at the price of generalizability and relevance. Aronson and Carlsmith (1986) have distinguished two senses in which laboratory experiments may lack realism which inhibits their generalizability:

1 Experimental realism – in this sense an experiment is realistic if the situation which it presents to the subject is realistic.
2 Mundane realism – subjects encounter events in the laboratory setting which are likely to occur in the real world.

Other issues which impact upon the success of laboratory experiments are that subjects know they are in experimental situations and are being observed (so that their response will be impacted upon by the experimental manipulation) and that their interpretation of what the impact of the manipulation is supposed to be will influence their behaviour.

Field experiments blur the distinction between the laboratory and the real world. Therefore they increase the possibility of generalization – in other words external validity. Examples of true field experiments in management research are rare though as it is obviously difficult for the researcher to have ultimate control over the situation. The classic study of the Hawthorne works of the Western General Electric Company is often put forward as an exemplar. This study highlighted one particular difficulty of conducting field experiments: the impact of being researched. These studies, investigating changes in length of working day, heating, lighting, and other variables, found increases in productivity during the study which were virtually irrespective of the specific changes. Workers were responding to the attention given by the experimenters, since labelled the 'Hawthorne Effect' (see Roethlisberger and Dickson (1939) for a detailed exposition of the Hawthorne Studies).

An alternative approach has been developed by Campbell and Stanley (1963). They advocate quasi-experimentation as a valuable approach to the development and analysis of studies in field settings. Quasi-experiments share the same ideals about scientific research as true experimentation. Hypotheses are tested and cause and effect investigated. The focus of quasi-experiments is upon naturally occurring events outside the laboratory. For example, in work organizations this may occur when change is being introduced to one business unit within a company and not another. Hence subjects cannot be randomly or systematically assigned to experimental or control groups. Thus, where the randomized assignment is used in true experiments to control for an infinite number of 'rival hypotheses', in quasi-experimentation each rival hypothesis has to be specified and specifically controlled for (Robson, 1993). For a more in-depth discussion of field experiments and quasi-experimentation see Gill and Johnson (1997), Chapters 4 and 5.

The commitment towards experimental method remains in areas of management research. In particular, researchers who have come from a social psychological background are more likely to operate field experiments and hence their use is most often seen in sub-disciplines such as organizational behaviour (see, for example, Luthans et al., 1985; Martinko et al., 1989; Orpen, 1979). It is particularly popular in areas such as team development and job design (see, for example, Cohen and Bailey, 1997; Cohen and Ledgford, 1994; Van den Bulte and Moenart, 1998; Ward, 1997). The derivation of this approach from the natural sciences means that in all attempts at experiments the aim is to establish a cause–effect relationship. The role of the researcher is as detached controller and observer, examining the impact of the stimuli on effect. The researcher's values and emotions are generally not discussed or, if they are, only in the sense of how these biases can be eliminated. This maintains the impression or possibility of a theory-neutral observational language and is also seen in the other commonly quoted positivistic approach towards management research – the survey.

Surveys place emphasis upon cross-sectional analyses, using standardized measures to compare across situations. They entail the collection of data on a number of respondents or units, usually at a single juncture in time. The aim is generally to collect systematically a body of quantifiable data in respect of a number of variables which can then be examined to discern patterns of association (Bryman, 1992: 104).

Although surveys generally supply correlations and not causations, this has not deterred survey researchers who have developed a wide variety of procedures for elucidating causality by means of a *post hoc* reconstruction of 'the logic of causal order' (Davis, 1985) that lies behind the cluster of variables generated by a particular investigation. Thus in order to establish causal relations from cross-sectional analyses, the following are required:

1   There must be a relationship (established, for example, using chi^2 correlation coefficients) which holds in various situations under varying conditions.
2   The relationship must be non-spurious. In other words, the relationship seen between two variables is not being caused by a third variable.
3   A temporal order must be established to the assembly of the variables in question. This could be seen as the most controversial aspect as most survey designs involve collecting data at one point in time; thus the establishment of temporal order requires a degree of intuition or common sense. (Bryman, 1993; Bulmer, 1984)

Marsh argues that much of the criticism of survey research as positivistic actually has little to do with assessing the epistemological basis of survey research and is often of a practical, technical nature or raises problems which concern all kinds of data collection in the social sciences (1979: 294). Hence it is clear that in trying to understand and evaluate different approaches to research we need to explore the epistemology underlying them and distinguish that from critique concerning how well a particular method has been applied.

It is beyond the scope of this book to engage in lengthy debate on the pros and cons of survey methodology or experimental method. The majority of management research textbooks provide discussions of these (see, for example, Bryman, 1993; Easterby Smith et al., 1992; Robson, 1993). Our focus instead is on the way in which these methods are idealized in management research because they are thought to reflect the methods utilized by natural scientists. Thus the next section examines some of the preoccupations of positivist management research and argues that these derive from a (misconceived) notion of the process of research in natural sciences.

Positivist preoccupations about conducting research

Causality or internal validity

The first preoccupation of positivist management research relates to causality or internal validity. As discussed earlier, this is concerned with the extent to which we can be sure that an independent variable causes a particular outcome (dependent variable). Cook and Campbell provide a list of threats to internal validity which might be posed by other extraneous variables, and which have to be overcome if researchers are aiming to prove that what they have identified as the cause is really impacting upon the effect. These are illustrated in Box 3.3.

Box 3.3 Threats to internal validity

1 *History*. Things that have changed in the participants' environments other than those forming a major part of the inquiry (e.g. occurrence of major air disaster during the study of effectiveness of desensitization programme of persons with fear of air travel).

2 *Testing*. Changes occurring as a result of practice and experience gained by participants on any pre-tests (e.g. asking opinions about factory farming of animals before some intervention may lead respondents to think about the issues and develop more negative attitudes).

3 *Instrumentation*. Some aspect(s) of the way participants are measured changes between pre-test and post-test (e.g. raters in observational study using a wider or narrower definition of particular behaviour as they get familiar with a situation).

4 *Regression*. If participants are chosen because they are unusual or atypical (e.g. high scorers), later testing will tend to give less unusual scores ('regression to the mean'); for example an intervention programme with pupils with learning difficulties where the ten highest-scoring pupils in a special unit are matched with ten of the lowest-scoring pupils in a mainstream school – regression effects will tend to show the former performing relatively worse on a subsequent test.

5 *Mortality*. Participants dropping out of the study (e.g. in a study of adult literacy programme – selective drop-out of those who are making little progress).

6 *Maturation*. Growth, change or development in participants unrelated to the treatment in the inquiry (e.g. evaluating extended athletics training programme with teenagers – intervening changes in height, weight and general maturity).

7 *Selection*. Initial differences between groups prior to involvement in the inquiry (e.g. through use of arbitrary non-random rule to produce two groups: ensures they differ in one respect which may correlate with others).

8 *Selection by maturation interaction*. Predisposition of groups to grow apart, or together if initially different (e.g. the use of a group of boys and girls initially matched in physical strength in a study of a fitness programme).

9 *Ambiguity about causal direction*. Does A cause B or B cause A? (e.g. in any correlational study, unless it is known that A precedes B or *vice versa* or some other logical analysis is possible).

10 *Diffusion of treatments*. When one group learns information or otherwise inadvertently receives aspects of a treatment intended only for a second group (e.g. in a quasi-experimental study of two classes in the same school).

11 *Compensatory equalization of treatments*. If one group receives 'special' treatment there will be organizational and other pressures for a control group to receive it (e.g. nurses in a hospital study may improve the treatment of a control group on the ground of fairness).

12 *Compensatory rivalry*. As above but an effect on the participants themselves (referred to as the 'John Henry effect' after the steel worker who killed himself through over-exertion to prove his superiority to the new steam drill); for example when a group in an organization sees itself as under threat from a planned change in another part of the organization and improves performance. (Cook and Campbell, 1979: 51–5 (quoted in Robson, 1993: 70–1). For a critique of this approach towards validity see Hammersley (1991))

The desire to maximize internal validity and provide tight causal links suggests an increasingly controlled environment. Whilst this may be the aim of researchers, more common is the use of survey methodologies. The extent to which these can be used to imply causation has been open to considerable question; for example the contingency approach to organizational design has been extensively criticized in this respect (Child, 1977; Miller and Friesen, 1984; Schoonhoven, 1981).

Reliability and replication

> Positivist notions of reliability assume an underlying universe where inquiry could, quite logically be replicated. This assumption of an unchanging social world is in direct contrast to the qualitative/ interpretative assumption that the social world is always changing and the concept of replication is itself problematic.
>
> (Marshall and Rossman, 1989: 147)

Regardless of whether one agrees with Marshall and Rossman that the world is in a state of constant flux, reliability is a key issue for those of a positivist persuasion. Essentially, reliability is concerned with the consistency of results obtained in research. Kirk and Miller differentiate between three different types of reliability: see Box 3.4.

Box 3.4   Different approaches to reliability

Quixotic reliability: the circumstances in which a single method of observation continually yields an unvarying measurement.

Diachronic reliability: the stability of an observation through time.

Synchronic reliability: the similarity of observation about the same time period. (Kirk and Miller, 1986: 41–2)

The concept of reliability thus impacts upon the extent to which we can be sure that what we have identified as 'cause' actually impacts upon 'effect' because reliability essentially enables us to be sure about the efficacy of our measures. Unless a measure is reliable it cannot be valid (Schriesheim et al., 1993).

Four threats to reliability can be identified (Robson, 1993): subject error; subject bias; observer error and observer bias. Positivists give much attention to reducing these in order to get to the 'truth'. Hence many research texts focus on the need to develop objective measures of organizational phenomena. There is an assumption that bias is a problem because of both poor researchers and poor respondents. Thus we hear about the inability of ten per cent of the adult population to fill out 'even simple questionnaires' (Selltiz et al., quoted in Silverman, 1993: 107).

The implication is that researchers should improve both the sophistication of the measures used and the ways in which they are applied. In particular, attention must be given to the standardization of measures in order to ensure that they can be replicated.

The replication of established findings is seen as one way of eliminating bias and ensuring reliability. This is given great credence in the management research literature. However sometimes there is a gulf between what is preached and what is practised. Podsakoff and Dalton (1987) analysed the content of journal articles from 1985 versions of *Academy of Management Journal*, *Journal of Management*, *Administrative Science Quarterly*, *Journal of Applied Psychology* and *Organisational Behaviour and Human Performance* and found that only around two-thirds of the empirical research reported reliability coefficients. They join other critics in calling for a more rigorous and well-documented approach towards replication, although, as will be discussed later, the extent to which replication is undertaken in the natural sciences is questionable.

Generalizability

As discussed earlier, one of the aims of positivist research is to generate causal laws which have predictive powers. Obviously, generalizability is fundamental to this. Quantitative methods, and in particular surveys, are considered superior to qualitative approaches in this respect due to the naturalistic settings and limited number of cases utilized in qualitative research.

Nevertheless the aim for generalizability in both experimental and survey research is problematic. Surveys are often carried out in a limited area and at one point in time and, as was noted earlier, experiments often require taking people out of their everyday contexts and thus impacting upon their behaviour. Le Compte and Goetz have highlighted the threats to external validity, as shown in Box 3.5 below.

Box 3.5   Threats to external validity

- Selection: Findings being specific to the group studied.
- Setting: Findings being specific to, or dependent on, the particular context in which the study took place.
- History: Specific and unique historical issues may determine or affect the findings.
- Construct effects: The particular constructs studied may be specific to the group studied. (Le Compte and Goetz, 1982, quoted in Robson, 1993: 73)

In order to try to overcome these threats in both experimental and survey research, a great deal of emphasis has been placed on probability sampling. The main aim here is to construct a sub-set of the population which is fully representative of the population from which it is drawn. It is then possible to infer statistically the likelihood that a pattern seen in the sample will be replicated in the population. A variety of probability sampling methods are available (for a detailed discussion of sampling see Baker, 1988: 146–56). However even when a probability sample has been achieved (which is very difficult, given the need for opportunism in gaining access for management research) this is often within a localized population which may impact on the extent of generalizability of the research findings. For example the extent to which Goldthorpe et al.'s 'Affluent Worker' studies (1968) could be generalized beyond the Luton area (where the studies were undertaken) has been debated (Clegg and Dunkerley, 1980). Thus the problem of generalizability remains a key issue for positivist management research.

Operationalism

> to do any research we must be able to measure the concepts we wish to study.
>
> (Kidder and Judd, 1986: 40)

Empirical observation is central to the traditional scientific method. However many of the constructs under study are not easily observed, for example motivation. Therefore researchers rely on observing things which are taken to represent those constructs. This process of letting something we can observe represent something we cannot observe is called 'operationalizing'. It is the reduction of concepts into indicators. The process of operationalization ideally involves gaining access to what Moser and Kalton (Marsh, 1979) call the 'individual true value' of concepts which methods measure with a greater or lesser degree of precision. Thus there is an obligation in research to specify what concepts mean and precisely how they will be measured.

Clegg and Dunkerley (1980) show how operationalizing organizations by using measurement and scaling techniques has the result of objectifying them because operational definition assumes

> that empirical categories can best be defined by the operations used to observe the experiences to be included in the categories. The purpose of operational procedures is to structure these operations so that different results can be assigned numerical values. When a succession of similar objects with each different result is assigned a different numerical scale, the aggregate of all of those possible values is called a scale. The scale in turn is supposed to represent a concept. (Willer and Willer, quoted in Clegg and Dunkerley, 1980: 258)

Hence any concept is reduced to a scale of observable indicators.

In discussions of translating concepts into observable entities most authors refer to the work of Lazarsfeld (1958). Lazarsfeld's scheme for measuring concepts involves four key steps: imagery, concept specification, selection of indicators and formation of indices. Bryman (1993) provides examples from the Aston research programme to illustrate each of these steps. He also demonstrates how the rigorous practices associated with Lazarsfeld's approach are far less widespread than might be imagined from the number of times he is referred to. Thus Marsh (1979) argues that the problem is not about converting complex and rich reality into variables; it is the crudity with which we generally measure concepts, owing to the even greater crudity with which many concepts are theorized. So, whilst for some the response to the crudity of quantification is to move towards qualitative research, for others it is to develop ever more sophisticated tools and techniques.

The validity of measurements is an important issue in operationalization. In this sense validity is concerned with the extent to which the measurement provides an accurate reflection of the concept. One way in which this can be assessed is to compare operationalizations of the same concept. For example, Sharfman and Dean (1991) compare the works of a variety of authors who have studied organizational environments. It is clear that authors have used a similar characterization of the concept's dimensions but a different approach towards operationalizing those dimensions, for example some focusing on perceptual measures and others on objective. Perhaps unsurprisingly, the studies then found different results concerning the relationship between environment and organization. This raises difficult issues concerning the validity of measures as, if we assume that there is an objective reality to be measured, then we would expect researchers, provided that they are using appropriate measures, to gather the same findings. Similarly, in reworkings of the Aston studies, where the measurements of both the Aston group and other approaches towards structure were combined, there was a disappointing level of agreement (Pennings, 1973). Hence there remains a search for variables which accurately reflect the objective reality assumed to exist outside the interpretations of onlookers – equating to Moser and Kalton's (1971) 'individual true value'.

Hence the quality of measurement in management research has been a concern for many management academics (see, for example, Schriesheim et al., 1993; Schwab, 1980; Simons and Thompson, 1998) and it has been argued that in general the attention paid to measurement adequacy has been no more than lip service (Schoenfeldt, 1984). There has also been expressed the concern that some academics focus too much on measurement and buy into the fallacy of misplaced precision which consists of believing that one can compensate for theoretical weakness by methodological strength. Thus Coser (1975: 296) suggests that too many researchers find themselves in the same situation as St Augustine when he wrote on the concept of time: 'For so it is O Lord, My God, I measure it but what it is I measure I do not know'.

The focus on measurement, reliability, generalizability and validity can be traced to a particular view of the way in which research is undertaken in the natural sciences. Whitley reviews the writings of a number of authors, critiquing their view that science is essentially a method of producing and validating knowledge which can be applied to management in a straightforward way (1984b: 370). A related issue concerns the extent to which the model of the natural sciences which is being followed actually operates in research in this arena. Our own involvement in a research project examining the ways in which scientists work in publicly funded research laboratories[2] (see Cohen et al., 1999a; 1999b for details) and the work of others (Mitroff, 1980; Mulkay and Gilbert, 1986) suggests this is not the case. For example Chalmers (in Robson, 1993: 58) argues that:

1 ultimately there is no fully proven scientific knowledge;
2 there is no foolproof or automatic method for deriving scientific theories from the 'facts' of experience;
3 science is not just based on what we can see, hear etc.;
4 the person of the scientist and her or his opinions, prejudices etc. loom large in science;
5 objectivity can not be guaranteed.

As we will discuss later in this chapter, a number of issues, such as publishing conventions and career structures, encourage natural scientists to present their work in a certain way with no discussion of the vagaries, ambiguities and subjective side of their work. Hence the practice of their research may differ dramatically from how they report it. Manicas (1987) notes this and raises a paradox that while

> the practices of physical scientists bear little resemblance to the dominant philosophy of science, it is no exaggeration to say that in consequence of their relatively late beginning as sciences the practices of mainstream social sciences have long since been constituted by it. (1987: 242–3)

Hammersley (1992) also questions which natural science we are using as a basis and during which period of its development, arguing that there are significant differences between different sciences and within each over time. In responding to this, Donaldson (1996: 55) suggests that Newtonian physics is the best model for organization theory. However his justification for this, that inquiries into management and organizations parallel studies of falling bodies more than they do the physics of black holes, is somewhat opaque!

In this section we have considered the preoccupation with causality, reliability, generalizability and operationalism. Underpinning these is a set of assumptions concerning the relationship between the researcher and the researched. It is to this that we will turn now. It is important to note, however, that whilst the emphasis of this section has been upon surveys and experiments as closest to the scientific ideal and most often used from a positivist perspective, this does not mean that they cannot be used from a more interpretative stance. Some surveys in particular focus upon how people make sense of their situation rather than the observable (for example, Goldthorpe et al., 1968) and in the field of social psychology there has been a great deal of research focusing on meanings using quantitative techniques. Where positivistic tendencies remain, these are often with regard to assumptions about the relationship between the researcher and the researched and the possibility of a theory-neutral observational language.

The relationship between the researcher and the researched

In this section we move on to address the underlying assumptions of a positivist approach towards management research with regard to the status of management and the role of the researcher in examining that concept.

The status of the subject under study – positivist assumptions about the role and functions of management

As discussed previously, positivist studies of management and organizations tend to focus on the observable. For example, positivist analyses of organizational structure change study macroscopic observed variables of an objective kind. This could be argued to negate the role of management and hence stand in contrast to strategic choice perspectives (Child, 1972). However Donaldson does not see these as incompatible. Instead he argues that choices are intervening factors 'in that they are caused by the material factors that compose the situation . . . choice and determinism are compatible in that the choices made by human actors are shaped and predetermined by situational imperatives' (1997: 80). This determinism can also be seen in the Aston studies and other contingency studies. In some respects the Aston researchers recognize that by focusing on the formal they do not get a picture of actual practice in the organizations, suggesting that they consider 'what is officially expected should be done and what is in practice allowed to be done; it does not include what is actually done; that is what really happens in the sense of behaviour beyond that instituted in (formal) organizational forms' (Pugh and Hickson, 1976: 69). This clearly raises questions over the level of determinism.

Studies such as these suggest that managers face an objective reality to which they themselves need only apply suitable methods for assessing in order to come up with the correct solution to organizational issues. It has been argued that this penchant for method reduces management to 'a bag of tools, technologies, analytical techniques and applied instruments' (Stillman, quoted in Miller and King, 1998: 44). Thus we see the underlying presumption that management itself can be scientific – a value-free activity, with the claim of management expertise being 'composed within the old hymn of value neutral competence' (*ibid.*: 46). Hammer and Champy (1993) provide an illustration of this when they discuss the value-free nature of business process re-engineering in that it 'begins with no assumptions and no givens' (quoted in Alvesson and Willmott, 1996: 46). In addition business process re-engineering, in common with a number of other technicist approaches to management, ignores the political aspect of organizations, utilizing a naively mechanistic conception of organizations and politics (Grint and Willcocks, 1995; Knights and McCabe, 1998).

The assumption underpinning business process re-engineering and a variety of other management prescriptions, that management can be conceptualized in a technical way, creates an illusion of neutrality (Alvesson and Willmott, 1996: 12) and has brought about a situation where insufficient attention is paid to ethical or moral issues in management (Anthony, 1977; MacIntyre, 1981). Hence while Donaldson (1996) discusses the need for effectiveness, there is no consideration of the question: effective for whom? Instead it is assumed that the environment or other contingencies will drive managers towards making the right, rational, business-oriented choices. Reed criticizes the Aston studies for adopting a similar line, arguing that 'it is guilty of assuming a transcultural, context free bias in favour of an ahistorical atemporal and value free commitment to organisations as the primary institutional carriers of a means–ends rationality' (Reed, 1992: 138). Similarly Child (1984), amongst others, has criticized the neglect of political issues in much contingency theory and other positivistic management research.

Thus there is a tendency to adopt a unitarist and functionalist approach. Managers are seen as rational technicians, dealing with technical issues which are resolvable through the application of superior knowledge. They are assumed to be neutral in their decisions which are aimed at achieving greater organizational effectiveness.

The role of the researcher

> through the denial of feelings, imagination and the human spirit, concealed assumptions, rigid, sterile and inappropriate methods of inquiry and the enlargement of trivia into problems of consequence, we, you and I preserve our employment prospects to the detriment of our souls, our fellow men and society.
>
> (Pym, 1993: 234)

The relationship between subject and researcher is an indicator of ontological and epistemological assumptions on which a given study is based.

Even the use of terms such as 'subject' suggests a particular view of those taking part in the research process. Thus the spectrum of researcher involvement can serve as an 'epistemic barometer' (Olson, 1995: 3).

The belief that science can produce objective knowledge rests on two key assumptions: first the ontological assumption that there is an objective reality 'out there' to be known and secondly that it is possible to remove all subjective bias in the assessment of that reality. These assumptions relate to the correspondence theory of truth which states that theory can be tested against irreducible statements of observation – the 'facts of the situation'. The aim of research is to produce accounts which correspond to this independent reality. Thus Donaldson (1996: 164) notes that 'The main antidote to fanciful theorizing is empirical testing'. The extent to which this assumption is inherent in our 'common sense' views of the world can be illustrated by comparing them to those of another culture. See Box 3.6 below which discusses the way the Wintu tribe perceives reality.

Box 3.6   A different perspective on reality

> Among the Wintu tribe there is a recurring attitude of humility and respect towards reality, toward nature and society . . . I cannot find an adequate term to apply to a habit of thought that is so alien to our culture. We are so aggressive towards reality. We say 'this is bread' . . . we do not say as do the Wintu 'I call this bread' or 'I feel' or 'I taste' or 'I see it to be bread' . . . The Wintu never say starkly 'this is'. (Lee, 1959: 129, quoted in Van Maanen, 1995b: 139)

The correspondence theory of truth can be seen to permeate a good deal of management research, with many researchers assuming that their data represent the truth about an objectively measured world. Kilduff and Mehra argue that such researchers 'rigorously exclude intuition or subjective experience from their research reports and signally distrust humour, irony and the paradoxical' (1997: 480), preferring instead the role of rational analyst.

In experimental and survey research the researcher remains a detached observer and, as discussed earlier, attempts are made to eliminate or at least minimize bias through the use of standardized tools for data collection and analysis and replication of the research. Thus the research is 'meticulously designed to put questions to "Nature Itself" in such a way that neither the questions, nor their colleagues, nor their superiors can affect the answer' (Campbell, 1969: 411). This detachment comes not just in the ways in which research is carried out but also from the assumption that the researcher is value-neutral when choosing what to study. Little consideration is given to political or emotional issues at either stage.

As discussed in the previous chapter, to assume that qualitative, inter-pretative research is necessarily anti-positivistic is flawed. Nevertheless, some researchers argue that the choice between quantitative and quali-tative methods represents a distinction between 'fundamentally different epistemological frameworks for conceptualising the nature of knowing social reality, and procedures for comprehending these phenomena' (Filstead, 1979: 45; Smith, 1984; 1989), for example, claims that the realist position underpinning quantitative research stands in direct con-trast to the idealist position underpinning qualitative research and that the two are incommensurable. Similarly Lacity and Janson (1994) discuss how researchers may hesitate to apply qualitative approaches because they equate qualitative research with non-positivist, anti-positivist or inter-pretativist research. That said, they go on to point out that many qualitative methods however are steeped in the positivist tradition (*ibid.*: 137) and categorize different approaches to text analysis as either posi-tivist, linguistic or interpretative, based on the underlying assumptions made about the data. These assumptions include:

1 the nature of the text data;
2 the relationship between the researcher and the text;
3 the prescribed method for understanding text data;
4 the evidence accepted to validate text interpretation.

Lacity and Janson suggest that a defining feature of positivistic text ana-lysis methods is that they presume that text material is 'isomorphic to a set of factors and that the reader can infer the meaning of text without interaction with the author or speaker' (1994: 142). Other differences between the three approaches are illustrated in Table 3.2 below.

Thus, as discussed earlier, the assumption in many research texts that positivism only applies to quantitative approaches to research is open to considerable question. We would agree with other researchers (for example, Martin, 1990b; Silverman, 1993) who argue that the dichotomy between quantitative and qualitative research is of limited use. Hammersley and Atkinson, for example, discuss how ethnography is often wedded to the notion of realism and thus whilst ethnographers might discuss how their subjects socially construct their realities, this constructivism is not applied to the ethnographic process itself: 'Once we come to see ethnographers as themselves constructing the social world through their interpretations of it there is a conflict with the naturalistic realism built into ethnographic methodology' (1995: 11). Often there is a failure to recognize that what is seen as real depends on current cultural codes as 'the most unapologetic realist styles foster an impression that ethnography is a clear unmediated record of a knowable world. It is washed by a thick spray of objectivity' (Van Maanen, 1995a: 7). Thus residual tensions remain in interpretative research between a subjectivist attentiveness to actors' meanings and an objectivist treatment of them as phenomena that exist out there independently of analysts' identification of them (Weiskopf and Willmott, 1996).

Table 3.2   Alternative approaches to textual analysis

	Positivist	Linguistic	Interpretative
Research method	Identification of non-random variation	Study language–reality relationship	Analyse the cultural influences of the writer or speaker and interpreter
Nature of text	Objective	Emergent	Subjective
Role of researcher	Outsider	Outsider	Insider
Validity checks	Quantitative	Primarily qualitative	Qualitative
Examples	Verbal protocol analysis Script analysis	Speech act analysis Discourse analysis	Hermeneutics Intentional analysis

(Adapted from Lacity and Janson, 1994: 153)

This approach has been criticized by those from a constructivist perspective who believe that there can be no 'pure' data as all data are mediated by our own reasoning as well as that of participants. Silverman (1993: 208) argues that 'to assume that naturally occurring data are unmediated details, is self evidently a fiction of the same kind as put about by survey researchers who argue that techniques and controls suffice to produce data which are not an artifact of the research setting'. Similar criticisms of ethnography come from Rosaldo (1986) who criticizes ethnographers for their unwarranted claims of objectivity and Denzin (1998) who complains that ethnographers maintain the scientific posturing of a more positivist style of research.

This is not to say that all ethnographers take such an objectivist stance. For example, Manning (1995) provides a comparison of three ethnographic studies and illustrates the different levels to which the authors reflect upon their own impact and interpretations. Similarly, in his illuminating account of management at ZTC Ryland, Watson (1994: 7) is clear that what he presents is his construction and that therefore it is important to 'reveal the hand behind the text. . . . I was no neutral fly on the wall in ZTC Ryland and I was not "collecting" attitudes and other data like a naturalist netting butterflies. Like any other social researcher I was influencing those I was researching'.

It becomes clear, then, that we should avoid falling into the trap of setting up quantitative and qualitative research as dichotomous, each underpinned by a particular epistemology. The picture seems somewhat more complex and requires recognition that quantitative versus qualitative does not capture the full range of options that we face and misrepresents the basis on which those decisions should be made instead: 'what is involved is not a crossroads where we go left or right. A better analogy is a complex maze where we are repeatedly faced with decisions and where paths wind back on one another' (Hammersley, 1992: 172).

Whether qualitative or quantitative methods are being utilized, management researches would do well to heed the words of Gouldner who has argued that in order for social science research to move forward there is a need for us to stop acting as if those who are studying (researchers) and those who are studied are two distinct breeds. He goes on to argue that organizational science is not 'a bundle of technical skills, it is a conception of how to live and a total praxis' (1976: 504).

Conclusions

When reviewing textbooks prescribing the conduct of management research and comparing this with practice, it becomes clear that there is often a mismatch between what is preached and what is practised. This is not just the case for management research. Even in the natural sciences the neat, linear way in which research is reported seems to reflect little of the confusion, complexity and shades of grey that permeate the research process (Van Maanen, 1995a, 1995b). However to be published, particularly in high-ranking American journals, it is argued that researchers have to follow a particular way of reporting which derives from a positivistic approach towards research.

This is not to suggest that it is purely in order to be published that researchers adhere to positivistic assumptions. Rather, some of these are ingrained in our common-sense understandings of research and thus often remain unchallenged. Unfortunately, much of what is considered positivistic management research may not actually represent positivism as it remains under-theorized and conceptually lacking, thus perhaps being better described as naïve empiricism. In future chapters we will examine the ways in which some management researchers have moved away from positivism (and empiricism) and have begun to challenge some of its fundamental tenets by examining conventionalist, postmodern and critical epistemologies.

This chapter may have focused largely on a critique of positivist management research. However, in defence of positivism, it is appropriate to consider its possible positive consequences for management research. For example, Bharadwaj (1998: 1) suggests that a salutary aspect of positivistic approach is that it has led to a focus on the 'need for good tools and methods that could safeguard against the fallibility of the human mind'. In a similar vein Marsh argues that many of the criticisms directed at positivism are actually criticisms of poor research and that therefore we must continue to search for more sophisticated statistical techniques to overcome current limitations (1979). Di Maggio also believes that the reductionism that is part and parcel of positivistic approaches is useful to a degree. He calls for 'strategic reduction' which involves abstracting away enough of the world's confusion and complexity to develop pointed explanations of organizational phenomena. However he admits that where one draws the line is still more art than science (1995).

Thus whilst the development of more interpretative, critical and post-modern approaches towards research have seriously injured positivism, we should pause before assuming that those injuries are fatal. Management researchers need to consider to what extent they have been unsuspectingly clinging to some of its central tenets with regard to assumptions concerning the relationship between themselves and the subject under study. Perhaps, in undertaking critical reflection, some researchers may agree with Behling who draws on Winston Churchill when he comments that the natural science model 'is the worst possible way to study organizations – except for all others' (1980: 489). Others, however, may seek to move towards alternative approaches which focus on the ways in which individuals construct their realities.

Further reading

Perhaps the most vocal exponent of positivism in management research is Lex Donaldson and readers may find it useful to look at his book, *For Positivist Organization Theory* (1996). Gill and Johnson's book, *Research Methods for Managers* (1997), considers in more depth the impact of some of these issues on research methodology. For an excellent overview of qualitative and quantitative approaches see Bryman (1993), *Quantity and Quality in Social Research*. Also, in his book *What's Wrong with Ethnography?* (1992), Hammersley attempts to deconstruct the quantitative–qualitative divide and posits a more complex view of the methodological and philosophical choices confronting the researcher. For a good review and critique of the Aston Studies see Clegg and Dunkerley (1980). Finally, the debate between Van Maanen and Pfeffer in *Organization Science* in 1995 is both entertaining and instructive, highlighting the different ways in which researchers from different traditions view management research.

Notes

1   There is debate about whether subjects should be randomly assigned or assigned according to particular characteristics in order to ensure the two groups are incomparable. Matching is considered inferior as it is impossible to know whether all variables have been covered. Some authorities (Kidder and Judd, 1986) refuse to accept studies as true experiments those studies where a matching approach has been used.
2   McAuley, J. and Duberley, J. (1995) 'Management in Scientific Establishments – How Scientists Construct this Reality'. ESRC grant reference R000221639.

4

Conventionalist Epistemology – The Socialization of Science?

A new scientific truth does not triumph by convincing its opponents and making them see the light, but rather because its opponents eventually die and a new generation grows up that is familiar with it.

(Max Planck, *Scientific Autobiography and Other Papers*, quoted in Kuhn, 1970a: 151)

As we have illustrated in Chapters 2 and 3, the different versions of positivism are united by the epistemological principle that warranted knowledge about the world emanates from the scientist's ability directly and objectively to access empirical data about that social and natural reality. So although positivists might disagree about what is observable and contest issues around the possibility of induction and verification, they are united by the view that warranted knowledge is that which has a correspondence with reality which has been established by the scientist's neutral and passive registration of various sensory inputs. Here it is assumed that, as in Wittgenstein's picture theory of language (1922), language reflects reality: the structure of reality provides the structure of language just as a picture provides an organized system of representation of what it portrays.

Most of the epistemological alternatives to positivism are most easily understood as developments of distinctive critiques of certain aspects of positivism's epistemological commitments – even where their philosophical history pre-dates the full elaboration of positivism during the nineteenth and twentieth centuries. With the first alternative, conventionalism, it is the possibility of a theory-neutral observational language and its consequent eradication of the role of *scientists'* subjective interpretation in the acquisition of warranted knowledge (see Box 4.1) which are undermined. This is accomplished by replacing positivism's passive conception of the scientist's apprehension of reality with that of the scientist as an active social agent conducting a value-laden enterprise in a particular historical context.

The aim of this chapter is to delineate the nature of conventionalism, initially through reference to the work of Immanuel Kant and Thomas Kuhn. We will then explore how this conventionalist position has been

Box 4.1

Keat and Urry (1982: 60–1) draw upon Kolakowski (1972) to characterize conventionalism in terms of three related elements:

1　Scientific statements are not seen as true or false descriptions of some external reality, but rather as creations of the scientist which are taken to be true.
2　The acceptability of a scientific statement is not the product of the application by scientists of some universally valid criteria or set of 'objective' standards of evaluation. Rather, such acceptability is construed by conventionalists as the product of the scientist's 'subjective' apprehension of reality which is usually derived from, or indeed determined by, the socially sanctioned *conventions* that dominate the scientific communities to which they belong.
3　The truth or falsity of statements is 'underdetermined' by their observations of empirical data – observation cannot provide objective control over scientific statements because a theory-neutral observational language is not available.

applied in the various management disciplines. Here we review the work of particular scholars such as Gibson Burrell and Gareth Morgan (1979). The latter demonstrates how different sets of *a priori* assumptions have been organized into distinctive modes of engagement which influence what 'we see' – whether 'we' are engaging in management research or management practice. Having considered Burrell and Morgan's focus upon the role of paradigms in knowledge production, we will then review Morgan's later work (for example, 1986) which emphasizes the role of metaphors in generating 'images' of management and organization.

Throughout, several key conventionalist themes arise directly from Keat and Urry's definition given in Box 4.1. As we have already indicated, important amongst these is the conventionalist view that we are active participants in the processes of perception. Although what we see as 'out there' appears to be independent from us, conventionalists argue that we are not passive receivers of external stimuli and data, as many empiricists assume. Instead they point to how our conventionally based and socially sanctioned modes of engagement are projected on to, and impose a logic and order on, what we 'see'. In effect we participate in creating what we experience as independent from, and external to, ourselves. Here a significant difference is only too evident between conventionalist critiques of positivism and the interpretative modifications of logical positivism reviewed in Chapters 2 and 3. The rhetorical force of the interpretative position largely depends upon their own agreement with a logical positivist account of natural science. This endorsement serves to legitimate their own account of social science which is grounded in how the methodological unity of the sciences cannot be sustained because of fundamental differences in their subject matters. In contrast, the conventionalist critique is concerned with the objectivist conception of science that underpins all forms of positivism. Unlike interpretivists, conventionalists dismiss the positivists' search for an overarching set of standards that genuinely specify objectivity as obsessive and futile. For the conventionalist, social and natural reality are not 'things' outside the discourse of science but are to varying degrees constructed by science itself.

In the natural sciences such conventionalist concerns have been expressed by Heisenberg's 'uncertainty principle' (1958) – that it is impossible to study something without that influencing what is seen. This has led Gribbin, for instance, to argue that 'the electron is created by our process of experimental probing . . . no elementary phenomenon is a phenomenon until it is a recorded phenomenon' (1985: 210). So what a scientist observes is not independent of the process of observing but is an outcome of the scientist's methodological interaction with, and conceptual constitution of, their objects of knowledge. A classical statement of this view is provided by Ludwik Flek's aptly named work 'Genesis and Development of a Scientific Fact' (1935–79). Flek argued that during inquiry scientists construct not only their accounts of the empirical facts but also the facts themselves. So for Flek and other conventionalists every scientific fact is the product of the collective thinking of a community united by a 'thought style', therefore every scientific fact is a social fact. Likewise other conventionalists, such as Duhem (1962) and Poincare (1952), reject a key positivist epistemological commitment – the possibility of a theory-neutral observational language. However rather than dismissing scientific theories because they referred to a cognitively contaminated or even inaccessible reality, Duhem and Poincare saw such knowledge as being negotiable fictions whose retention and revision depended on their coherence, elegance, simplicity and utility rather than their fundamental (i.e. correspondence) truth.

So for conventionalists the role of language changes from the younger Wittgenstein's 'picture' theory, which defended the possibility of a universal scientific language, to that of the older Wittgenstein's theory based upon 'forms of life'. In the latter theory Wittgenstein (1958) demonstrated how, far from reflecting reality, language shapes or socially constructs reality. This shift effectively demolishes any claims to objectivity since our renditions of reality are located in language itself rather than anything independent of it. Scientists' 'representations' of reality are thus the product of 'language games' through which they construct their realities by deploying their particular game's concepts and theories. For Hanson (1958: 8) this meant that 'there is more to seeing than meets the eyeball' – there cannot be any neutral foundation for science located in the passive registration of sensory inputs since the scientist's language-in-use, their theories and hypotheses influence what will be observed *before* any observations are made – a thesis which in effect socializes science and which was subsequently highly influential upon Thomas Kuhn.

Immanuel Kant

The themes in conventionalist epistemology outlined above can be related to aspects of Immanuel Kant's undermining of empiricism in his work *Critique of Pure Reason* which was first published in 1781. Here Kant distanced himself from naive empiricist epistemology by arguing that our minds are not passive receivers of sense-data. Rather we automatically select, limit, organize and interpret our experience of external reality. We endow the world with meaning, and not *vice versa* as the empiricists claimed. Kant tried to show how our knowledge always contained components deriving from ourselves prior to any experience. Although the categories, concepts and meanings we use seem to originate in what we take to be the external world, Kant claimed that they naturally derive from our innate *a priori* (i.e. prior to experience) cognitive structures. Hence Kant rejects the Cartesian dualism – that it was possible for the mind neutrally to access and contemplate the objects of external reality. Instead, for Kant, the so-called external world is a construction of the mind working on our sensory inputs. Any separation between the knower (i.e. the subject) and what is known (the object), as proposed by a Cartesian dualism and accepted by all forms of positivism, is undermined by Kant.

For Kant, we cannot have direct knowledge of reality: things-in-themselves, which he called '*noumena*', are by definition unperceivable and therefore unknowable. Hence Kant's view is a type of *phenomenalism* in two respects: first in that this noumenal reality exists independently of human cognition, since a condition of our consciousness is that there must be something out there to be conscious about, and secondly in that Kant claimed that the *a priori* contents of the human mind anticipated and organized every sensory experience. Because our experience is therefore always shaped or mediated by our mental structures (e.g. space, time and causal necessity), we can only know this external world through those cognitive structures. Hence all we can have is knowledge of how the world appears in our consciousness via the filtration and order imposed by our *a priori* mental forms – which are themselves independent of reality itself. Kant called these *a priori* mental forms *transcendentals* – factors that are always present in any system or discipline. He called the resultant thought objects '*phenomena*'. In other words, things-in-themselves aren't knowable in themselves but only as phenomena – things-for-us.

So for Kant 'pure reason' entailed rationalist claims to knowledge beyond knowable phenomena. Hence his 'critique of pure reason' on the one hand delimited scientific knowledge to knowledge of phenomena, while on the other hand it critiqued the rationalist's movement beyond those limits. However some rationalist elements were retained in Kant's perspective which lead him to argue that while the action of our mental *a priori* forms structure our perceptions of reality, these innate grounds of experience were also accessible to us. Through rational reflection we can *know* what the *a priori* grounds of experience are and understand *how* we organize our sensory inputs. As we will show, this Kantian emphasis upon rational reflection, or reflexivity, that entails us thinking about our own thinking, is a key theme of conventionalist management scholars and is expressed in their search for how knowledge is variably constituted according to the paradigm and metaphor deployed.

However because we cannot engage with the noumenal world without some deployment of *a priori* forms it follows that despite our rational reflexive capacities we are still stuck in a phenomenal world from which there is no escape. Hence Kant believed that scientific knowledge was knowledge of phenomena created out of our sensitivity and understanding – the action of the structures of our minds upon an ultimately unknowable noumenal reality. Thus the aim of philosophy was to explain how

> subjective conditions of thought can have objective validity, that is, can furnish conditions of possibility of all knowledge of objects. (Kant, quoted in Callinicos, 1983: 12)

Kant's views raise two important sets of questions with regard to conventionalism.

First, where do Kant's cognitive structures come from? Are they a fixed property shared by, and innate to all, people (i.e. anthropological); or do they derive from the different social contexts in which we live and thereby vary according to history and culture? With regard to this question, many conventionalists emphasize a social derivation. They accept that we are trapped within a *'hermeneutic circle'* – that we always engage with the world via our socialized pre-understandings. There is no escape from these processes, hence there is no observation free from the observer's interpretation based upon presuppositions that derive from their initiation into the 'know how' of a particular socio-historical culture.

Secondly, if all knowledge is phenomenal, how can we ever be certain that a cognitively independent reality exists? After all, if Kant's noumenal world can only be postulated in thought itself – what are the grounds for thinking that such metaphysical entities exist? Indeed how can we know that our cognitive structures merely *mediate* and shape an independent reality? Surely from a Kantian perspective there are no epistemological grounds for asserting that anything exists beyond thought itself? It follows that our cognitive structures actually *create* conceptually dependent realities – figments of our imagination which we externalize and thereby accord the status of reality. With regard to this question we shall demonstrate how it has bedeviled conventionalism with its proponents, such as Kuhn and Morgan, oscillating between reality mediation and reality creation. In reality mediation a realist ontology is retained whereas in reality creation a subjectivist ontology is adopted (see Box 4.2 below).

In a nutshell, like Kant, conventionalists argue that *any observer*, implicitly or explicitly, influences what is observed. An observer's prior

Box 4.2

Ontology is derived from the Greek words 'ontos' (being) and 'logos' (theory or knowledge). It is a branch of metaphysics dealing with the essence of phenomena and the nature of their existence. Hence to consider the onto-logical status of something is to ask whether it is real or illusory. Here we are primarily concerned with the ontological status of social and natural reality.

A *realist ontology* assumes that social and natural reality exist inde-pendently of our cognitive structures: an extra-mental reality exists whether or not human beings can actually gain cognitive access to it. In other words, Kant's noumenal reality exists.

A *subjectivist ontology* assumes that what we take to be external social and natural reality is merely a creation of our consciousness and cognitions: reality is a projection of our cognitive structures with no independent status. In other words, the existence of Kant's noumenal world is rejected – all that exists is the phenomenal world.

beliefs, sentiments, theories, background knowledge and expectations mould what they assume to be 'out there'. Any conclusions about external reality cannot be separated from the cognitive, social and emotional pro-cesses that have led them to those conclusions in which language is regarded as a vehicle for creating rather than reflecting reality. Because the acquisition of warranted knowledge cannot be based upon empiricist claims as to how things 'out there' really are, the role of the observer's inevitably subjective interpretation of experience becomes a central epi-stemological concern to conventionalists. But of equal importance are the issues raised by conventionalism about ontology, or more precisely the ontological status of social and natural reality.

When conventionalists deny the possibility of a theory-neutral obser-vational language, a common inference is that what we often assume to be an external reality is actually a *product* of our use of conventionally sanc-tioned concepts and language etc. Although it is by no means inevitable, this inference can lead to the implicit and explicit adoption of a subjec-tivist ontology and the consequent eradication of any independent check upon knowledge claims – the relativistic implications of which will be considered later in this chapter (see Box 4.4 for a definition of relativism).

For conventionalists, what we routinely and for them naively assume to be an independent external social and natural reality is a variable human artefact – it is not something which can be discovered through the exercise of our sense-making faculties. Indeed the positivist's questions about how to generate or test theories through accessing reality are replaced by questions about why and how particular versions of reality have arisen or have changed. Indeed

instead of being glued to objects, terms and their concepts are glued together into a solid structure and they lack any constraints in their terms of reference. Instead of theory-neutral observation, we have observation neutral-theory:

instead of truth as a simple 'mirroring' of reality, it becomes a matter of convention. Change in knowledge can then only be an all or nothing affair, the replacement of one rigid structure by another. (Sayer, 1992: 75)

The underpinnings and implications of this epistemological orientation for the management disciplines are best illustrated in the work of the most accessible of its exemplars – Thomas Kuhn. As we shall illustrate, Kuhn also confronts one of the most significant problems of a conventionalist position – the relativism Sayer alludes to above.

Kuhn's thesis

In 1962 Thomas Kuhn, who had begun his career as a physicist, published a book entitled *The Structure of Scientific Revolutions*. This book and its enlarged second edition (1970a) caused a storm of controversy which still persists today. Besides the continuing confusion caused by Kuhn's own ambiguities, the controversy arose because Kuhn's thesis used historical examples to demonstrate how, in practice, science proceeds neither inductively, through verification, nor deductively, through falsification. From these observations Kuhn developed a theory of science which presented a devastating anti-empiricist critique of positivism's key epistemological commitments and what amounted to a conventionalist alternative to Popper's reformulation of positivism.

Central to Kuhn's thesis is the concept 'paradigm' which derives from the Greek word '*paradeigma*' which means a pattern, model or plan. His use of this concept, particularly in the 1962 edition, is at times both equivocal and confusing since he uses it in at least 22 different senses (see Masterman, 1970). Nevertheless it is evident that by the term 'paradigm' he is referring to a set of beliefs, values, assumptions and techniques, centred around successive exemplars of successful practical application. A paradigm serves as a regulative framework of metaphysical assumptions 'shared by members of a given community' (Kuhn, 1970a: 175) which specifies the character of the world and its constituent objects and processes and which acts as a 'disciplinary matrix' by drawing the boundaries for what the community's work is to look like. As such, paradigms are 'universally recognized scientific achievements that for a time provide model problems and solutions to a community of practitioners' (Kuhn, 1970a: viii). Each 'practitioner community' is characterized by a consensus, into which neophytes are socialized through their disciplinary training. This consensus is grounded in a tradition that bases their work around a shared way of thinking and working within an established network of ideas, theories and methods. Each paradigm therefore has its own distinctive language which offers a unique means of classifying and construing the objects encountered during scientists' engagements with

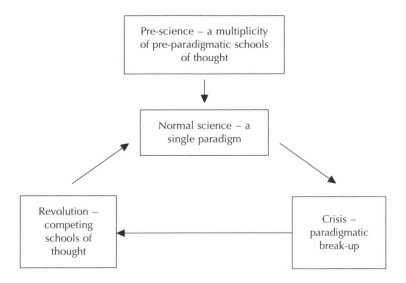

Figure 4.1   Kuhn's view of scientific development

the world. In order fully to explicate the epistemological implications of Kuhn's thesis it is now necessary to outline his approach to a central issue for all conventionalists – how he understood paradigm development and change (see Figure 4.1).

For Kuhn the early stages of the development of a science are characterized by diversity in that there is no universally accepted set of theoretical and methodological commitments organized into a received paradigm. Various competing pre-paradigmatic schools of thought disagree over basic methodological and theoretical assumptions while interpreting the same areas of interest in divergent ways. None of these pre-scientific schools of thought as yet constitutes a paradigm since no single school is prepotent and thereby dominant (see Kuhn, 1977: 295). For instance in ancient Greece some astronomers saw the earth as a stationary sphere at the centre of a larger rotating sphere which carried the stars, while some Egyptian astronomers thought that the earth was shaped like a plate, with water beneath and a dome of sky above. Eventually one school of thought becomes dominant and drives out its rivals which gradually disappear. In astronomy it was Aristotle's views, systematically refined and mathematically organized by Ptolemy in the second century A.D., which emerged as the triumphant paradigm (Kuhn, 1957). This located a spherical earth at the centre of an incorruptible and unchanging universe and placed the planets and stars on transparent crystalline spheres rotating about the earth. When such a single paradigm becomes accepted by a scientific group, what Kuhn calls 'pre-science' ends and 'normal science' can begin. So once the governance of a single former school is established it then acts as a paradigm and allows the following to happen:

1   the basics of the paradigm are expressed in textbooks and scientists
     can take them for granted by no longer having to justify the use of
     major concepts;
2   the paradigm sets standards for, and defines, legitimate scientific work;
3   the paradigm supplies a conceptual framework, within which normal
     science can be developed, which forces 'nature into a preformed and
     relatively inflexible box' (Kuhn, 1970a: 24);
4   the paradigm guides research in a purposeful manner by directing
     scientists' 'puzzle-solving' activities through the establishment of
     criteria for choosing problems 'that, while the paradigm is taken for
     granted, can be assumed to have solutions' (*ibid.*: 37).

Kuhn (1957: 45–85; 1970a: 25–34) identifies three types of problem
which are investigated during the 'mopping-up' operations of normal
science. First there is the determination of significant facts. For instance,
with the acceptance of Aristotle's two-sphere cosmology, scientists
observed the movements of heavenly bodies and placed the location of
the planets' orbits between the Earth and the stars. Secondly there is the
matching of facts with theory. For instance, within the two-sphere
cosmology, the orbits of the planets should preserve the Earth-centred
circular motion observed in the stars. However observation did not
confirm this expected symmetry; rather it showed irregularities in the
motions of the planets. Far from taking this as evidence which would cast
doubt upon their basic cosmology, usually astronomers instead tried to
explain away these unexpected observations – at least until Copernicus.
Thirdly, there is the articulation of theory. For instance, the geocentric
view of the cosmos is supported by Aristotle's theory of motion which
stated that without the intervention of external force, Earth, the heaviest
element, would move naturally towards the centre of the universe.

So for Kuhn, because of action of their paradigmatic framework during
normal science, scientists assume that they will be able to find solutions to
what their paradigm defines as acceptable problems. In this the scientist is

> a solver of puzzles, not a tester of paradigms . . . he is like the chess player who,
> with a problem stated and the board physically or mentally before him, tries out
> various alternative moves in the search for a solution. These trial attempts,
> whether by the chess player or by the scientist, are trials only of themselves, not
> the rules of the game. They are possible only as long as the paradigm itself is
> taken for granted. (Kuhn, 1970a: 37)

However such puzzle-solving precludes investigation of those problems
which cannot be allowed, nor expressed, by the 'rules of the game'. For
example Aristotelian cosmology saw the universe, by definition, as
unchanging. Hence the appearance of comets or new stars posed severe
problems but these problems were not investigated because they could
not be expressed in terms of the 'rules of the game'. Instead such problems were rationalized away as being 'metaphysical, as the concern of

another discipline, or sometimes just as too problematic to be worth the time' (1970a: 37).

So while normal science persists, research is constrained by the boundaries of the paradigm. However these boundaries are not necessarily always fixed, especially when scientists eventually become aware that the results of observation do not conform to what should be expected. Where such 'anomalies' persist, they are sometimes set aside and left for better-equipped future researchers to deal with, or they are explained away as being the result of incompetence. But some anomalies resist these tactics and have to be explored. Here the scientist will initially follow normal paradigmatic rules – but if this puzzle-solving is unsuccessful in explaining the anomaly then some aspects of the paradigm itself may be reviewed and its conceptual categories adjusted so that the paradigm can anticipate and explain the anomaly. This leads to what Kuhn calls 'extraordinary research' which stretches the rules of normal science and entails philosophical introspection which makes the rules of the paradigm more explicit. However some anomalies cannot be accommodated or ignored – they come 'to seem more than just another puzzle of normal science' (Kuhn, 1970a: 82). For instance Copernicus in his *De Revolutionibus Orbium* argued that the Aristotelian–Ptolemiac framework was unable to resolve fundamental problems. He described one particular failure that led him to reject it and develop an alternative: 'The mathematicians are so unsure of the movements of the sun and the moon that they cannot even explain or observe the constant length of the seasonal year' (quoted in Kuhn, 1957: 137). Copernicus claimed that his new heliocentric cosmology solved the problem of the length of the calendar year. For Kuhn the problems caused by such significant and persistent anomalies can result in a crisis in which the failure of the existing paradigm causes it to break up. Out of, and in effect exacerbating, this chaos emerges a new paradigm which enables new observations to be made.

For Kuhn the new paradigm, despite rearguard actions by defenders of the old paradigm, attracts more and more scientists – particularly those who are young and uncommitted. Eventually the old and increasingly discredited paradigm is abandoned. In Kuhn's terms these changes constitute a 'scientific revolution'. For an individual scientist he likens the change to a 'gestalt switch' or a 'religious conversion' in which there is no purely rational argument that demonstrates the superiority of the new paradigm justifying the change of allegiance. A reason for this is that proponents of different paradigms will not only deploy different languages to describe the world; they will also subscribe to different methodological and evaluative principles. Scientists cannot choose between paradigms through their evaluation of the facts since what counts as the facts will have changed. Hence the choice between paradigms is like 'a choice between incompatible modes of community life . . . which can never be unequivocally settled by logic and experimentation alone' (1970a: 93–4).

Those who adopt the new paradigm see the world differently from how it had been seen previously.

For example, during the 50 years after Copernicus Western astronomers began to see change (e.g. the appearance of comets, sunspots, new stars etc.) occurring in what previously had been known as an immutable cosmos. However such a drastic reorientation can take a long time. As Kuhn observes, both Newton and Copernicus were generally not accepted until 50 years after their deaths and he refers to how Darwin did not expect to convince

> experienced naturalists whose minds are stocked with a multitude of facts all viewed, during a long course of years, from a point of view directly opposite to mine. (Charles Darwin, quoted in Kuhn, 1970a: 51)

However with the victory of the new paradigm normal science then resumes with a new set of problems, since 'many of the puzzles of contemporary normal science did not exist until after the most recent scientific revolution' (*ibid.*: 141). The cycle illustrated in Figure 4.1 recommences with a period of normal science until it too is challenged by a new period of revolutionary instability.

The epistemological and ontological implications of Kuhn's thesis

At any given time, scientific ideas are acceptable as long as they conform to the existing paradigm adhered to by a scientific community which determines the boundary between orthodoxy and heterodoxy. Scientific change depends upon the persuasive power of scientists to convince others of their assumptions and findings. Therefore scientists cannot go out to falsify other scientists' claims by applying Popper's 'critical attitude'. Neither do they attempt to discover the unknown. Rather, their shared paradigm tells them what to expect and to discard unanticipated results either as methodological artefacts or as anomalies which should be ignored until they are resolved by better-equipped future generations of scientists. Therefore what we take to be science cannot be said to conform to some asocial pre-given standard of rationality since definitions of science and good science amount to *social conventions* into which members of the scientific community are socialized. Adherence to a position is the result of psychological and sociological factors such as conformity arising from socialization and/or obedience to authority and hierarchy. Because every scientist is trapped in their own culturally derived paradigm, they cannot claim to have a neutral standpoint from which they can objectively observe and assess knowledge claims since, to paraphrase Kuhn's intellectual forerunner Ludwik Flek, scientific facts are social facts (1935–79). This means that a theory-neutral observational language is impossible – rather, observations and their meaning are determined by the paradigm deployed by the socialized scientist.

To illustrate this point it is helpful to turn to Hanson (1958) where he asks the reader to imagine the astronomers Tycho Brahe and Johannes Kepler observing the sun at dawn. He poses the question: what do they see? According to Hanson (*ibid.*: 23–4) Tycho Brahe, because he has a geocentric cosmology, would 'see the sun beginning its journey from horizon to horizon. He sees that from some celestial vantage point the sun . . . could be watched circling our fixed earth'. However Johannes Kepler, because he has a heliocentric cosmology, 'will see the horizon dipping, or turning away, from our local fixed star. The shift from sunrise to horizon turn . . . is occasioned by *differences between what Tycho and Kepler think they know*'. The implication is that all knowledge is founded upon assumptions which are arbitrary since whatever paradigm is adopted is a matter of social convention. Without a neutral observational language positivistic commitments to a correspondence theory of truth must be abandoned in favour of a consensus theory of truth (see Box 4.3).

Box 4.3

Correspondence theory argues that the truthfulness of an account or theory is determinable by direct comparison with the indisputable facts of a neutrally accessible reality. If they fail to correspond then the theory, or account, must be rejected.

Consensus theory argues that any judgement as to the truthfulness of an account or theory is the outcome of, and is nothing more than, socially established agreement, or convention, between those who share a particular paradigm or frame of reference. 'Truth', therefore, is a term attached to a set of beliefs that have managed to prevail in a particular social context. Although scientists will usually claim correspondence as a basis for their truth-claims, this is regarded by conventionalists as either naive or a strategic and rhetorical ploy that masks how truth can only be a matter of social convention because scientists do not have, and cannot have, access to the empirical facts upon which they could inductively build their theories or deductively test their theories. During normal science such agreements are the product of conformity to the uncontested authority of tradition and hierarchy within the paradigm rather than the outcome of participation in democratic debate.

Kuhn's rejection of a theory-neutral observational language leads to two very different sets of implications which are both tacitly invoked by his statement that after a scientific revolution 'scientists are responding to a different world' (1970a: 135). Although it is evident that he means that any scientific statement may be seen as the social constructions of the scientist, are these statements just different versions of an independently existing noumenal reality which we can never fully know because our theories are always under-determined, or does it mean that reality is created and determined by the socially constructed theory? In other words

– what does Kuhn mean by 'scientist . . . responding' in the above quotation? The question is whether those 'responses' are grounded in an intersubjective consensus based upon *either* the paradigm's reactive mediation of an independently existing reality *or* the paradigm's proactive creation of a reality that has no independent ontological status. Here Kuhn's incommensurability thesis implies the latter view and by implication the adoption of a subjectivist ontology.

Kuhn's incommensurability thesis is usually taken to mean that scientists cannot have a rational dialogue across the boundaries between two or more paradigms. The concepts, the interpretations and the epistemological standards deployed by scientists depend upon the paradigmatic context in which they occur. Hence a paradigm cannot be compared or criticized from the standpoint of an alternative paradigm since

> the proponents of competing paradigms practice their trades in different worlds . . . Practicing in different worlds, the two groups of scientists see different things when they look from the same point in the same direction. (*ibid.*: 150)

Thus for Kuhn there is no framework of paradigm-independent epistemological criteria by which it is possible to decide between the competing knowledge claims of different paradigms. Keat and Urry draw attention to the subjectivist ontological implications by arguing that paradigm incommensurability means that 'theories are determinative of what is real, and when they change in a fundamental way, we are not faced with a different conception of the same world, but a different world' (Keat and Urry, 1982: 60). It follows that Kuhn adopts what amounts to a relativistic position (see Box 4.4). Kuhn's relativistic voice is amplified by his observation that 'as in political revolutions so in paradigm choice there is no standard higher than the assent of the relevant community' (1970a: 94) or his view that the choice between paradigms is between 'incommensurable modes of community life' (*ibid.*: 93). For Lakatos this meant that 'there is no way of judging a theory save by assessing the number, faith and vocal energy of its supporters' (1970: 93) – a matter of 'mob psychology' (*ibid.*: 178). While Lakatos disapproves of the incipient relativism created by the incommensurability thesis, Feyerabend (1978) in contrast welcomes its rejection of rationalism and its emphasis upon the role of the subjective in the choice between incommensurable theories. While he argues that incommensurable theories can be refuted individually by discovering the internal contradictions from which they might suffer

> their contents cannot be compared. None of the methods which Carnap, Hempel, Nagel, Popper or even Lakatos want to use for rationalizing scientific changes can be applied, and the one that can be applied, refutation, is greatly reduced in strength. What remains are aesthetic judgements, judgements of taste, metaphysical prejudices, religious desires, in short, *what remains are our subjective wishes.* (1978: 284–5) (emphasis in the original)

Box 4.4

Generally, *relativism* is the doctrine that no absolutes exist. It is expressed by Protagoras' dictum that 'Man is the measure of all things; that are that they are, and of things that are not that they are not'. In its epistemological application relativism holds that what counts as warranted knowledge, truth and reason are always relative to (i.e. conditioned by) some historical epoch and/or place and/or cultural context and/or (as in Kuhn's case) paradigm. For instance Bernstein defines relativism as

> The basic conviction that when we turn to the examination of those concepts that philosophers have taken to be the most fundamental . . . we are forced to recognize that . . . all such concepts must be understood as relative to a specific conceptual scheme, theoretical framework, paradigm, form of life, society, or culture. Since the relativist believes that there is or can be a non reducible plurality of such conceptual schemes, he or she challenges the claim that these concepts can have a determinate or univocal significance. For the relativist, there is no substantive overarching framework or single metalanguage by which we can rationally adjudicate or univocally evaluate competing claims or alternative paradigms. (1983: 8)

Thus relativism asserts:

1   that there are no neutral, or independent, ahistorical criteria for judging knowledge- or truth-claims because we cannot stand outside our own socio-historical milieux;
2   we can only talk about truth being relative to the socially established assent of some community, paradigm, language-game, culture and so on;
3   any empirical observation is only intelligible in terms of this prevailing consensus;
4   reality cannot intervene as an independent arbiter of truth because our sense-making activities create reality.

Of course a problem which arises with relativism is that

> Every single truth-claim that was ever entertained by a community of like-minded knowers must count as valid when referred to the language-game, vocabulary or belief-system then in place. Thus for instance it was once true – not just an artefact of limited knowledge or erroneous 'commonsense' perception – that the fixed planets were seven in number; that the Sun rotated about the Earth; that the process of combustion involved the release of a colourless, odourless, intangible substance called phlogiston, rather than the uptake of oxygen; that no fixed-wing aircraft could possibly get off the ground since the necessary lift could be generated only by a bird-like flapping motion, or perhaps – as Leonardo was the first to suggest – a rotary-blade arrangement helicopter type. (Norris, 1996: 172)

In effect, Kuhn's relativistic voice reduces epistemology to a descriptive survey of varying scientific practices that can have no neutral evaluative standpoint since there are no grounds for evaluation that aren't relative to a particular set of paradigmatic predispositions located in the socially established norms of a particular scientific community. Hence any appeal to 'rationality', 'reason' and 'objectivity' etc. as universal epistemic standards for scientific activities cannot be made. Instead epistemic standards encoded into paradigms are seen as culturally specific and express preferences for, and surreptitiously privilege, particular cultural traditions. It follows that the selection of one paradigm over others must be based upon sentiment, taste, habituation and power rather than a rationally defensible choice. These concerns lead Feyerabend to advocate what amounts to an epistemological anarchism in which 'the only principle that does not inhibit progress is: anything goes' (*ibid.*: 23).

Conventionalism and management research

In the management disciplines a conventionalist focus upon how the *a priori* contents of the human mind anticipate and organize sensory experience has been accomplished primarily through the enthusiastic appropriation of Kuhn's concept of paradigm so as to critique what is seen as mainstream (i.e. positivist) management theory. Usually Kuhn's view that the social sciences were pre-paradigmatic (1970a: 160) proto-sciences (1970b: 245) is downplayed. In doing so, various scholars have attempted to develop what amounts to a metatheory (see Box 4.5) of their particular discipline to create, in effect, a paradigm of paradigms. On the one hand such meta-thoretical endeavours often resonate with Kuhn's relativistic voice, while on the other hand they often ambiguously articulate a Kantian emphasis upon ability to be rationally reflexive. The result has been the reduction of management research to the reflexive analysis of the dominant modes of thinking deployed by management scholars and practitioners alike.

Within management and organization theory a key example of such a metatheoretical development is Gibson Burrell and Gareth Morgan's analysis of the influence of sociological paradigms upon organizational analysis (1979). Throughout the 1980s their approach was subsequently applied to a variety of management disciplines which included accounting (Chua, 1986; Hopper and Powell, 1985), marketing (Arndt, 1985), information systems (Hirschheim, 1985; Hirschheim and Klein, 1989), personnel and human resource management (Gowler and Legge, 1986; Kamoche, 1991) – a trend which still persists, as exemplified by Collins' metatheory of organizational change (1998). Here we shall concentrate upon Burrell and Morgan's seminal work as well as some of its later developments and applications by Morgan (1980; 1983a; 1983b; 1986; 1993) who is largely responsible for the current popularity attained by metatheoretical thinking in management and organization theory.

Burrell and Morgan's paradigms

Burrell and Morgan (*ibid.*) invite us to consider that various sociologists are the social scientific counterparts of Aristotle and Copernicus, or

Box 4.5

'Metatheory' literally means 'beyond, above, before or after (meta) theory'. It entails the systematic analysis of the overarching structures of thought within a substantive domain so as to specify the conditions under which particular theoretical perspectives are deemed appropriate. In effect metatheories uncover and open up to critical reflexive inspection what Kant would understand as innate, transcendental grounds of experience – the pre-understandings, assumptions and connections which are expressed as conventions that organize, for instance, organizational analysis. The result of metatheoretical analysis is usually a more general theory which describes and explains why and how theoretical variation and development occurs within, for instance, management theory. However the problems of epistemological circularity noted in Chapter 1 are starkly illustrated by metatheoretical analyses. For instance any metatheory inevitably simplifies the relationships it reveals by only focusing on the influence of certain variables upon the theories within the chosen substantive domain. So while metatheory points to how any mode of engagement with the world is laden with *a priori* commitments, since metatheories are theories about theories they are in themselves also laden with *a priori* selectivity and partiality. Ironically, conventionalists who propose metatheoretical analyses of particular management domains confront problems around justifying their own analyses without contradicting themselves by privileging their own accounts through either a tacit appeal to a neutral observational language, or through asserting what amounts to a rationalist stance.

Newton and Einstein, since they have inspired very different ways of understanding and analysing Burrell and Morgan's own focus of interest – organizations. Here Burrell and Morgan apply Kuhn's notion of paradigm in a very broad sense to refer to mutually exclusive social constructions which generate distinctive analyses of social life. So while they agree with Kuhn that meaningful communication between paradigms is impossible, they also consider that several paradigms, characterized by permanent incommensurability, can exist simultaneously. This synchronic view of social science paradigms – where the normal state of affairs is pluralistic – is in stark contrast to Kuhn's diachronic view of paradigm development in the natural sciences. As we have shown previously, Kuhn's view was that incommensurability only exists when an established paradigm is confronted by revolutionary science taking place – a temporary situation which is diachronically resolved through the eventual re-establishment of normal science through the supercession and hegemony of a new paradigm.

Central to Burrell and Morgan's thesis is that social theory in general and organizational analysis in particular can be understood in terms of a matrix of four paradigms whose two axes are based upon different metatheoretical assumptions about the nature of social science and the nature of society. They argue that all social scientific theory will inevitably

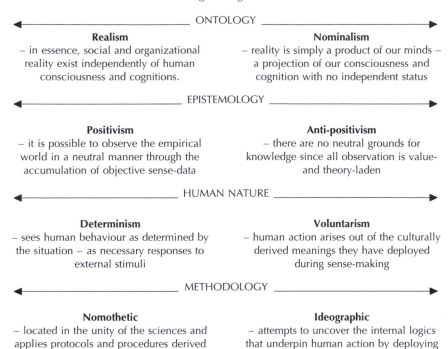

ONTOLOGY

Realism
– in essence, social and organizational reality exist independently of human consciousness and cognitions.

Nominalism
– reality is simply a product of our minds – a projection of our consciousness and cognition with no independent status

EPISTEMOLOGY

Positivism
– it is possible to observe the empirical world in a neutral manner through the accumulation of objective sense-data

Anti-positivism
– there are no neutral grounds for knowledge since all observation is value- and theory-laden

HUMAN NATURE

Determinism
– sees human behaviour as determined by the situation – as necessary responses to external stimuli

Voluntarism
– human action arises out of the culturally derived meanings they have deployed during sense-making

METHODOLOGY

Nomothetic
– located in the unity of the sciences and applies protocols and procedures derived from the natural sciences

Ideographic
– attempts to uncover the internal logics that underpin human action by deploying methods that access cultures

Figure 4.2 Burrell and Morgan's metatheoretical assumptions about the nature of social science

make implicit or explicit assumptions along these dimensions – if the theory in question does not, then it isn't social science. The horizontal axis is constituted by social science metatheory which is expressed in social scientists' assumptions about the nature of the social world and how it might best be investigated. They conceive this bi-polar dimension in terms of a dualism: a choice between the incommensurable alternatives of subjectivist versus objectivist assumptions about ontology, epistemology, human nature and methodology (see Figure 4.2). By accepting one set of metatheoretical assumptions, the social scientist denies the alternative.

In a similar manner the assumptions about the nature of society provide the vertical axis of the matrix. These are construed by Burrell and Morgan as two bi-polar extremes: the sociology of regulation versus the sociology of radical change. The former assumes that society and its institutions are characterized by underlying equilibrium, consensus and cohesiveness without fundamental differences of interest between different sections and is concerned to analyse how the *status quo* is maintained. When conflict happens it is viewed as a temporary aberration necessary for adaptation to changed circumstances. In contrast, the sociology of radical change assumes that society is riddled with fundamental conflicts, modes of domination, exploitation and deprivation. It is therefore concerned with human change of, and emancipation from, a society which stunts human development. By accepting the assumptions that underpin the sociology of regulation, those assumptions that constitute the sociology of radical change are denied – and *vice versa*.

The two dimensions are combined to produce the four paradigms illustrated in Figure 4.3 below. Burrell and Morgan argue that the four paradigms are

> contiguous but separate – contiguous because of the shared characteristics, but separate because the differentiation is . . . of sufficient importance to warrant treatment. . .as 4 distinct entities . . . [which] . . . generate quite different concepts and analytical tools. (1979: 23)

This situation is illustrated by Hassard's (1991) use of Burrell and Morgan as a framework for producing four accounts of work behaviour in the British Fire Service. Each account was based upon a theory and methodology consistent with a particular paradigm. Thus the functionalist account used psychometric techniques and a quasi-experimental methodology to understand the changing nature of the fireman's orientation towards work. In contrast, the interpretative account deploys an ethnography which 'de-concretizes the view of organizational reality created in the . . . [functionalist] . . . paradigm; it suggests that (Fire Service) organization is a cultural phenomenon which is subject to a continuous process of enactment' (*ibid.*: 288). In the radical humanist study a 'central notion is that human consciousness is corrupted by tacit ideological influences . . . to drive a wedge of false-consciousness between the known self and the true self . . . [where] . . . the hegemony of organization is dependent upon the reproduction of social arrangements which serve to constrain human expression' (*ibid.*: 291–2). The radical structuralist account analyses 'the strategic relations between Capital and Labour . . . and describes the role of State agencies in seeking to mediate contradictory forces and restore system equilibrium' (*ibid.*: 294). While Hassard's work is helpful in that it reveals key aspects of each metatheoretical quadrant of Burrell and Morgan's scheme, it also shows how certain problems and topics cannot be addressed from the point of view of particular paradigms – an observation which, despite Hassard's own denials, further demonstrates the incommensurability of paradigms.

Throughout their work Burrell and Morgan are adamant that the four paradigms are mutually exclusive and incommensurable and that interparadigm journeys are rare. This is because

> they offer different ways of seeing. A synthesis is not possible, since in their pure forms they are contradictory, being based on at least one set of opposing metatheoretical assumptions. They are alternatives, in the sense that one can operate in different paradigms sequentially over time, but mutually exclusive, in the sense that one cannot operate in more than one paradigm at any given point in time, since in accepting the assumptions of one, we defy the assumptions of all the others. (1979: 25)

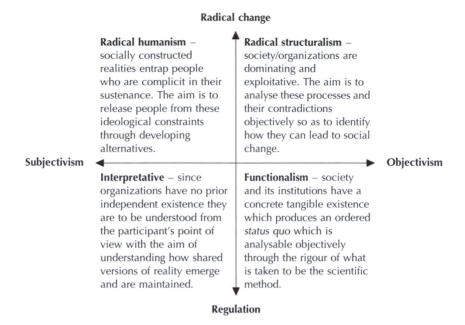

Figure 4.3   Burrell and Morgan's four paradigms

Because the metatheoretical norms of one paradigm are not translatable into those of an alternative, there cannot be any *a priori*, independent, neutral or rational grounds for debate or for deciding upon which paradigm has the better problem-solving capacity. Thus the conduct of organizational analysis cannot be resolved by appeal to the 'correct' epistemological rules. Any epistemological rules, no matter what form they take, are always specific to the norms of a particular scientific community. Indeed as Hassard (*ibid.*) shows, the issue of incommensurability pervades even the choice of topics and the perception of problems since these issues are not independent of the variable processes of social construction produced by different paradigms. Therefore so as to protect the weaker, emergent paradigms (for example, radical humanism), Burrell and Morgan emphasize the need to defend incommensurability and recommend that

> each paradigm needs to be developed in its own terms . . . a form of isolationism . . . Contrary to the widely held belief that synthesis and mediation between paradigms is what is required we argue that the real need is for paradigmatic closure. In order to avoid emasculation and incorporation within the functionalist problematic the paradigms need to provide a basis for their self preservation by developing on their own account. (1979: 397–8)

It is their version of the incommensurability thesis and their recommendation for separate intellectual development that has become the most contentious aspects of Burrell and Morgan's approach. The ensuing debate continues with on one side those (for example, Carter and Jackson, 1993) who defend incommensurability and advocate paradigmatic closure as means of survival for the less established paradigms. In opposition Reed (1985; 1990), for example, proposes a pluralistic view of knowledge production grounded in a consensus which dissolves the objectivist–subjectivist metatheoretical boundaries between paradigms. He believes that this objective–subjective dualism 'grossly overstates the philosophical and ideological incompatibilities between different conceptual frameworks' (1985: 205) and articulates an incipient relativism which ultimately denies the possibility of scientific progress. The problems created by incommensurability and relativism equally bedevil Morgan's subsequent writing – a body of work which perhaps is largely responsible for the current prominence of metatheoretical thinking in management and organization theory.

Morgan's metaphors

Morgan elaborates his earlier work with Burrell by developing the concept of metaphor as a metatheoretical tool (1980; 1983a; 1983b; 1986; 1993) for analysing organizations and management. In doing so Morgan repositions metaphor as central to the ways in which anyone understands and reasons about their experience. According to Morgan (1983a: 21), while paradigms inevitably shape and bound our understandings of organizations and management, knowledge is further shaped by the ways in which we tacitly 'concretize' our more fundamental paradigmatic assumptions. During such concretization people will deploy images of social phenomena, generated by and linguistically expressed as metaphors, which allow the structuring of inquiry by favouring particular insights, forms of explanation, and modes of puzzle-solving. For Morgan, metaphors are deeply embedded in our cognitive structures and are the vehicles by which paradigms are operationalized in our minds:

> images of a social phenomenon, usually expressed in terms of a favoured metaphor, provide a means of structuring scientific inquiry, guiding attention in distinctive ways . . . in suggesting that certain kinds of insight, understanding, and explanation may be more appropriate than others. (1983a: 21)

So when a metaphor is used it enables a person to understand and experience a phenomenon (e.g. an organization) in terms of another (e.g. a machine) which is better known to them (Lakoff and Johnson, 1980: 5; Morgan, 1993: 5). In this manner the use of metaphors allow us to draw upon pre-existing knowledge about the familiar and transfer this knowledge to relatively new domains thereby creating similarities between two different phenomena by prefiguring one in terms of the other. For Tsoukas (1991) it follows that metaphors do not merely 'describe' external reality; rather they help 'constitute' reality and 'prescribe' how it should be

Box 4.6

In his book *Images of Organization* (1986) Morgan presents and analyses eight metaphorical representations that have been used as a means of constituting management and organization. In commenting on four of the metaphors reviewed in this work he later observes that:

> while a 'machine view' of organization focuses on organization as the relationship between structures, roles, and technology, the 'culture view' shows how organization rests in shared meanings. The psychic prison metaphor shows how structures and shared meanings can become conscious and unconscious traps. The political perspective shows how these characteristics are often shaped by clashes of interest and power plays – and so on . . . each metaphor offers specific ideas for the design and management of organizations in practice. (1993: 280)

For Morgan each metaphor derives from a particular paradigm: the machine metaphor from the functionalist; the culture metaphor from the interpretative; the psychic prison metaphor from the radical humanist; the domination metaphor from the radical structuralist, and so on.

'viewed'. In so doing they provide a 'missing link' between more abstract scientific discourses and 'lay' organizational applications – between the macro-level of paradigm and the micro-level of theory and organizational practices (see Box 4.6).

Moreover, as Kuhn himself has observed, during scientific revolutions, the metaphors deployed by scientists change and are 'central to the process by which science and other language is acquired' (1987: 21). So by invoking amongst others Wittgenstein (1958) and Ortony (1979) Morgan's basic point is to reject the possibility of a theory-neutral observational language and emphasize how phenomena are interpreted through the medium of language – 'a creative process in which scientists view the world metaphorically' (1980: 611).

The response of positivists to Morgan's views was to try to preserve the objective foundations of management by defending the possibility of a theory-neutral observational language through calls to purge metaphors from scientific language since their use distorts meaning and obscures the facts of reality (for example, Bourgeois and Pinder, 1983; Pinder and Bourgeois, 1982). Morgan's various responses to this attack (for example, 1983b) might be summarized by his view that metaphor is a 'primal generative process' through which we forge our relationships with (organizational) reality and which is 'fundamental to the creation of human understanding and meaning in all aspects of life' (1996: 228) – we therefore cannot eradicate metaphors but we can be reflexive and sceptical about their use and thereby change them. Indeed the role of metaphors provides an explanation of how 'highly conventionalized social constructions of reality emerge . . . and how we can deliberately stretch the conventional' (1996: 234). By opening to inspection the usually sub-limated taken-for-granted assumptions which metaphors tacitly articulate and by pointing to their arbitrariness and partiality, Morgan attempts to facilitate our own reflexive understanding of how researchers and practitioners variably construct and act in relation to organizations and management.

The immediate message from Morgan's work is that reality is always experienced subjectively through the lens of the particular paradigm which has been operationalized through the deployment of certain metaphors. Different metaphors may be used to 'generate alternative social realities' (Tsoukas, 1993: 324). The conceptualization of reality resulting from the deployment of a particular metaphor can become reified in the sense that it has become cognitively entrenched yet experienced as existing independently of the people who continue to reproduce it through their being engaged in the understandings and courses of action it sanctions. The result may be what Tsoukas calls a 'dead' metaphor which 'is so familiar and habitual that we have ceased to become aware of their metaphorical nature and use them as literal terms' (1991: 568). As Alvesson and Willmott observe, a lack of reflexive self-understanding with regard to the metaphors we use will result in management researchers' and practitioners' analyses being conditioned by 'a few dominant metaphors and associated value-orientations for conceptualizing management and organization' (1996: 93).

So while the awareness of new metaphors can give researchers and practitioners alternative ways of understanding organizations, or the processes of managing them, the irony is that their unnoticed acceptance into everyday speech can also rigidify our linguistically based meaning systems by becoming normal, unchallenged, representations of our worlds – processes which create interesting insights 'yet obliterate others' (Morgan, 1993: 277). Indeed as Chia (1996a: 143) points out, the very claim to the deployment of a theory-neutral observational language is merely 'the momentarily arrested, stabilized (and conventionalized) sense of a metaphorical expression'. So while metaphors are pivotal in enabling the development of new management knowledge because of the creative insight they bestow, they can also constrain knowledge by creating conceptual inertia. Moreover, at the risk of mixing our metaphors, one metaphorical queen may die only to be succeeded by yet another metaphorical queen – the queen is dead, long live the queen!

It follows from Morgan's various metatheoretical analyses that, usually, the process of metaphorical engagement is done in circumstances where we don't voluntarily choose the metaphors we deploy – we thus become entrapped by those metaphors into particular partial ways of seeing the world. Here two important themes can be identified within Morgan's work. The first focuses upon detailing the different metaphors already in use in management and organization theory where the reader is advised on their application and partiality. This inductive emphasis on the already available has led Reed (1990) to suggest that Morgan's off-the-shelf approach tries to transform organization theory into a 'supermarket of metaphors' where passive consumers can at will 'visit to purchase and consume its conceptual wares according to their brand preferences and purchasing power' (*ibid.*: 38).

The second theme in Morgan's work focuses attention more upon the processes of metaphorical thinking which undermines the mistaken attribution of concreteness to our conceptual schemes and attempts to stimulate the development of new, provisional, metaphorical insights which apparently are pivotal in 'empowering' individuals to see beyond the particular 'images' into which they have been socialized, thereby engendering 'creative action', 'organizational change' and 'reflexive practice' (for example, 1993: 275–6; 286–7). The implication for Morgan is by drawing people's attention to the role of metaphors, and by inference what he construes as paradigms, we can transform our worlds by dismantling the received wisdoms generated by our habitual use of dead metaphors and problematize and dislodge their underlying paradigms. An integral part of this process is the creation of conceptual space which allows the reflexive application of alternative metaphors that articulate new ways of seeing the world and thereby provide new frameworks for action. For instance what managers need are 'fresh metaphors' to help their reflexive thinking about how they engage with reality that move them beyond traditional positivistic emphasis upon foundations and objective truth (1993: 279). Presumably, besides practitioners themselves, the providers of these fresh metaphors are management researchers, writers, consultants and the like.

Some problems with conventionalism

The application of Kuhn's work by Burrell and Morgan and others counters the picture of science which has been accepted by many positivistically inclined management theorists, researchers and practitioners. At first sight conventionalism in its various guises presents a distinctive epistemological alternative to positivism. This alternative is grounded in the rejection of a key positivistic commitment – the possibility of a theory-neutral observational language. The result is an adoption of a subjectivist epistemology in which there are no extra-discursive means of arbitrating knowledge claims since the scientist's apprehension of reality is the product of socially derived conventions which are deployed prior to observation. In effect these socializing conventions are understood as webs of knowledge-constituting assumptions that either create reality or mediate an independently existing reality.

The implication is that management knowledge and authority, along with the practices they legitimize, cannot be grounded in access to an uncontaminated source of privileged knowledge: any claim to privileged knowledge is construed as a rhetorical ploy to support discursively a particular conventionally derived perspective. Obviously this dismissal of privileged knowledge equally applies to management and organizational research: hence the perceived need to undertake research into *both* metaphors-in-use by organizational actors and reflexively to uncover those metaphors used by researchers in making sense of, and constituting knowledge about, management and organizational phenomena.

The ambiguity is that to avoid self-contradiction such a dismissal of privilege must apply equally to conventionalism itself. For instance, earlier in this chapter (see Box 4.5) we pointed to how any metatheoretical scheme is inevitably partial in its own right and throws problems of epistemic circularity into sharp relief. For instance Burrell and Morgan's own stance, which underpins their metatheoretical models and consideration of metaphors, is in itself on the subjectivist side and would seem to be an expression of radical humanism. Indeed they describe radical humanism as understanding that human consciousness is

> dominated by the ideological superstructures with which [we] interact . . . The major concern . . . is with release from the constraints which existing social arrangements place upon human development. (1979: 32)

Given its repeated emancipatory overtones, their work seems to coincide with the concerns of radical humanism more than any other paradigm. The result is a paradigm of paradigms, an overarching metaphor (e.g. psychic prison) of metaphors, an example of conventionalism that in itself inevitably deploys particular conventions. This is an ambiguity which pervades all conventionalist thought: if all knowledge is conventional then conventionalist metatheoretical analyses themselves cannot stand apart – they too must also express particular conventions. This begs the question of why should we accept any conventionalist's own particular conventionalist stance – perhaps it is all a question of mob psychology?

So it is evident that the conventionalist's subjectivism can 'throw the baby out with the bath water' in the sense that it leads to a relativistic position. This happens in two distinct ways which, to paraphrase Hollis and Lukes (1982), are each a rosy path paved with plausible assumptions. The first path is paved through combining a subjectivist epistemology with a subjectivist ontology – that reality is merely a *creation* of our cognitive structures and has no independent status. The second path takes a particular phenomenalist route. This entails the adoption of a subjectivist epistemology, while retaining a realist ontology, but denying the possibility of any epistemic impact of that noumenal reality upon our socially constructed phenomenal realities. In other words, reality-in-itself exists but there is no means of assessing its impact upon our schemes of knowledge so as to assess their veracity. Thus we have different phenomenal versions of reality but no extra-discursive means of judging their accuracy through reference to noumenal reality.

The destination of either conventionalist path is in effect a view of science as a closed meaning system with no possible reference to an external reality. The result is a relativistic stance which is riddled with fundamental epistemological contradictions. As Mannheim has observed, 'the assertion of relativity itself claims absolute validity and hence its very form presupposes a principle which its manifest content rejects' (1952: 130). What this means is that because relativism contends that notions of truth are socially and historically derived, then it follows that the doctrine of relativism itself cannot be valid since it too must be relative to particular socio-historical conditions. Indeed, assertions of relativism require the presupposition of universally applicable neutral standards of evaluation but they deny the possibility of such standards since everything is relative. In other words, any relativistic approach seems incoherent in that it is unable to cope with its own critique of itself and thereby cannot justify its approach on its own grounds – it is thus incapable of defending itself (see also Siegel, 1987).

If we accept the relativistic claim that all knowledge is the outcome of what amounts to social construction whereby the cultural dispositions of scientists act to create knowledge and in which there are no extra-discursive checks over knowledge claims, then one has to also question: the epistemological status of Kuhn's own historical 'description' of different scientific practices and his theory of scientific change; Burrell and Morgan's metatheoretical model of sociology and organizational analysis; and Morgan's account of metaphors as epistemic bridges between paradigms and theory/action. If, as they all argue, there is no independent critical rationality then surely they too must deploy some paradigmatic stance in their engagement with historic accounts? Is there a danger that they inadvertently, and contradictorily, assert some 'Archimedian fulcrum' through either a tacit claim to a theory-neutral observational language or to a rationalist position so as to substantiate the veracity of their own meta-theoretical accounts of other scientists' epistemological orientations?

For instance Morgan's use of metaphor denies the possibility of language being used to produce neutral engagements with reality, yet, as Chia cogently shows, Morgan does 'presuppose the possibility of conveying the meaning of metaphors literally' (1996a: 127), an ambiguity that Morgan fails to resolve. If they avoid such an tacit assertion of privilege for their own accounts then a conventionalist spiral of a paradigm of paradigms must ensue. So if Kuhn, for instance, wishes to be epistemologically consistent and avoid contradicting himself he must adopt a relativistic argument that concludes that since all knowledge is the outcome of socio-historical processes, there are no extra-discursive reasons for preferring one theory over another – including, presumably, his own metatheory! It would seem that such epistemological tangles cause both Kuhn and Morgan to oscillate inadvertently between subjectivist and objectivist ontologies and thereby vary in their orientations towards relativism.

After the collaboration with Burrell, Morgan seems to have two meta-theoretical positions which resonate throughout his work, though which is amplified the most varies. One voice, which is louder in his popular work

Images of Organization (1986), expresses the view that different metaphors provide different snapshots of the same independently existing reality. For instance, where he invokes the Indian tale of the six blind men trying to understand the elephant, he concludes that

> there is a difference between the full and rich reality of an organization, and the knowledge we are able to gain about that organization . . . We can use metaphors and theories to grasp and express this knowledge . . . but we can never be sure that we are absolutely right. (1986: 341)

He exhorts the reader to sample, experiment and ultimately combine different metaphors so as to develop a better, more comprehensive, 'reading' of organizations. In reflection, Morgan observes that

> *Images of Organization* is a book that is itself rooted in a dominant metaphorical frame stressing the social construction of reality. But it is not a 'solipsist' work that denies an objective reality. Rather, its position is that objective reality can only be grasped subjectively through metaphors that shape our thinking. (1996: 239)

The implication is that, grounded in an ontological realism, all the eight metaphors he reviews, and presumably the different underlying paradigms which they operationalize, are commensurable in that they can be synthesized so as to represent reality better. Morgan's advice is that management and organization theory, research and practice can be improved by the use of multiple metaphors which highlight different aspects of the *same* already formed underlying social reality. Metaphorically (!), metaphors become like searchlights which light up particular parts of our (organizational) night-time horizon yet while doing so leave other parts of the horizon in darkness and thereby unavailable for inspection.

Elsewhere (for example, 1980; 1983a; 1983b; 1993) Morgan's relativistic voice seems to be amplified by a preference for paradigmatic incommensurability. Different groups of metaphors belong to different, incommensurable paradigms and can only be assessed within the relevant paradigmatic terms of reference. Here a subjectivist ontology is tacitly deployed – where different organizational realities are the *outcomes* of the deployment of metaphors embedded in the shared norms of different scientific communities, where reality is a 'living text' that is simultaneously 'written' and 'read' (1993: 283). Social reality has no independent existence and remains unformed until the act of cognition. It follows that there can be no recourse to extra-paradigmatic standards to adjudicate between metaphors since organizational analysis is a 'subjective enterprise concerned with the production of one-sided analyses' (1980: 612) because there can be no appeal to the intervention of an independent reality so as to justify a metaphorical synthesis as argued elsewhere – in other words, the night-time horizon doesn't exist until a searchlight is switched on by someone!

A similar oscillation between objectivist and subjectivist ontologies is to be found in the work of Kuhn who, despite his loud relativistic voice, does at times deny the charge of being a relativist:

> Later scientific theories are better than earlier ones for solving puzzles in the often quite different environments to which they are applied. That is not a relativist position, and it displays the sense in which I am a convinced believer in scientific progress. (1970b: 206)

The above observations need to be contextualized by Kuhn's implicit appeals to a realist ontology elsewhere in his work. For instance in reflecting upon his early position Kuhn simultaneously alludes to the impossibility of a theory-neutral observational language and to the possibility of an ontological realism. He claims that

> a vast amount of neural processing takes place between our receipt of a stimulus and the sensory response which is our . . . [given] . . . datum . . . the production of data from stimuli is a learned procedure . . . In *The Structure of Scientific Revolutions* . . . I repeatedly insist that members of different scientific communities live in different worlds . . . I would now want to say that members of different communities are presented with different data by the same stimuli. Notice, however, that change does not make phrases like a 'different world' inappropriate. The given world, whether everyday or scientific, is not a world of stimuli. (1977: 308–9)

From these two quotes it would seem first that scientific revolutions entail progress but that this progress entails better problem-solving capabilities and not, as is commonly supposed, a more accurate representation of reality; secondly, the source of stimuli is an independently existing noumenal reality but we have no access to this reality – instead it is mediated by our community membership to produce phenomenal realities. As with Morgan, what Kuhn does not explore is how this alternative position can avoid relativism by allowing external reality to intervene in our social construction and adjudication of knowledge while maintaining the impossibility of a theory-neutral observational language.

Conclusions

Recently the use of the term 'paradigm' has become promiscuous in the management disciplines. Often claims are made that paradigm shifts have either occurred (for example, Bessant, 1991; Mink, 1992) or are required (for example, Burnes, 1992; Ouchi, 1981). We hope that this chapter will have convinced the reader that while the term 'paradigm' is problematic even in Kuhn's work, such extravagant claims for management are fundamentally misguided as they merely refer to what amount to readjustments within functionalism rather than one of Burrell and Morgan's alternatives gaining the status of normal science amongst academics or practitioners.

So what must be emphasized here is that the conventionalist's rejection of a theory-neutral observational language only leads to relativism when those embarking upon this journey also accept that there are no extra-discursive means of arbitrating knowledge claims. As we shall demonstrate, particularly in Chapter 7 where we deal with pragmatism and critical realism, there are alternative means of arbitrating knowledge claims which are extra-discursive and do not rely upon a theory-neutral observational language. These alternatives promise a non-relativistic and non-positivistic set of epistemological commitments – but these necessitate the maintenance of a realist ontology and the articulation of how reality can still intervene so that anything does not go.

In sum, the rejection of a theory-neutral observational language is a necessary, but not a sufficient, condition for relativism. Sufficiency can derive from, but not exclusively so, the adoption of a subjectivist ontology. As implied by Kant, albeit in a very different idiom, the rejection of a theory-neutral observational language does not inevitably lead to a subjectivist ontology. So where Kuhn gets frightened by the spectre of relativism he lays out some ontological and epistemological commitments that promise an escape from relativism but the actual route is not overtly mapped out. To exonerate himself fully from the charge of relativism, Kuhn would *not* necessarily have to contradict himself by re-establishing what he had so effectively destroyed – the possibility of a theory-neutral observational language. Rather he would have to:

1 assert that there is a mind-independent reality to which our truth-claims are ultimately answerable;
2 indicate how such answerability might be achieved without the presupposition of a theory-neutral observational language.

It is precisely the two issues above which we shall return to in Chapter 7. However before encountering such a non-relativistic position we will consider in Chapter 5 the contribution of the postmodernists who, far from fearing the implications of relativism, celebrate it – while in Chapter 6 we shall review the contribution of Habermas and the critical theorists to dealing with some of the issues posed by relativism.

Further reading

Kant's original works are notoriously difficult so we advise readers interested in pursuing their study of Kant to consult Broad's book, *Kant: An Introduction* (1978). Meanwhile most of Kuhn's own work is written in an engaging manner and is relatively easy to follow – unlike much of the commentary on Kuhn – so we advise readers to refer to *The Structure of Scientific Revolutions* (1970a).

Besides their own seminal original work (1979) there is an accessible literature covering the application of Burrell and Morgan's ideas to a variety of management disciplines. These include accounting (Chua, 1986; Hopper and Powell, 1985), marketing (Arndt, 1985), information systems (Hirschheim, 1985; Hirschheim and Klein, 1989), personnel and human resource management (Gowler and Legge, 1986; Kamoche, 1991) and organizational change (Collins, 1998). These accounts should be contrasted with Gioia and Pitre's (1989) evaluation of multiparadigm perspectives and Hassard's (1991) analysis of the Fire Service. An interesting critique of Hassard is to be found in Parker and McHugh (1991). For an important edited collection upon the role of metaphor which influenced Morgan's work see Ortony's edited volume (1979). All of Morgan's work cited here is particularly readable and informative. Readers might be quite familiar with his more popular work (e.g. 1986; 1993), however we would also recommend Morgan's (1983b) debate with Pinder and Bourgeois (1982; Bourgeois and Pinder, 1983) which is particularly helpful in illuminating the differences between convention-alists and positivists in organizational theory and analysis. Two collections edited by Oswick and Grant (Grant and Oswick, 1996; Oswick and Grant, 1996) provide useful examples of the application and use of metaphor and interesting discussions of the role of metaphor in manage-ment theory generation. Thorough reviews of the issues posed by relativ-ism are to be found in Siegel (1987) and Hollis and Lukes (1982).

5
Postmodernist Epistemology – Relativism Unleashed?

> The consequence of a postmodern stance is that we are advised to stop attempting to systematically define or impose a logic on events and instead recognise the limitations of all our projects.
>
> (DeCock, 1998: 5)

Since the early 1980s 'postmodernism' has attracted considerable interest, particularly in the social sciences. Despite this attention, the term 'postmodernism' remains notoriously difficult to define. This is partially due to the complexity of the language used by postmodernists. However, what makes the term particularly opaque is that at first sight it appears to refer to a diffuse body of work in which postmodernists themselves reject a single correct position in favour of a multiplicity of perspectives which emphasize ambivalence and indeterminacy.

Nevertheless the aim of this chapter is to present the main themes of postmodernism by identifying the unifying epistemological assumptions which underpin and sanction this ambiguity. The implications of these epistemic common denominators for how we understand science and how we undertake management research will then be considered. Finally this epistemology will be subject to a critique that focuses upon its relativistic tendencies. While conventionalists and (as we will show in Chapter 6) critical theorists fear and attempt to avoid relativism, postmodernists disavow their escape attempts and instead willingly embrace, celebrate and reinvigorate relativism. As critical theorists strive to achieve consensus, postmodernists encourage dissensus. In effect truth, whether in terms of rationally grounded consensus or correspondence to an independent reality, is no longer a worthwhile goal. It could be argued that some postmodernists contradict themselves here by presenting a relativist 'totality' aimed at ending all 'totalities'. We will return to this point later. First, however, we have some conceptual ambiguity to resolve.

Postmodern: period or epistemology

Originally the term 'postmodernism' referred to a particular style of fine art, literature, architecture, film, dance etc. which was characterized by randomness, anarchy and fragmentation. In the past decade or so, the term's usage has gradually spread into various cultural areas and many academic disciplines. Regardless of context, the postmodern was usually seen as culturally innovative representing a move away from the ordered structures associated with modernism, towards something explicitly eclectic and indeterminate. In this sense the 'post' in 'postmodern' means 'after' the modern, but it can also mean 'against', or a 'denial', or a 'transcendence' of the modern tradition. Of course this begs the question – what is signified by the terms 'modern' or 'modernism'? Here, following the norm set by Kellner (1988), Berg (1989) and Parker (1992), we can identify two somewhat different yet interrelated answers: first one that relates to the historical period we ostensibly now live in; and a second that relates to an epistemological position that engenders a distinctive theoretical perspective.

The periodization view noted above claims that there have been fundamental changes in society and its institutions in the latter part of this century. The precise timing of this break is hard to pinpoint, although Charles Jencks (1984) suggests that the postmodern epoch began on 15 July 1972 at 3.22 p.m. when the Pruitt-Igoes public housing development in St Louis, Missouri, previously billed as LeCorbusier's 'machine for modern living', was knocked down, having been recognized as uninhabitable. The starting point of the new epoch is perhaps unimportant: what matters is that the current period of postmodernity represents an evolution from, or break with, a modern past. Here the term 'modernity' is associated with the dramatic changes to society which followed the Enlightenment. This was a period when industrialization, urbanism and scientific and technological development promised our emancipation from the terrors inflicted by the vagaries of the world. Progress was assured by our increasing ability to exercise control over our natural and social environments, allowed by our development of a newly enhanced reason. As Harvey observes, this Enlightenment project

> took it as axiomatic that there was only one possible answer to any question. From this it followed that the world could be controlled and rationally ordered if we could only picture and represent it rightly. (1989: 27)

The argument here is that social and economic reality has changed: we have left behind this optimistic modernist past and entered a new stage in the development of capitalism. For example the current levels of accelerated social economic and technological change have been labelled as the postmodern 'condition' (for example, Clegg, 1990) or 'era' (for example, Gergen, 1992). Elsewhere alternative labels have been developed, such as 'postindustrialism' (Bell, 1973); 'the end of organized capitalism' (Lash and Urry, 1987); 'the age of unreason' (Handy, 1989) and 'postcapitalism' (Drucker, 1993). Regardless of the label used, the unifying theme is one of tremendous change; a sense that we are entering a new historical configuration. For instance it is argued that the processes of production, distribution, exchange and consumption have not just dramatically accelerated but have also become increasingly diverse, specialized and temporary: a destabilized 'casino capitalism' (Bluestone and Harrison, 1988), of 'globalization and relativization' (Robertson, 1992), of 'intensified risk' (Beck, 1992), of 'heterogenization' (Daudi, 1990) and 'time–space compression' (Harvey, 1989).

This new reality of disorder and uncertainty that signifies a break with a more certain and stable modernist past, has spawned new social and institutional forms (Bauman, 1988) which, for instance, require post-modern political leadership (*Newsweek*, 1994). Nevertheless for some commentators (for example, Clegg, 1990; Handy, 1989) it is still possible to pursue the Enlightenment foundationalist project which, as we have illustrated, assumes the capacity to deploy a detached scientific reason to analyse objectively and reveal the underlying dynamics and implications of this new reality. This suggests a social science of postmodernity which, as far as management theory is concerned, does not look much different from contingency theory (Johnson and Gill, 1993; Tsoukas, 1992).

Clearly the periodization debate emphasizes that it is the world that has changed rather than notions about how we acquire warranted knowledge of it. As Parker has noted, postmodernist 'epistemological baggage is left behind and the modernist project continues unhindered' (1992: 12). In contrast, the second approach noted above overtly entails the elaboration of Parker's postmodernist epistemological baggage – a change in how we engage with and know reality which constitutes a decisive break with the Enlightenment project, the essence of modernity. Here epistemic suspicion abounds to the extent that, because any form of foundationalism is renounced, Kant's noumenal reality becomes ontologically annihilated. Postmodern epistemology thereby constitutes a philosophical break with the dominant epistemology of modernity – positivism.

Best and Kellner observe that postmodernism 'abandons the rational and unified subject postulated by much modern theory in favour of a socially and linguistically decentred and fragmented subject' (1991: 4). As we illustrated in Chapter 1, positivist epistemology sanctions and locates the authority of science in the ability to access a body of privileged and uncontaminated knowledge which reveals the essentials of the world and guarantees explanation, prediction and control. Whilst the postmodernity–periodization debate may question the fulfilment of such promises in the social sciences, because conditions of instability and unpredictability make analysis difficult, it is postmodernist epistemology which directly challenges modernism's positivistic certainty in the possibility of epistemic privilege and progress. Postmodernist epistemology dismisses the positivist's rational certainty in the attainability of epistemic privilege and replaces it with a relativist view of science and knowledge. If all science is understood as the product of social construction, rather than the outcome of rational investigation, its authority is undermined. Indeed an outcome of the deployment of postmodernist epistemology is the exposure of the social processes that underpin ostensibly neutral scientific practices. Therefore it is hardly surprising that postmodernist epistemology is not usually shared by those concerned to analyse the implications of the postmodern era for society and its institutions. Moreover postmodernist epistemology would cast suspicion upon, and ultimately negate, the aims of those who wish to categorize observable social and historical developments 'that support the hypothesis that society is moving towards a new postmodern era' (Hassard, 1993: 2).

Ironically, the seeds of this postmodernist epistemological challenge were sown by positivism itself. By extolling the power of human reason and holding out the promise of progress, the Enlightenment project of positivism had paradoxically institutionalized criticism and uncertainty concerning what the criteria of progress should be, the methods by which it might be obtained, and whether it is even desirable. Everything became open to the critique spawned by positivism's articulation of a sceptical, calculating reason – ultimately that reason itself became open to critique. In this manner positivism–modernism eroded the versions of reality that it promulgated and which had made the fragility of the human condition easier to bear (Berger et al., 1973: 166). As Giddens (1991: 3) argues, 'doubt, a pervasive feature of modern critical reason, permeates into every life as well as philosophical consciousness, and forms a general existential dimension of the contemporary social world' (1991: 2). Indeed the increasing secularization of Western society, as a product of the Enlightenment rationalist dictum 'dare to know', may have only replaced the premodern belief in the providence of an immutable God-given order to life with a growing realization of the uncertainty and fallibility of the very human reason it propagated. In other words, positivism began to exhaust itself. It is in this realization that the development of postmodernist epistemology lies.

Postmodernist writers such as Foucault, Lyotard and Baudrillard have all found avid audiences in many of the social science disciplines. In part this is due to a growing disillusion with the positivistic assumptions which still dominate these disciplines and the apparent demise of traditional critical alternatives, such as Marxism. Moreover, as Alvesson wryly observes, postmodernism constitutes 'a new brand image . . . on the edge of the intellectual frontier', a fad which has advantages for those concerned to market their 'knowledge products' by 'defining out earlier work and creating space for new careers' (1995: 1068). Thus postmodernism may be seen as offering a new and distinctive means of understanding science that, at first sight, has some radical cachet yet may also be seen as something of a bandwagon for aspiring academics.

Postmodernism, grand narratives and the linguistic turn

A recurrent theme in postmodern epistemology is a rejection of the modernist or the positivist (the terms are generally used interchangeably) 'grand' or 'meta' narrative (see Berg, 1989; Parker, 1992) and that it is possible to develop a rational and generalizable basis to scientific inquiry which explains the world from an objective standpoint. For instance, Lyotard defines the postmodern 'as an incredulity towards metanarratives' (1984: xxiv), while Harvey (1989: 10) suggests that it entails a rejection of overarching propositions that assume the validity of their own truth-claims. In particular Lyotard (*ibid.*) and Bauman (1989) attack the 'fallen' Enlightenment metanarrative of science as the source of human progress and emancipation through rational control located in reliable knowledge. For Lyotard the promise of the Enlightenment to emancipate humanity from poverty and ignorance died in the Nazi concentration camps and the Stalinist gulags. Indeed Bauman (*ibid.*) argues that it was the modern rational bureaucracy which allowed and enabled the holocaust, therefore how can rationality guarantee its promises? Accordingly progress and emancipation are seen by postmodernists as self-legitimizing myths, as delusions based upon yet another metanarrative.

So postmodernists point to the disrepute into which modernism has fallen, and use this revelation to legitimate an attack upon positivist epistemological assumptions and ultimately replace them with an anti-empiricist position which argues that all knowledge is indeterminate. From this perspective there can only be narratives based upon particular perspectives and points of view. It follows that there is a need for a 'war on totality' (Lyotard, 1984: 81) and its pretentious search for the 'true' dynamics of change (*ibid.*: 37). Here the target is the positivist claim that 'truth' is to be found in the observer's sensory registration of the facts that constitute external reality through the application of a neutral observational language. The truthfulness of various competing accounts of reality may be adjudicated through reference to their *correspondence* with the facts. It is only the positivists' claim to be able to stand outside their own cultural tradition, and thereby neutrally apprehend the facts of the world, that can justify their knowledge-claims. It is precisely this epistemological maxim, and its notion that a neutral observational language is possible, that has been challenged by the postmodernists' 'linguistic turn'. The linguistic turn suggests that language is never innocent; that no meaning exists beyond language; that knowledge and truth are linguistic entities constantly open to revision; that the 'social bond is linguistic but it is not woven with a single thread' (Lyotard, 1984: 40). With the linguistic turn the relationship between a concept (the signifier) and its mental concept (the signified) is seen as arbitrary – for the postmodernist nothing exists outside the articulation of arbitrary signs which manufacture a profusion of images. The justification for this view usually draws upon Derrida's critique of structuralism (1973).

According to structuralists like Saussure (1966), meaning is a product of a system of representation based upon the relationships between signifiers and signifieds. Saussure defined the linguistic sign as a two-sided entity; one side was called the signifier (e.g. a word). Inseparable from the signifier, and indeed engendered by the signifier, is what Saussure called the signified (a mental concept). Signification is the process which binds the signifier and signified together to produce a sign. Writers, such as Lacan (1977), attack Saussure's assumptions concerning the relationship between signifiers and signifieds. This is because for Saussure the signified has primacy. The human relation involved in this version of the sign is one where a pure signified exists in the mind of the sign user. In other words the sign is conceived as 'an arbitrary notation for referring to the mental concepts already harboured by the sign user' (Cobley and Jansz, 1997: 70). Derrida also critiques what he sees as Saussure's logo-centric tendencies, arguing that Saussure privileges speech over writing by giving the impression that the spoken signifier is somehow closer to the signified.

Derrida's critique of structuralism is perhaps best seen in his argument (*ibid.*) that meaning includes identity (what something is) and difference (what something is not). He combines two senses of the term 'difference' – to differ in space and to defer in time – to produce what he calls differance: that the meaning of a word 'is derived from a process of deferral to other words . . . that differ from itself' (Gergen, 1992: 219). If meaning can only be attained by looking at the relationship of one word to others (e.g. in a dictionary) then the accomplishment of meaning is continually deferred as each consultation of the dictionary merely leads to further words which in turn have to be looked up (see Box 5.1). According to Derrida, such unending deferral means that communication is polysemous. Any signifier can relate to many signifieds and hence its meaning cannot be pinned down. Thus, there are always deferred and marginalized meanings within any communication which can be revealed in a text by a reader.

The result of this linguistic turn is the 'fundamental uncontrollability of meaning' which implies that the '"out there" is constructed by our discursive conceptions of it and these concepts are collectively sustained and continually renegotiated in the process of making sense' (Parker, 1992: 3). Therefore there is no single discoverable true meaning, only numerous different interpretations. In sum this free-play of signifiers means that they get their meaning only from other signfiers within language and do not refer to anything outside themselves such as an independent reality. The language of science cannot represent or illuminate some external reality.

Thus the postmodernists' acknowledgement of the linguistic turn means that what we take to be knowledge is constructed in and through language. Knowledge has no secure vantage point outside such socio-linguistic processes. Whatever knowledge is, it cannot be justified through metaphors which commit us to thinking that it is an accurate representation of the external world. Hence what Vattimo calls the 'myth of transparency' (1992: 18), of unmediated access to reality, is an illusion. Rather it is language and the social negotiation of meaning themselves

Box 5.1

Gergen (1992: 219) provides the following example of corporate rationality whose meaning at first sight seems self-evident but whose polysemous aspects means that it could mean virtually anything:

'Lets be logical about this; the bottom line would be the closing of the Portsmouth division' does not carry with it a transparent meaning. Rather, its meaning depends on what we make words like 'logical', 'bottom line' 'closing' and the like. These meanings require that we defer to still other words. What does the speaker mean by the term 'logical' for example? To answer we must defer to other words like 'rational', 'systematic' or 'coherent' . . . at the outset it is clear that there are many meanings for such terms . . . they have been used in many contexts and thus bear 'the trace' (in Derrida's terms) of many terms. For example 'logical' can also mean 'right thinking', 'conventional' or 'superior'. Which does the speaker really intend? . . . each term employed for clarifying the initial statement is itself opaque until the process of *differance* is again set in motion. 'Right thinking' can also mean 'morally' correct, 'conventional' can also mean 'banal', and so on. And in turn these terms bear the traces of numerous others in an ever-expanding network of significations.

that need to be illuminated to display their constructive properties and processes.

Likewise Rorty (1979: 357–61) dismisses the possibility of a theory-neutral observational language and argues that whatever counts as truth, or reality, is a changeable socio-linguistic artefact where justification lies in the consensus arising out of the culturally specific 'language games' of a 'form of life'. For Rorty different language games constructed in diverse forms of life are incommensurable. Therefore the knowledge of one community cannot be judged by the standards of another community (1982: 188–9). It follows that there is a need to focus attention upon the arguments that are reasonable and persuasive to members of a particular community. In such a project Rorty suggests that philosophy can no longer perform its traditional role which was to 'underwrite or debunk claims to knowledge made by science' (1979: 3). This is because philosophers can no longer presume to rise above the language-games of different traditions since philosophers themselves are merely engaging in their own community-specific language-games. There is no Archimedian position outside all life forms and their language-games which enables philosophers to adjudicate knowledge claims.

In a similar vein Lyotard (1984, 1988) sees knowledge as being produced by particular language-games which, via their own rules and structures, produce a plurality of localized understandings. He uses the term 'agon' to refer to the unresolvable contest between different communities' language-games and he argues that postmodernists must accept this diversity and be concerned to gain knowledge of these variable and socially contingent understandings. Thus Lyotard differentiates modernism's 'expert's homology' from what he calls postmodern science which 'refines our sensitivity to differences and reinforces our ability to tolerate the incommensurable' (1984: xxv). The inevitability of incommensur-ability means that consensus as a generalizable epistemic standard 'has become an outmoded and suspect value' (*ibid*.: 66). Indeed it is toleration of dissensus amid the incommensurable which is essential for the postmodernist since any consensus implies the hegemony of a particular narrative or language-game which serves to silence alternative possible voices and prevent the heteroglossia which would otherwise ensue (see Gergen, 1992: 222–4).

Rorty's attack upon positivism's epistemological premises is replicated in other postmodernists' shared concern to advocate a de-differentiation of relations between subject and object (for example, Chia, 1995; Jeffcutt, 1994; Kilduff and Mehra, 1997). De-differentiation (see Box 5.2 below) dissolves positivism's dualism between subject and object into a duality and thereby postmodernism challenges positivism's certainty in the attainability of epistemic privilege and replaces it with a social construc-tivist view of science and knowledge in which the role of language is crucial.

Box 5.2

Generally de-differentiation means the erosion of boundaries between things. Here it is being used in a philosophical sense where positivism's Cartesian subject–object dualism proposes the separation, or differentiation, of the knower/observer from the known/observed. Postmodernist de-differentiation puts back together what positivists claimed to be separate: in knowing/ observing the knower/observer creates what is known/observed. The result of de-differentiation in postmodernism is the deployment of a subjectivist ontology. De-differentiation dissolves the distinction between reality and its representation in the sense that our linguistic representations are seen to *create* reality. For Baudrillard all that we are left with are 'simulacra' – images which refer to nothing but themselves: a 'hyper-reality', divorced from extra-linguistic reference points, in which there is nothing to see save simulations which appear to be real. Reality as an independently existing reference point is thereby destroyed and 'the boundary between hyper-reality and everyday life is erased' (Best and Kellner, 1991: 120). To paraphrase Derrida, nothing exists outside the text.

So because of the linguistic turn and its implications for de-differentiation, postmodernists think that language does not, and cannot, re-present an external reality. Instead, it creates what positivists assume to be an inde-pendent external reality (see Latour, 1990). For instance, Chia draws upon Woolgar (1988a and b) to argue that there is a tendency to reify, invert and then forget built into the positivist's differentiated mind-set. This is similar to Berger and Luckmann's view that man (*sic*) forgets 'his own authorship of the world . . . and . . . the dialectical relationship between man the producer and his products is lost to consciousness' (1971: 106). In what amounts to a deconstruction of scientific processes (see Box 5.3), Chia argues that what passes for scientific research

> often begins with the production of documents speculating on notions about how the world around us might be. This step is used to project the existence of a particular object which then forms the legitimate focus of investigation. At this stage the speculated object begins to take on a life of its own (reification) and is increasingly perceived as being separate and independent of our apprehension of it. Next a reversal of relationship occurs so that the impression is given that it is in fact the existence of the object which first stimulated our attention towards it. Finally researchers become so accustomed to talking in these inverted terms that the initial states of conceiving, reifying and inverting of the observer/ observed relationship are forgotten or strongly denied. This process is so subtle and insidious that it often goes undetected and, hence, leads to the impression of a pregiveness in the object of analysis. (1995: 589)

For Chia (*ibid.*) this movement from the socially constructed and overtly precarious to the fixed and independent means that the postmodern always precedes the modern's 'false concreteness' – its antecedence is merely forgotten and/or denied.

Hence for postmodernists 'reality' can have an infinite number of attributes, since there are as many realities as there are ways of perceiving and explaining. For instance, by stressing the indeterminacy of language, Derrida dismisses the view that 'the truth' could be discovered by either rationalist or empiricist methods as an example of modernist '*logocentricism*'. Derrida critiques logocentricism by arguing that for every 'fixed' idea, there is also an 'absent' idea. In other words, how we make sense of the world inevitably entails partiality as by interpreting experience in a particular way we inadvertently exclude alternative renditions. Here he is pointing to how a 'logos', because it has a fixed point of origin with a preformulated structure of metaphysical assumptions (such as the positivist's subject–object dualism), legitimates and stabilizes particular modes of engagement and action while excluding other possibilities. Unity and consistency are maintained at the expense of separation and contradiction. A key analytical approach associated with this critique and postmodernism generally is called *deconstruction* (see Box 5.3 below).

So postmodernists, in dismissing the possibility of privileged knowledge, argue that if one assumes that it is possible for an observer passively to register the facts of reality, that assumption ignores the possibility that the observer's linguistic apparatus is proactive and creative in influencing what we apprehend. Influential upon our linguistically derived sense-making are our social interactions in various cultural milieux which bias us towards particular constellations of collective meaning located in received stocks of knowledge. Usually we remain blithely unaware of these constructive socio-linguistic processes as we do these things rapidly, automatically and unconsciously. Thus, although the ontological result may appear as objective and separate from ourselves, as 'out there', through language we

Box 5.3

As the term implies, 'deconstruction' is the dismantling of constructions – or more precisely linguistic constructions. It derives from literary criticism where texts are analysed so as to reveal their inherent contradictions, assumptions and different layers of meaning. All texts therefore contain elements that counter their authors' assertions. In an epistemological sense any body of knowledge can be treated as a text that can be deconstructed. Here deconstruction attempts to demonstrate how any claim to truth, whether made by scientists or theologians, is always the product of social construction and therefore relative. This is attempted by showing how their texts contain taken-for-granted ideas which depend upon the exclusion of something. Often this will involve identifying the assumptions which underpin and thereby produce the 'fixed' truth-claim. These assumptions are then disrupted through their denial and the identification of the 'absent' alternatives whose articulation produces an alternative rendition, or re-reading, of reality. Hence deconstruction denies that any text is ever settled or stable: it can always be questioned as layers of meaning are removed to reveal those meanings which have been suppressed. It leads to questions about *how* something becomes seen as factual and about the consequences of such privileging. The result is that a relativistic position for deconstruction does not get the deconstructor closer to a 'fixed', or privileged, truth. At most it only offers alternative social constructions of reality within a text which are themselves then available to deconstruction and thereby are not allowed to rest in any finalized truth. In these respects postmodernism is parasitic in that it can only feed off existing texts.

are active participants in creating what we apprehend. In Chia's terms (1995), postmodern deconstruction is about remembering these epistemically formative socio-linguistic processes that attribute a false concreteness to our objects of analysis and which modernists have subliminated or forgotten.

Postmodern analysis of management

> In organisation and management science today it is not important whether a statement is true or false, but whether the fact or statement is accepted, saleable or valid for a larger audience.
>
> (Berg, 1989: 195)

Since all science is understood to be the product of socio-linguistic construction, postmodernists undermine science's authority by pointing to how notions of truth, objectivity, facticity and science are merely prestigious discursive, or linguistic, constructs. As Jeffcutt observes, '"reality" or "truth" becomes an "effect" and not an absolute position, an outcome of a particular reading . . . of a text' (1993: 27). Because there can be 'no standards worthy of universal respect dictating what to think or how to act' (Shweder, 1984: 47), those who argue that epistemic privilege is still possible are dismissed as 'cultural overseers' (Rorty, 1979: 317). Hence for Gergen (1990), the postmodernists' mission is to deploy their rhetorical skills so as to: unsettle and reconstitute the language of representation; erode epistemic hegemony and undermine traditions and orthodoxies; and carve out the new domains of intelligibility thereby giving voice to 'truths' previously suppressed. This mission focuses upon 'what is non obvious, left out, and generally forgotten in a text and examines what is unsaid, overlooked, understated and never overtly recognized' (Rosenau, 1992: 168). At first sight this programme of erosion seems also to entail emancipation as previously silenced voices are given audibility. As such, postmodernist epistemology has devastating implications for how we understand management and management practices.

First, postmodernists would reject any analysis of management which posits its development in terms of a progressive accumulation of knowl-edge – such a modernist-positivist grand narrative would be seen as dependent upon a privileging of the truth-claims of managers. Thus a postmodern approach would challenge management's positivistic ortho-doxy by treating its constituent disciplines not as resources for analysing different aspects of reality but as discourses (see Box 5.4 below) which socially construct and certify particular meaningful versions of reality that are taken to be neutral and thereby accorded scientific status. Through its discursive activity, science produces the behaviour it seeks to describe (Turner, 1987: 61) since empirical findings 'reflect pre-existing intel-lectual categories' (Hassard, 1993: 12). Management knowledge, as such, is seen as the outcome of distinct discourses each with its own mode of engagement constituted by its own rules, structures and epistemic criteria. If management's legitimacy is primarily located in its claim to articulate rationality and ensure progress, postmodernism must question this appar-ently self-evident legitimacy.

Secondly, postmodernists de-centre the subject. Here the individual knower is rejected as the autonomous origin of meanings and as the focus of analysis. Instead, through the language we use in and gain through social interaction we obtain and propagate shared discourses which enable us to make sense of the world. The individual is thereby constituted through exposure to historically and socially contingent discourses. The result is that people are not free to make their own interpretations; rather they are constrained by existing discourses. Human beings are thereby construed not as self-directing but deterministically – as mere conduits for discourses which produce the individual. Thus particular webs of mean-ing are seen as being historically and socially distributed through parti-cular scientific discourses. As such, any management discipline would be seen as a particular historical and social mode of engagement that restricts

Box 5.4

Central to Foucault's approach is the notion of *discourse*. Discourses are sets of ideas and practices which condition our ways of relating to and acting upon particular phenomena: a discourse will be expressed in all that can be thought, written or said about a particular topic, which by constituting the phenomenon in a particular way influences behaviour. In these respects discourses constrain and stabilize the free-play of signifiers into a particular gaze. Thus discourses are similar to Kuhn's paradigms in that they structure knowledge and practice by producing rules which systematically delimit what can be articulated. Discourses are social constructions and the existence of a reality independent of their knowledge constitution is at best precarious. For Foucault, all aspects of life are subject to observation, investigation and regulation through the media of discourse. In effect the history of science is one of how particular discourses have come to dominate particular socio-historical contexts and thereby dictate what counts as knowledge and what does not. Over time discourses therefore change and *genealogy* is the analysis of the conditions which make it possible for a particular discourse to develop and the analysis of the processes by which discourses change and adapt. The point is, however, that we can never attain any knowledge save that constructed in and by some discourse.

what is thinkable, knowable and doable within its disciplinary domain. Through their education and training, managers learn to speak this discourse and the discourse speaks to them by structuring their experiences and definitions of who they are.

Hence different management disciplines would be understood as a set of ideas and practices which structure our ways of understanding and behaving, which act as a grid for the perception and evaluation of reality. Here the development of any management discipline as a discourse would be the focus of a genealogical analysis (see Box 5.4 above) by examining the underlying discursive rules and categories which socially construct subjectivity by enabling and limiting what is thought, said or written about a particular disciplinary domain. In this deconstruction of the taken-for-granteds that underpin a discipline, a key focus would be to analyse the socio-historical conditions which have made it possible for a particular discourse to be developed and through which it might change.

Thirdly, central to a postmodern analysis would be power. Power is not seen as being possessed by conscious agents, whether they be individuals or collectivities. Rather, like knowledge, power is seen to be the outcome of and to reside in discourses themselves. In Cooper's (1989) terminology knowledge and power 'inhabit each other'. For Foucault, 'the exercise of power perpetually creates knowledge and, conversely, knowledge constantly induces effects of power' (1980: 52). For instance the ability to deploy a particular scientific discourse reflects a command of knowledge of a particular domain. In the case of management this ability is employed in relation to people who lack such a command and who have no socially legitimate claim to such knowledge. In a sense the deployment of any discourse is seen as empowering those people with the right to speak and analyse while subordinating others who are the object of the knowledge and disciplinary practices produced by the discourse. Thus not all people are equal within the web of power relations which defines them. Here claims to detached reason and objective analysis merely serve to mask the self-aggrandizement of the 'speaker' who, through the discourse, dominates and oppresses those who they analyse and categorize. The disempowered collude in the establishment of this power relationship in two ways. First they accept the authority of discourse speakers to analyse and categorize thereby empowering them. Secondly the discourse defines and constrains the identities of the disempowered to the extent that they engage in self-surveillance and correction of their behaviour towards the norms it articulates. Likewise those with privileged access to the relevant discourse gain a sense of meaning and identity from the practices it sanctions. In this manner individuals and collectivities become constructed, classified, known and transformed into self-disciplining subjects through power that they don't possess.

Thus human subjectivity is portrayed as an outcome of the exercise of power – 'a game in which the rules are never revealed or understood by the players' (Delanty, 1997: 106). In this sense postmodernists see power as being everywhere yet nowhere – as a relationship between subjects yet also independent of subjects where, 'it is not possible for power to be exercised without knowledge, it is impossible for knowledge not to engender power' (Foucault, 1980: 52). The result is that the positivist basis of any scientific discipline is challenged with science being viewed as a power–knowledge technology for regulation which 'produces reality . . . domains of objects and rituals of truth' (Foucault, 1977: 194) and which in effect suppresses the articulation of alternative possible 'truth-effects'.

Postmodernism and research methodology

all that I have tried to do here is to remind the reader that our methods are not gifts from the gods. The methods are our own construction and we need not accept them uncritically; in fact we need not accept them at all. Let us abandon method, let us take ourselves and our lives more seriously. George Orwell (1954: 177) once wrote 'political language . . . is designed to make lies sound truthful and murder respectable and to give an appearance of solidity to pure wind' perhaps this is a fitting epitaph to the eventual death of sociological method: it gave an appearance of solidity to pure wind.

(Phillips, 1973: 179)

The implications of postmodernism for how management research is conducted obviously differ according to the mode of postmodernism under consideration. When viewed as an era or period in time, the implications are few. Essentially traditional methods can be used to attempt to capture the nature of the new and the implications that has for individuals and organizations. In contrast, postmodernist epistemology clearly has important challenges for the way that management research is undertaken.

The anti-empiricist stance adopted by epistemological postmodernists (particularly those classified as sceptical by Rosenau, 1992 and Kilduff and Mehra, 1997) means that the importance which has traditionally been attached to research methodology by positivists becomes suspect. Indeed sceptical postmodernists rarely do empirical work of any kind as they deny the possibility of an empirical social science (Kilduff and Mehra, 1997). Thus they engage largely in deconstructing and critiquing existing work rather than undertaking new empirical approaches, causing some writers to characterize the approach as parasitic (Alvesson, 1995). For some this means postmodernism destroys the thing it most reveres as the identity of subjects which is carefully constructed through postmodern analysis is lost as writers seek the safety of philosophical theorizing. Thus many postmodernists could be characterized as armchair researchers, preferring to theorize and philosophize, critiquing from afar. In doing so, they can be just as guilty as positivists of mystifying what they do and marginalizing others through their use of jargonistic language which makes them look clever and prevents others from gaining a clear understanding. Even those who do empirical work have been criticized for taking a minimalist approach. For example Feldman (1998) critiques Joanne Martin (1990a) for using 'a single paragraph from a speech to make far ranging assertions about the suppression of feminism in an organization and organizations in general without any attempt to demonstrate the assertions empirically. Deconstruction thus licences generalization independent of empirical evidence, making it impossible to evaluate the logic and coherence of the argument' (Feldman, 1998: 70).

Whilst there has been a tendency for postmodernist writers in organization and management studies to maintain a distance from empirical research, this does not have to be the case – although they would maintain a scepticisim about the ability of empirical investigation to determine the actual nature of organizations. Empirical research from this perspective would focus on gaining an understanding of a situation at a particular point in time, recognizing that this is only one of a number of possible understandings. Just as science loses its authority from a postmodern perspective, so too scientific methodology 'loses its status as the chief arbiter of truth' (Gergen, 1996: 12). While research technologies produce data, the process of production and interpretation of data must inevitably rely on forms of language embedded within cultural relationships. Hence, the language that is produced by the empirical process does not equate with an increasingly accurate correspondence with reality (Hassard,

1993). Instead, 'theories of organizing are self justifying narratives rather than systematic attempts at making transcendental truth claims' (DeCock, 1998: 5). No research method is considered to have a privileged status in terms of providing access to reality. Any debate over which methods enable us better to observe and capture reality becomes pointless, as the postmodernist context of doubt recognizes the limitations of this project and distrusts all methods equally (Richardson, 1998).

Nevertheless Gergen points out that at the same time there is nothing in postmodernism that argues against the use of empirical technologies – suggesting that whilst there is scepticism of the grand narrative of progressive science it is impossible to deny that the means by which we now do things called transmitting information, automating production and quality control were not available to us in the last century. Thus 'Traditional research methods may very well be used to produce results that sensitize the readership to alternative modes of understanding. So long as one does not objectify terms such as team, values, competencies and the like but instead remains sensitive to parochial forms of reality that these terms sustain and to the valuational implications of such work, then such technologies are not inconsistent with most postmodern arguments' (Gergen and Thatchenkerry, 1996: 12). Hence the researcher has to maintain a suspicion and deconstruct the results produced through research.

Thus, instead of negating the importance of research methodology, some management researchers have focused on the liberating potential of the postmodern perspective, arguing that it frees researchers to mix and match various perspectives or research styles in order to challenge conventional wisdom (Kilduff and Mehra, 1997; Gergen and Thatchenkerry, 1996). This freedom to combine styles follows from the belief that all research approaches are embodied in cultural practice and no particular method grants privileged access to truth – therefore

> the hypothetico-deductive method and the preference for quantitative analysis characteristic of positivist research are elements available to the researcher to be combined possibly with other elements such as ethnography, biography, textual deconstruction and semiotic interpretation. The placement of hypotheses in a text for example does not necessarily signal the researchers commitment to apriori predictions. Hypotheses are rhetorical devices that can be used as helpful summaries of theory and as guide posts for the reader. (Kilduff and Mehra, 1997: 465)

In this way Kilduff and Mehra adopt an inclusive approach which they feel attempts to go beyond dualities such as modernist/anti-modernists, or positivist/anti-positivist championing the simultaneous availability of apparently incongruous research methods including laboratory experiments, deconstruction, ethnography and sophisticated statistical analyses.

However, whilst these writers stress the opportunity for a 'mix and match' approach, others see postmodernist methodology as largely qualitative and the majority of studies which could be classed as postmodern seem to adopt a qualitative approach towards methodology (Cassell, 1996; Kondo, 1990;

Martin, 1990b). This has caused consternation amongst some academics who feel that postmodernists have privileged certain methods as their own and that qualitative analyses focusing on narrative or drawing on interviews, participant observations, and multiple perspectives are too often assumed to be postmodern (Kahn and Lourenco, 1999). Ethnography in particular is popular with some postmodernists. Writers such as Linstead see ethnography as '*the* language of postmodernism' as it 'has the capacity to embody a variety of perspectives and settings; it can be regarded as the natural methodological and discursive response to epistemological and existential fragmentation; as a qualitative account its strength has been its theoretical description; it adapts easily to the "linguistic turn" in social analysis and incorporates an awareness of subjectivity; and it offers the possibility of "ethical" social science' (Linstead, 1993b: 98). Where positivistic ethnography focuses on representation, giving an accurate picture of reality, postmodern ethnography is more concerned with deconstructing that version of reality to identify other alternatives. The power of ethnography here comes from its ability to evoke, rather than describe – which apparently requires both poetic and conceptual rigour from the author so that they can produce an account 'poised in the space between "fact" and "fiction"' (Linstead, 1993a: 70). That is not to suggest that there is only one postmodern approach to ethnography. On the contrary, Linstead (1993a) identifies a number of possible approaches, each of which has a slightly different slant – see Box 5.5 below.

Box 5.5

Postmodern and Rortian ethnography

Interrogates traditional practice, asking of every representation 'is this a fact?' and refusing to come to any final conclusions.

Lyotardian ethnography

Provides detailed studies of fragmented information networks, clarifying linguistic practices and adding to the store of accessible data that would contribute to preformativity and the development of the aims of knowledge.

Baudrillardian ethnography

Could do nothing more or less than record experience as the flickering of images on a television monitor . . . whatever is caught by such means is fleeting ephemeral and misleading, appearance rather than essence.

Deconstructive ethnography

Rather than asking 'is this a fact?', focuses on how this could come to be considered as a fact and the consequences of treating it as a fact. Looks for internal contradiction and drives to demystify traditional theoretical concepts and the workings of common sense or naturalized perception. (Linstead, 1993a: 65–8)

The attraction of ethnography comes, in part, from its ability to focus on the micro aspects of organizational life. From a postmodern perspective the aim is to increase understanding of local practices, not to develop universal, generalizable theory. Quoting studies such as Zimmerman's study of social workers, and Boden's examination of the 'business of talk', Reed (1997) groups ethnomethodology, actor network theory and post-structuralism under the heading of postmodernism as they 'occupy a shared epistemological niche' in which the study of 'the local, the decentred, the marginal and the excluded is superior to examining what is at the centre' (Rosenau, 1992: 136). Ethnography as a method enables the researcher to give voice to those not represented in the dominant discourses (Giroux, 1992: 56), and amplify voices which have struggled to be heard (Kilduff and Mehra, 1997). In that sense it could be argued to be emancipatory, and certainly some avowed postmodernists see it this way as the quote from Boje, discussing postmodern approaches towards understanding the learning organization, below highlights:

> the postmodern rebel (Boje, 1993) deconstructs the modernist learning con-versation to reveal the muck and mire being smeared across our minds, the regimentation of the commodification programming that we are passively absorbing, the way in which our own values are neutered . . . postmodern critique reveals the story of humanity locked within gilded cages, perched upon velvet cushions above the minorities' children labouring on the cage floor, looking between the bars of commodification to the natural, unterritorialized spaces that are being chainsawed, strip mined and toxified. (Boje, 1994: 450–1)

The extent to which the implicit relativism of postmodernism constrains its ability to provide emancipatory potential is a point to which we will return to later.

It would be easy to imagine that theory has no place in postmodernist approaches. This is not the case according to Linstead who argues that theory can be used as 'a device to resuscitate the subordinate terms, to elevate them, to amplify the silenced voices in order to problematise the dominant understanding and, rather than create a new hierarchy, to re-construct a duality of awareness within conventional consciousness' (Linstead, 1993b: 116). This enables postmodern ethnography to be used to develop the capacity for reflection and reflexivity in managers and citizens (Gephart et al., 1996: 359). And, rather paradoxically, it can enable us to simultaneously 'know more and doubt what we know' (Richardson, 1998: 358). Postmodern ethnographies focusing on critically examining organizational discourses and providing the basis for such reflexivity are becoming more popular. Examples include Linstead's (1985) work using Levi Strauss' methodology for analysing myths to analyse everyday discourse on the shopfloor, Ely's (1995) study of sex roles in organizations and Kondo's (1990) examination of the production of identity in a Japanese workplace.

Whilst these authors may be utilizing postmodern approaches to empirical work, the focus of others has remained on the deconstruction of existing works. Examples include Kilduff's (1993) deconstruction of the March and Simon classic *Organizations* to identify the gaps and silences and show the Tayloristic assumptions underpinning it and Carter and Jackson's (1993) examination of motivation theory in general and expectancy theory in particular. They highlight well the aim of this kind of deconstruction when they make the point that they 'are not particularly concerned with validity of any theory of motivation to work but with their logics and contradictions' (*ibid.*: 90).

Cooper (1989) makes the point that when undertaking this kind of deconstruction the search is for gaps and instabilities in time, space and text. Typically this follows two movements of overturning, where terms are shown to suppress their binary opposites, and metaphorization which involves recognition that positively and negatively valued terms are defined in relation to each other and interpenetrate each other. Linstead (1993a) sees this process as consistent with Foucault's genealogical method where the aim is to uncover the social processes in the making of totalizing narratives or essentialist discourses. This Foucauldian approach is also working its way into research on management and examples include Knights and Morgan's (1991) examination of corporate strategy and Townley's (1994) study of Human Resource Management.

Role of the researcher

The researcher comes to the fore in postmodern research with the recognition that no methodology is capable of achieving an unmediated objective representation of the facts. As discussed earlier, methodology can be seen as a rhetorical attempt to persuade the reader of the scientific authenticity of the document. Positivists, using the language of the natural sciences and removing themselves from the research process, seek to persuade others that their research is objective and valid. From a postmodern perspective, instead of trying to erase all traces of themselves from their work, researchers should seek to demystify technology of mediation by explicitly detailing their involvement (Kilduff and Mehra, 1997). Researchers should also be humble about their findings, recognizing their role in the construction of those findings.

This has been seen as liberating by some researchers as they 'don't have to try to play god, writing as disembodied omniscient narrators claiming universal, atemporal general knowledge; they can eschew the questionable metanarrative of scientific objectivity and still have plenty to say as situated speakers, subjectivities engaged in knowing/telling about the world as they perceive it' (Richardson, 1998: 348). Others (for example, Linstead, 1993a; 1993b) point to the responsibilities this places on the researcher to be able to deconstruct the practices of others and oneself. Clearly there is a danger that this deconstruction becomes an endless, and perhaps paralysing activity (Ashmore, 1989). As there is no basis from which to be able to adjudicate, the deconstructors find themselves with no solid ground on which to stand and thus the method must be turned back upon itself (Linstead, 1993a: 57–8). Alternatively, it could be argued from a postmodern perspective that reflexivity is impossible as it requires the ability of the researcher to stand back and rationally reflect on their own assumptions – an ability to step outside false consciousness and examine the logic of their approach. Clearly this is problematic and reflexivity is a subject to which we will return in our final chapter.

Whilst, as we have mentioned, the researcher's role is more visible in postmodern research, the role of the reader is also explicitly recognized. Authors from this perspective deny responsibility for how their work is read and interpreted, recognizing that any reader brings to bear their own assumptions and taken-for-granteds when examining a piece of research, or other text (Burrell, 1997; Linstead, 1993a; Parker, 1993). Thus reading is recognized as a creative process, a recognition which adds to the impossibility of identifying an overarching reality or truth.

Postmodernism and relativism

> Should postmodernism be seen as practically useless since it offers nothing but a plurality of competing representational vocabularies in a world where facticity has disappeared or should it be neutered, tamed, harnessed further to imbue consultancy speak with another argot upon which to draw?
>
> (Burrell, 1993: 82)

At first sight postmodernist epistemology poses a significant sceptical challenge to positivism or indeed any other totalizing metanarrrative. It demands that people should think about and be suspicious of: how they engage with the world; the categories they deploy; the assumptions that they impose and the interpretations that they make. By 'not finding answers to problems, but . . . [by] . . . problematizing answers' (Cooper and Burrell, 1988: 107) postmodernism can make people think about their own thinking and question the familiar and taken-for-granted. Amongst researchers it encourages irony and humility as well as rebellion against the imposition of any unitary scientific discourse which imperialistically expunges plurality and forces epistemic closure.

So while postmodernism's reflexive value should not be underestimated, since it can at least sensitize us to alternative ways of apprehending the world, it also does sanction relativism through an articulation of what amounts to a subjectivist epistemology and a subjectivist ontology. Here truth is relative to one's mode of engagement with the 'world' for which no independently existing evaluative criteria exist. Moreover as Jeffcutt (1994: 228) argues, postmodernist epistemology suggests that '"reality" is not separate from its reconstitution, and the world we know is the world as represented'. In a similar vein, Wakefield (1990) likens postmodernism to 'the twilight of the real', while Gergen (1992) talks about reality's erasure. It follows that postmodernism is based upon the relativist view that the world is the *result* of representational practices. Through what Thompson calls 'a retreat into the text' (1993: 202), epistemology is collapsed into ontology, resulting in the world becoming whatever we wish to make it. The intellectual mirroring of reality that underpins positivism is thereby replaced by the relativist's intellectual production of reality. As Parker (1995) reports, the result of relativism can be what appear as absurd claims such as Baudrillard's denial that the Gulf War took place – apparently it was a media simulation. While such excesses appear as easy targets, what is more important is to consider how relativism creates severe epistemic contradictions within postmodernism.

If we take Townley's Foucauldian analysis (1994) as an example, she portrays human resource management as involving the social constitution of knowledge and order – a process of representation in which organizational worlds are rendered 'known, visible and potentially manageable' (*ibid.*: 144). Power is made invisible by the presentation of information as objective facts ostensibly 'independent of the interests of those who produce it' (*ibid.*: 145). But if we accept this postmodernist claim that all knowledge is the outcome of such partial constructivist processes, what therefore is the epistemological status of Townley's, and other postmodernists', own accounts? Can they really manage without invoking a metanarrative of epistemic privilege for their own accounts? Through their deconstructions is there a danger that they construct discourses about discourses that tacitly assert a claim to privilege for their own accounts through some rationalist epistemological back door? As we have illustrated, postmodernists see science as a mere rhetorical construction ripe for deconstruction. However such a postmodernist enterprise can only be carried out through language which, unless some tacit claim to epistemic privilege is deployed, should be in turn also deconstructed in terms of rhetoric. Therefore do postmodernists assume that their deconstructing intellectual stands outside the discursive knowledge–power relations which embed everyone else and that we should complacently accept their truth-effects?

For Habermas (1987) they cannot avoid the above charges – thus he accuses postmodernists of surreptitiously deploying positivistic metanarratives – a veritable performative contradiction! For Kellner (1988) this contradiction is evident in the work of both Baudrillard and Lyotard who make general statements about external cultural conditions and then deny the possibility of reality and its representation. Indeed the tacit notion that we should accept the 'truth-effects' of postmodernists' accounts is expressed by default in Townley's work (1994) – otherwise how can she justify her own ending of deconstruction and reflexivity through the closure of her own account? So if we accept that much of the post-modernist genre publicly deploys a relativistic metanarrative then the outcome is a double standard in that postmodernists apply their relativism only to the knowledge of others. For instance the totalizing metanarratives of science are the targets that give postmodernists themselves some voice as they are parasitically fed-upon and deconstructed. In accomplishing such deconstruction a double standard appears: postmodernists can only immunize themselves from the implications of their own epistemology by tacitly assuming an alternative metanarrative of epistemic privilege for their own accounts.

Alternatively, if postmodernists remain faithful to their relativism there remains the problem that the assertion of relativity, like positivism's notions of privilege, is still a metanarrative. Indeed it is a self-contradictory metanarrative which 'itself claims absolute validity and hence by its very form presupposes a principle which its manifest content rejects' (Mannheim, 1952: 130). The paradox here is that if we agree with the postmodernists' epistemic commitment that all knowledge claims are untrustworthy, why should we trust their claims about the relativity of knowledge? In other words, the nihilistic anti-dogmatic dogmatism of postmodernism's relativistic metanarrative nullifies itself since why should anyone accept a metanarrative that denies its own foundations? An outcome is a contradiction: the articulation an anti-totalizing relativistic discourse which imperialistically seeks to ban all metanarratives but its own totalizations. The postmodernists' response is that their theory is only one of many possible explanations: 'it is not universalizing although it may appeal to the universal' (Montagna, 1997: 132). This does not, however, solve all of their problems.

Even if it were possible to avoid the contradiction noted above, postmodernism must adopt a relativistic argument that concludes that since all knowledge is socially constructed, there are no good reasons for preferring one representation over another – including, presumably, their own genealogies and reconstructions. This adoption means that post-modernists must accept that we cannot and should not judge others and their discursively produced realities and truths. Such judgement would illegitimately limit the discursive power of others who have modes of engagement equally as valid as our own. While deconstruction might facilitate the articulation of heterodoxies and oppositional meaning systems which serve to undermine the rhetorical hegemony of the orthodox, the underlying socially produced significance of these liberated alternative voices is of no higher epistemic standard than orthodox meaning systems which they corrode.

In the fashion noted above the naïveté of positivism's rationalist and empiricist grand narrative gives way to the idea that knowledge is not subject to any extra-discursive checks. In many respects anything goes save that the text must provoke some pleasure, interest and excitement in terms of aesthetic appeal and rhetorical play (Kilduff and Mehra, 1997: 465). So despite the optimistic assertions of Bauman (1995) and others (for example, Rojek, 1995; Simons, 1995) that relativism can provide a 'liberating potential' based upon Rabinow's (1986) 'utopia of plural authorship', it is also evident that, by denying and eroding any basis to epistemic authority, it must also undermine the basis of critique and by implication the subsequent choice of interventions to change things. Paradoxically, postmodernism could thereby promote the aesthetic dis-interestedness and emotional detachment of Bauman's (1995) 'flanneur', who:

> is the man of the public who knows himself to be of the public. The flanneur is the individual sovereign of the order of things who, as the poet or as the artist, is able to transform faces and things so that for him they have only that meaning which he attributes to them . . . The flanneur is the secret spectator of the spectacles of the spaces and places of the city. Consequently flanerie can, after Baudelaire, be understood as the activity of the sovereign spectator. (Tester, 1994: 6–7)

If there is no possibility of adjudicating between different realities because there are no independent criteria upon which to judge, then it follows that there are no criteria through which we can engage in any form of criticism of the *status quo*. Critique becomes either a contentious exercise, since all that happens is a pointless juxtaposition of incommensurable narratives or the critic's unsustainable assertion of an epistemologically privileged metanarrative. Indeed under the mantle of relativism it is difficult to see how anyone can have anything to say which is significant, never mind critical. The practical effect is that 'the problems of (fictional) individuals in (mythical) organizations are safely placed behind philosophical double glazing and their cries are treated as interesting examples of discourse' (Parker, 1992: 11). Any intervention, organizational or otherwise, implies the exercise of choice based upon some kind of evaluative criteria. But, as Newton observes, the problem for a postmodernist would be 'in deter-mining that basis, since this implies the end of endless reflexivity and a move towards the postmodernity abhorrent notion of closure' (1996: 15).

So where does postmodernism's relativism leave us? Rather than critique and intervention, it would seem that the postmodern imperative is a mandatory non-judgemental rhetorical skill where multivocal authors playfully manipulate signifiers to create new textual domains of intelli-gibility redolent with 'poetic awe' and 'linguistic tension' (Tsoukas, 1992: 645), where scientists become 'balloon craftsmen – setting aloft vehicles for public amusement' (Gergen, 1992: 216). While such a jolly imperative might serve overtly to relativize everyone's account, what it ignores is the likelihood that claims to epistemic authority will not suddenly disappear (Berg, 1989: 205–6). The result may be that any (re)presentation of reality becomes a matter of taste where knowledge is commodified and reason is replaced by subtle forms of seduction where 'truth' is a matter of socially manipulable credibility awarded to the disseminators of knowledge by their audiences. Postmodernism could thereby promote a conservative disinterestedness that tacitly supports the *status quo* by engendering a disempowering silence about current practices as this relativistic dimension denies any possible grounds for critique. As Harvey (1989) has argued, the postmodern image of individuals manufacturing their own identities and realities is not a critique of capitalism but its apotheosis!

Conclusion

Hence current debates about epistemology seem to present us with two equally problematic alternatives. On the one hand the epistemological trauma created by postmodernism's inherent relativism may debilitate our confidence in the utility and ethicality of any kind of empirical research or organizational intervention. This could drive us either into a cynical passivity or into disabling philosophical introspection. Fearful of any discursive closure which would imply the construction of a metanarrative, the latter would be characterized by a relativist agenda of endless reflexive loops (for example, Ashmore, 1989) as we become self-absorbed in examining our own examinations of our own modes of engagement. Both passivity and introspection are particularly unappealing prospects for management research.

Alternatively the understandable fear of relativism could engender a conservative reaction in the form of a rejuvenation of positivism. This option would encourage the suppression of epistemological issues and the uncertainties they provoke along with a concomitant reassertion of a unreflexive empiricism. In this, positivism 'by making a dogma out of scientists' belief in themselves, . . . assures the prohibitive function of protecting scientific inquiry from epistemological self-reflection' (Habermas, 1972: 67). Such a head-in-the-sand approach is equally unappealing since, as Giddens has commented, 'the social sciences are lost if they are not directly related to philosophical approaches by those who practice them' (1984: xviii). In sum, the most important point here is that while postmodernists may be correct to reject positivism and its foundationalist truth claims, it is not axiomatic to infer that such a rejection justifies a flight into a postmodern epistemological, moral and political relativism. To paraphrase Bernstein (1983), what is needed, therefore, is a sustainable epistemology which avoids the Scylla of positivism and Charybdis constituted by the incipient relativism of postmodernism. As Bernstein puts it:

> with a chilling clarity Descartes leads us with an apparent and ineluctable necessity to a grand and seductive Either/Or. Either there is some support for our being, a fixed foundation for our knowledge, or we cannot escape the forces of darkness that envelop us with madness, with intellectual and moral chaos. (1983: 18)

It is the aim of the next two chapters to explore epistemological courses that attempt to deal with the 'Cartesian anxiety' described by Bernstein. It is precisely the relativistic problems created by the rejection of a theory-neutral observational language which Habermas confronts in his early work. In the following chapter we will outline and assess his attempted solution to these problems and consider how this has lead to a distinctive form of management research orientated towards critical theory. Meanwhile in Chapter 7 we will explore the pragmatic–critical realist course that attempts to provide a non-positivistic foundation for our knowledge which avoids Descartes' ostensibly ineluctable either/or dichotomy – a neither absolute nor relative epistemic stance that acknowledges both the relevance and limitations of postmodernism.

Further reading

Much of the work of postmodernists is pretty hard going. Best and Kellner (1991) and Harvey (1989) provide good starting points, giving a good critical introduction to the approach. The edited collection from Hassard and Parker (1993) also covers a good deal of ground. Kilduff and Mehra (1997) provide a brief overview of the application of postmodernist ideas to management in general, whereas Townley (1994) gives an insight into their use in human resource management. For an interesting genealogical analysis readers should look at Knights and Morgan (1991) whose examination of the way in which corporate strategy has developed as a discourse is fascinating. Those interested in deconstruction should find Martin (1990a), Linstead (1993a) and Cooper (1989) instructive.

6

Critical Theory and Management – The Return to Rationalism and the Promise of Progress?

We can be against critical theory or for it, but, especially at the present historical juncture, we cannot be without it. Indeed qualitative research that frames its purpose in the context of critical theoretical concerns still produces, in our view, undeniably dangerous knowledge, the kind of information and insight that upsets institutions and threatens to over-turn sovereign regimes of truth.

(Kincheloe and McLaren, 1998: 260)

In the last chapter we examined postmodernism and pointed to some of the inherent difficulties of relativism. For postmodernists all knowledge is partial and value-laden, thus any attempt at developing overarching theory is suspect. Whilst on the one hand postmodern theorists give an important insight into the dangers of instrumental reason and encourage researchers to be humble about their truth-claims, from a critical theory perspective a postmodern approach has three main problems: 'it fails to provide a language to articulate what are arguably indispensable concerns with autonomy, rights and justice; it is individualist in its emphasis on desire and pleasure; and it is irrationalist in its rejection of theory and rational critique' (Best and Kellner, 1991: 290). As we will show, whilst critical theory has some similarities with postmodernism (see Box 6.1 below), a key difference is that it maintains hope that knowledge can lead to emancipation and progress.

Critical theory focuses upon the inherent connection between politics, values and knowledge and, thereby, provokes a deeper consideration of the politics and values which underpin and legitimize the authority of 'scientific' knowledge (Alvesson and Willmott, 1988). Sometimes critical theory is given a broad meaning and includes all works taking a basically radical stance on contemporary society. These works tend to have an orientation towards investigating issues such as exploitation, asymmetrical power relations, distorted communication, and false consciousness. However, it has been argued that critical theory should not be treated as 'a universal grammar of revolutionary thought, objectified and reduced to discrete formulaic pronouncements or strategies' (Kincheloe and

Box 6.1   Similarities between postmodernism and critical theory

- Both attack the traditional division of labour which establishes fixed boundaries between regions of social reality and both utilize supra-disciplinary discourses
- Both carry out sharp critiques of modernity and its forms of social domination and rationalization
- Both combine social theory, philosophy, cultural critique and political concerns in their theories and unlike more academic theories some versions of both attempt to orient theory, practice and discourse towards politics
- Both have engaged in heated polemics against each other and have been synthesized with feminist theory. (Best and Kellner, 1991: 215)

McLaren, 1998: 263). Instead, following authors like Alvesson and Deetz (1996), we use the term with a more restrictive meaning, referring to studies that draw concepts primarily though not exclusively from the Frankfurt School.

The three leading theorists of the original Frankfurt School were Max Horkheimer, Theodor Adorno and Herbert Marcuse who originally operated within an avowedly Marxist framework. Although they later abandoned a specifically Marxist position, they maintained opposition to the destructive effects of Capitalism. A number of important research topics were addressed in the early works of the Frankfurt School, including the nature and emergence of Fascism, authority and the family, and art and popular culture (Pusey, 1987). Linking the work of the various representatives of the School was a concern with human freedom and the ways in which it is constrained through various forms of domination and social repression in the modern world. The critical theory which emerged was aimed at diagnosing the problems of modern society and identifying the nature of the social changes necessary to produce a just and democratic society (Layder, 1994).

The Frankfurt School also offered a critique of Cartesian-based epistemologies although the main target for both Adorno and Horkheimer was what they called 'instrumental reason' and the Enlightenment belief in the necessary connection between knowledge and freedom. Instrumental reason, as we will discuss, allows only for means–ends calculations and posits itself as politically neutral. Adorno and Horkheimer's major insight was to see this objectivist stance as founded on a desire for mastery and implicated in the practice of domination in the West (Alcoff, 1997). Horkheimer (1972) argued that rather than occupying a neutral position over the object, which serves to conceal the values and interests of the knower, we should see ourselves as embedded within social locations and understand reality as the product of an interaction between society and nature. For Adorno and Horkheimer (1987), what is needed from within the dialectic of Enlightenment reason is a negative critique which will break the systematically circular confirmations of instrumental reason, enabling the rearticulation and reinvigoration of Enlightenment ideals.

In this chapter we will focus particularly on the work of Habermas who is one of the second generation of the Frankfurt School. Whilst Habermas has built upon the ideas of previous critical theorists, it is important to realize that his work is not merely an extension of the work of Horkheimer, Adorno and Marcuse. Instead he sets out to 'reconstitute the whole paradigm of critical theory' (Pusey, 1987: 33).

Habermas

Like Kuhn, discussed in the previous chapter, Habermas (1972; 1974a; 1974b) presents a powerful critique of positivist epistemology. He argues that a correspondence theory of truth obfuscates the relationship between 'knowledge' and 'interest' by presupposing the possibility of a theory-neutral observational language that unproblematically reconstitutes reality for examination. While Habermas admits that positivism's limitation of the sciences to entities that were assumed to be immediately available to sensory experience has helped to remove metaphysical and religious dogmas from the realm of science, he also sees such empiricist commitments as problematic.

Positivism's presupposition of a theory-neutral observational language allows positivists to ignore the effects of the epistemic subject (i.e. the knower) upon what is known. For Habermas, knowledge is contaminated at source by the influence of socio-cultural factors upon sensory experience:

> even the simplest perception is not only performed pre-categorically by the physiological apparatus – it is just as determined by previous experience through what has been handed down and through what has been learned as by what has been anticipated through the horizon of expectations. (1974b: 199)

Habermas eschews positivism's 'objectivist illusions', which conceal the processes by which knowledge is constituted, by drawing attention to the socio-cultural factors that influence sensory experience. In this manner he substitutes the naïve empiricism of the correspondence approach to truth with a constructivism based upon the object–constituting activity of epistemic human beings. In this Habermas accepts the existence of a reality independent of human subjectivity which imposes limitations upon human endeavours. Thus, like Kant, Habermas puts forward a *phenomenalist* position that human cognition shapes reality through its imposition of *a priori* cognitive principles. This 'externality' can only become an object of human knowledge through our imposition of object-constituting epistemological 'categories' which derive from our fundamental 'interests' (1974a: 8). For Habermas, it is only through reference to fundamental interests that it becomes possible to understand: first, the criteria which are applied in identifying what is taken to be 'real' and, secondly, the criteria by which the validity of such propositions may be evaluated. Hence he identifies two 'object-constituting' epistemological categories, each of which involve specific interests and constitute the object-domains of two forms of knowledge:

> in the functional sphere of instrumental action we encounter objects of the type of moving bodies; here we experience things, events, and conditions which are, in principle, capable of being manipulated. In . . . [social] . . . interaction we encounter objects of the type of speaking and acting subjects; here we experience persons, utterances and conditions which in principle are structured and understood symbolically. (1974a: 8)

Following on from this, Habermas identifies two forms of knowledge with their attendant ontological domains, each deriving from specific human interests that he suggests have naturally developed during human evolution.

The first knowledge-domain, that of empirical–analytical science, emphasizes the human interest in our creative interplay with and attempts at exerting control over, the natural environment. This can be linked to evolution in that the need for physical survival leads to the development of knowledge about and control over the environment. This is 'not only a fundamental category of human existence but also an epistemological category . . . [which] . . . signifies a scheme both of action and apprehending the world' (1972: 28). For Habermas this instrumental interest in '*technical*' control over nature sets limits upon how we apprehend nature by placing parameters upon the theoretical concepts of the empirical–analytical sciences. For instance, because empirical–analytical science is oriented towards the establishment of technical control over nature, warranted knowledge becomes restricted to procedures that 'permit the deduction of law-like hypotheses with empirical content . . . [which] . . . make predictions possible' (1972: 308).

The second knowledge-domain, that of historical–hermeneutic science, emphasizes the human '*practical*' interest that arises out of the need for inter-personal communication where humans encounter other speaking, thinking and acting subjects who have to be understood symbolically. This interest is 'designed to guarantee, within cultural traditions, . . . self understanding of individuals and groups as well as reciprocal understanding between different individuals and groups' (1972: 176). Where communication fails, a condition for human survival is disturbed. Thus the historical–hermeneutic sciences are structured so as facilitate the apprehension of the meanings of actions and communications.

So for Habermas, although there exists an independent reality, this externality only becomes knowable to people through the action and mediation of our 'anthropologically deep seated interests'. In other words, these interests determine the aspects under which reality is objectified and can thus be made accessible to experience to begin with. They are conditions which are necessary in order that subjects capable of speech and action may have experience which can lay claim to objectivity. (1974a: 9)

To his taxonomy of interests and sciences Habermas adds what he calls 'critical science' which derives from 'emancipatory interest'. This third form of science is best illustrated by Habermas' critique of Gadamer.

Gadamer (1975) rejects the possibility of an ahistorical neutral position on the part of the observer/knower. He argues that any attempt at assuming the possibility of an 'infinite intellect' or 'transcendental' position devoid of our own 'historicity' are self-delusions. Instead he articulates what amounts to a conventionalist view of truth/knowledge and as such considers that our knowledge is socio-historically context-bound. What Habermas (1977) specifically objects to in Gadamer's perspective is the relativist outcome of his brand of conventionalism that produces the contention that there is no independent ground from which it is possible to criticize ongoing tradition. Habermas clearly thinks that this relativism leads to the uncritical acceptance of the underlying consensus of tradition and of repressive authority and power relations.

Habermas therefore identifies a third knowledge constitutive interest – an emancipatory interest that seeks to free people from domination – the systematic distortion of interaction and communication – and liberate their rational capabilities. The form of knowledge for this project is self-knowledge and understanding generated through self-reflection. When accomplished this self-reflection

> leads to insight due to the fact that what was previously unconscious is made conscious in a manner rich in consequences: analytic insights intervene in life. (1974a: 23)

Self-reflection demystifies previously unacknowledged distortions and enables awareness of the link between knowledge and interest. However the status of this third interest is ambiguous. Sometimes, as with practical and technical interests, Habermas accords fundamental anthropological status to the emancipatory. For instance he seems to think that it is formed alongside the other interests 'through the action of the "invariant" imperatives of a socio-cultural life form dependent upon work and communication' (1972: 13). However elsewhere he argues that the emancipatory interest is 'derivative' in that it can only exist under conditions of 'systematically distorted communication and thinly legitimated repression' (1973: 176). So usually he seems to think that the emancipatory interest can only develop to the degree that

> repressive force, in the form of the normative exercise of power, presents itself permanently in structures of distorted communication – that is, the extent that domination is institutionalized. (1974a: 22)

Table 6.1   The three knowledge-constitutive interests

Type of science	Cognitive interest	Social domain	Purpose
Natural science (empirical–analytical)	Technical	Work	Prediction control
Cultural science (hermeneutics)	Practical	Language/culture	Understanding/ consensus
Critical science	Emancipatory	Power/authority	Enlightenment

Source: Mingers, 1992

Thus critical science seeks to free people from overt and covert forms of domination. It unites aspects of the empirical–analytical and the historical–hermeneutical sciences within a project aimed at self-reflective understanding. Table 6.1 highlights the differences between the three categories of knowledge-constitutive interests.

Perhaps the prototype for critical science is psychoanalysis. This is because psychoanalysis involves 'depth-hermeneutics' (1972: 218) in which the distorted texts of the patient's behaviour become intelligible to them through self-reflection. This self-reflection is facilitated by the analyst's attempts at interpreting the patient's speech, behaviour and experiences in terms of unconscious causal variables that are identifiable through reference to the Freudian theory of neurosis. Through reflection upon the analyst's interpretations during therapy, the patient may begin to see 'himself through the eyes of another and learns to reflect on these symptoms as off shoots of his own behaviour' (1972: 32). In this fashion emancipation occurs as the patient becomes liberated from the terror of their own unconscious as previously suppressed and latent determinants of behaviour are revealed and thereby lose their power.

In sum, as with Kuhn's conventionalism, Habermas challenges positivism by attacking its claims to a theory-neutral observational language. This is accomplished by arguing that the object domains of forms of knowledge and their criteria of validity are constituted by interest. Therefore reality is only knowable through the operation of interest-laden modes of engagement. Subsequent accounts of reality are not objective or neutral but rather express interest – an expression obfuscated by appeals to neutrality and objectivity. But as McCarthy points out (1978: 295), by tying knowledge to the imperatives of human life, Habermas effectively undercuts notions of objectivity and encounters relativism. Therefore, as we have seen with Kuhn, 'how can Habermas claim anything more than an interest-relative truth for his own theories?' (*ibid.*: 293). It is evident that Habermas was aware of this problem and he tries to rescue the status of his own critique by finding an epistemological refuge from which that very critique might be pursued and defended.

As we have already pointed out, Habermas does admit to the existence of a mind-independent reality. Indeed this is a reality that remains unrevealed though it does apparently manifest itself through what Habermas calls 'the contingency of its ultimate constants' (1972: 33). However rather than allowing reality to play any part in the evaluation of knowledge claims through those manifestations, Habermas' attempted escape from relativism entails the proposition of a consensus theory of truth.

Habermas (1970a; 1970b; 1971) asserts that universal unconstrained consensus is implicit in human communication. He argues that when two speakers engage with one another, even if only to disagree, they take for granted certain assumptions about the organization of speech, and necessarily assume that they could reach an agreement, if they were to debate specific issues with one another under conditions free of distorting factors – in other words, free from domination (Morrow and Brown, 1994: 337–8). The ability to communicate linguistically in a fashion that satisfies what he calls 'validity claims' produces 'communicative competence'. These validity claims are: that the sentences speakers utter are comprehensive and their propositions are true; their overtly expressed intentions are honest; and the norms referred to in speech are correct. In everyday communication the validity claims which are inevitably made by speakers are usually accepted unquestioningly by hearers. This consensus is disturbed either by a misunderstanding or by a challenge to these claims. Such a situation may be remedied by clearing away misunderstanding, or by testing out the 'validity claims' through speakers and hearers undertaking analysis. Discourse occurs where this analysis is made explicit and entails the application of canons of argument and evidence with the intention of coming to agreement over the validity claims which have been disputed or misunderstood.

According to Habermas any communication rests upon the assumption that speakers can justify their tacit validity claims through recourse to argument and discourse. However, in what he calls 'systematically distorted communication', validity claims are maintained through the exercise of power which prevents justification through engagement in discourse and produces a pretence of consensus. Habermas uses the concept of the lifeworld to explain the general background context in which these validity claims (informed by different kinds of 'rationality' or reasoning) take place. Thus, while claim-making and the everyday practice of conversation goes on in the foreground this all depends on a background of assumptions. The two together form what Habermas means by the lifeworld. In this sense the lifeworld refers to the way in which our activities and ideas are related to the institutional, economic and cultural structure of the society in which we live (Layder, 1994: 192). The problem for Habermas is to elucidate how we might differentiate between systematically distorted communication and discursively produced 'rational' consensus.

Habermas attempts to resolve this question through his notion of the 'ideal speech situation'. Here rational consensus occurs when agreement derives from argument and analysis without resort to force, coercion, distortion or duplicity. This is characterized by all participants having an equal chance to initiate and participate in discourse, with all validity claims being open to discursive examination free from the constraints imposed by disparities in power (see Box 6.2).

Box 6.2   The ideal speech situation

The *ideal speech situation* is interpreted by McCarthy as freedom from internal and external constraint:

> that there must be for all participants a symmetrical distribution of chances to select and employ speech acts, that is an effective equality of chances to assume dialogue roles. If this is not the case, the resultant agreement is open to the charge of being less than rational, of being the result not of the force of the better argument but, for example, of open or latent relations of domination, of conscious or unconscious strategic motivations. Thus the ideal of truth points ultimately to a form of interaction that is free from all distorting influences. (1978: 308)

For Habermas, although such a consensus is not attained in everyday social interaction due to the operation of power and domination, it is both presupposed in, and a potential in, any communication. Thus the extent to which actual communication deviates from the ideal, and hence from the truth, depends upon the degree of repression in society. Hence the goal of Habermas' critical theory is 'a form of life free from unnecessary domination in all its forms is inherent in the notion of truth' (McCarthy, 1978: 273). So through his development of the ideal speech situation it is evident that Habermas adopts a conventionalist position that deploys a consensus theory of truth, as a regulative standard, to assess the extent of systematically distorted communication.

In this sense, critical theory seeks to show the practical, moral and political significance of particular communicative actions. It also investigates how a particular social structure may produce and reinforce distorted communicative actions that practically and subtly shape its members' lives:

> critical theory can thus be seen as a structural phenomenology. It is a phenomenology because it attends to the skilled and contingent social construction and negotiation of intersubjective meanings. It is structural because it attends to the historical stage on which social actors meet, speak, conflict, listen, or engage with one another. Ontologically it marries subjectivist and objectivist positions. Human actors make sense of daily life subjectively, through communicative interaction but 'sense' depends on context or setting – the objective social structure in which those actors work and live. (Forrester, 1983: 235)

Critical theory and management research

> it is because organisational research is conducted in the interests of management that such research does not account and provide for social structural change.

(Rosen, 1987: 575)

Given the stance of critical theory, it may seem at first that it has little to offer management research. Indeed some writers point to the fundamental contradiction between critical theory and the aims of management, with the former 'fundamentally opposed to alienation and exploitation', and the latter 'implicitly directed towards structuring organizational and societal relationships by means of oppression and exploitation' (Grice and Humphries, 1997: 417). Others would argue, though, that critical theory provides a platform from which it is possible to gain an understanding of the political and negotiated aspects of management and thus undermine the masquerade of management as a neutral activity (see, for example, Alvesson and Willmott, 1988; 1992a; 1996; Jermier, 1998; Nord and Jermier, 1992).

The various ways in which management is constructed has developed into an area of importance from this perspective. As we will discuss, this has led some writers to challenge the ways in which critical theory has in the past either ignored or else constituted managers as a homogeneous group (Alvesson and Willmott, 1992a; Clegg and Hardy, 1996; Nord and Jermier, 1992), seeing them very much as the agents of capitalism oppressing the workers in order to maximize returns to the owners of capital. These writers argue that (some) managers themselves can also be viewed as oppressed and that there is a wide disparity between different levels of management. Thus critical theory warns us that 'what passes for "ordinary work" in professional-bureaucratic settings is a thickly layered texture of political struggles concerning power and authority, cultural negotiations over identity and social constructions of the problem at hand' (Forrester, 1992: 47).

A criticism that has been levelled at Habermas and others from the critical tradition, however, is an insufficient level of concern with empirical research (Morrow and Brown, 1994). There has been a tendency to focus at a more abstract, esoteric level and to write in such a way that it can be difficult to judge the implications for doing research from this perspective. Perhaps this is no surprise as it could be argued that researchers from a critical perspective are stuck between a proverbial rock and hard place 'in the paradoxical context of the cross fire of attacks from positivists who claim it is antiscientific, on the one hand, and the postmodernists who declare its scientific and rationalistic aspirations to an Enlightenment illusion on the other hand' (Morrow and Brown, 1994: 23).

At a general level, the aim of critical theoretic approaches to management studies is to understand how the practices and institutions of management are developed and legitimized within relations of power and domination such as capitalism. Fundamental to this approach is the belief that these systems can be transformed to enable emancipation. Thus

> The point of doing critical management studies must be more than simply being different, simply having another way of looking at the world. It must be about making a difference. (Grice and Humphries, 1997: 422)

This involves a process through which individuals and groups become freed from repressive social and ideological conditions that restrict the development and expression of human consciousness. However emancipation is not about the re-engineering of work practices by management to give workers greater autonomy and thereby increase their motivation. This would merely represent an alternative way of privileging the aims of management. Rather, the process of emancipation must involve a continuing process of critical self-reflection and associated self-transformation.

It has been argued that this departs dramatically from conventional approaches to the generation of knowledge about management which fail to question the rationality of established power and authority. The aim of traditional approaches has been to produce more accurate knowledge of the reality of management so that resources can be allocated and organized in a more effective way. By subjecting the rationality of such understandings and objectives to close scrutiny, critical theorists show how much management research has ignored or remained silent about many aspects of organizational life such as inequality, domination and politics and has instead focused upon 'preserving the status quo to the detriment of advancing a more rational society in which socially unnecessary forms of domination are addressed and eliminated' (Alvesson and Willmott, 1996: 51).

Thus the instrumental rationalism which underpins much management research is exposed. From a critical theory perspective, though, the aim is not to remove values in order to make the process of management research more objective as it would be from a positivist approach (Donaldson, 1996; Pugh, 1983). This would not be possible as facts cannot be separated from values. Rather, it is to make the values underpinning any piece of research explicit. The researcher does not sit on the sidelines as a neutral observer, but is very clear about their own values and objectives in undertaking the research. As Parker (1995) contends, because truth is seen as a temporary consensus, values become of central importance when adopting a critical perspective. Thus, Habermas argues, knowledge must discard the illusion of objectivism which 'prevents consciousness of the interlocking of knowledge with interests from the lifeworld' (Habermas, 1971: 305–6). Nor does critical theory advocate the abandonment of epistemological questions. Instead, as Habermas has argued, different kinds of science are understood to be embedded in different kinds of human interests (Alvesson and Willmott, 1996: 65). For emancipation to take place there is a need to counter the influence of 'scientism' which occurs when 'we no longer understand science as one form of possible knowledge but rather identify knowledge with science' (Habermas, 1971: 4).

At this point it is important to distinguish between critical theory and critical thinking. Whilst many researchers of management may consider themselves to be critical, in that they attempt to stand back from their work and interrogate their findings with a critical eye, this does not necessarily mean they are operating within a critical theory perspective.

Prasad and Caproni (1997) distinguish between critical theory and critical thinking by focusing on four broad themes that are integral to critical theory:

1 an emphasis on the social construction of reality;
2 a focus on issues of power and ideology whereby there is an awareness that social constructions are influenced by power relations and a consideration of the role of ideology in preventing individuals from living fulfilling lives by masking social contradictions and creating false expectations;
3 the need to understand any social or organizational phenomenon with respect to its multiple interconnections and its location within holistic historical contexts;
4 the importance of praxis, the ongoing construction of social arrangements that are conducive to the flourishing of the human condition. Prasad and Caproni see the achievement of praxis as difficult but the most important part of critical theory, as 'without sustained commitment to praxis, critical theory restricts itself to becoming a self indulgent academic effort and thus risks losing its emancipatory potential' (1997: 3).

Similarly Calhoun (1995: 35) argues that 'a theoretically serious critical engagement with one's social world calls for an account of that world in terms of its salient features for practical action, and an ability to place it in relation to other basic patterns of activity (e.g. other epochs as well as culturally or socially different contemporary settings)'. As a result, critical social theory should be seen as an interpenetrating body of work which demands and produces critique in four senses:

1 a critical engagement with the theorist's contemporary social world, recognizing that the existing state of affairs does not exhaust all possibilities and offering positive implications for social action;
2 a critical account of the historical and cultural conditions (both social and personal) on which the theorist's own intellectual activity depends;
3 a continuous critical re-examination of the constitutive categories and conceptual frameworks of the theorist's understanding, including the historical construction of these frameworks;
4 a critical confrontation with other works of social explanation that not only establishes their good and bad points but shows the reasons behind their blind spots and misunderstandings and demonstrates the capacity to incorporate their insights on stronger foundations. (Calhoun, 1995: 35)

In the field of management and organization studies, Alvesson and Deetz (1996) indicate two different approaches which have been used towards developing critical theory. The first of these falls into the category of *ideology critique* and can be traced back to the more traditional work of the early Frankfurt School. This can be seen in the critique of managerial ideology which was particularly popular in the 1970s and early 1980s. A good example is Labour Process Theory, where much of the work undertaken was derived from Marxist principles and often focused on the exploitation of workers by managers (see, for example, Braverman, 1974; Clegg and Dunkerley, 1980; Salaman, 1981). Alvesson and Deetz discuss how this approach to critical theory has evolved to address systemic processes that produced active consent and cultural control mechanisms (examples of this type of work include Burawoy, 1979; Czarniawska-Joerges, 1988; Willmott, 1993). The main focus of traditional ideology critique approaches towards critical theory has been upon four processes: naturalization, the universalization of management interests, the primacy of instrumental reasoning and the notion of hegemony (see Table 6.2 below).

Ideology critique has also been subject to some criticism that it often appears *ad hoc* and reactive, seeking to explain what has happened in the past rather than predict the future. Notions of false consciousness can also make it appear elitist as they presume a basic weakness in insight in those it wishes to empower. Thirdly Alvesson and Deetz (1996) argue that early accounts are often too simplistic, with the dominant group appearing singular. Thus managers are assumed to be a homogeneous grouping when clearly their experiences of work organizations can differ dramatically.

The second approach to critical management research has been inspired by the reformulation of critical theory by Habermas. Whilst there is some similarity with ideology critique, the focus changes to address the processes through which individuals might attempt to reform institutions through an ethically driven discourse which is arrived at in an ideal speech situation. In particular, patterns of communication are examined in the hope of removing 'systematic communicative distortions of jargon, misrepresentation, deceit and illegitimacy' (Alvesson and Willmott, 1992a: 11), thus developing conditions suitable for the ideal speech situation where accurate, honest and legitimate communication provides the basis for rational, reflective and moral decision-making (Lawrence and Philips, 1998).

On the basis of this free, open and rational discussion it is assumed that consensus can be achieved about both the present and the future. As discussed earlier, the validity claims made in such discussion can be assessed on the basis of criteria of comprehensibility, sincerity, truthfulness and legitimacy (Habermas, 1971). By studying the ways in which communication fails to meet this ideal and the systemic distortion of communication, critical theory offers an approach to understanding the structure of organizations. According to Forrester (1983: 239–40), such an approach would investigate the process by which a particular mode of organization shapes, offers, encourages, blocks, or makes credible criticism and learning (possible forms of discourse) regarding the fundamental communicative claims (truth, rightness, sincerity, clarity of meaning) that

Table 6.2 Major themes in ideology critique approaches

Naturalization	The reification of institutional arrangements so that their features are no longer seen as choices but as the natural way of being. Ideology critique exposes this tendency and focuses on the processes by which they are formed, sustained and transformed.
Universalization of management interests	Ideology critique confronts the ways in which management goals are perceived as the interests of everyone in the corporation.
The primacy of instrumental reasoning	The tendency to focus on the means rather than the ends. Thus debate about fundamental issues such as the purposes of organizations is stifled. This has been a major issue for critical theory.
Hegemony	The complex web of conceptual and material arrangements which produce the fabric of everyday life. This includes the processes through which the dominant group and the dominated manufacture consent.

(See Alvesson and Deetz (1996) for more in-depth discussion.)

constitute its very identity. Thus, for example, Lawrence and Philips (1998) show how the application of critical theory to an analysis of TQM/BPR (Total Quality Management or Business Process Re-engineering) would examine the manner in which these programmes work to reproduce or subvert managerial ideology, and distort or idealize organizational communication.

Fundamental to both approaches to critical theory is the focus on the emancipatory power of reason. Through this it 'offers the possibility for us to intervene in the evolution of society rather than to be merely swept along as non reflective and passive participants reproducing a social order without being aware of our role in the process' (Gephart, 1993). The implications of this for the ways in which management is conceptualized and the process of management research are explored below.

Conceptualizations of management

As we discussed in Chapter 2, much research into management has tended to obscure the political aspect of organizations, treating management as a technical, neutral activity (for critiques of this see Alvesson and Willmott, 1996; Anthony, 1977; MacIntyre, 1981; Whittington, 1992). As a result of this functionalist approach, organizations are often assumed to be unified wholes with management goals representing everyone within the organization. Willmott (1995) discusses how this rational, technicist notion of management is best seen in the representation of management knowledge as science, arguing that this helps in securing the exercise of managerial prerogative.

Critical theory fights against this tendency and, whilst research from this perspective is oriented towards practice, there is no attempt to provide quick fixes for management problems. Indeed there is a tendency to dismiss existing management theory as an expression of technocratic thinking that seeks to constrain human potential and desire in order to reinforce the *status quo* (Alvesson and Willmott, 1996). Traditional management theorists are also criticized for failing to appreciate 'the historical, socially constructed nature of existing work processes and for interpreting individual employees needs (e.g. money, security and self actualization) as essential to human nature rather than as a manifestation of the structure of social relations' (Alvesson and Willmott, 1992b: 438).

Thus the underlying metaphors of much traditional management theory are functionalist. The importance of organizational survival is often stressed and vested interests are something to be eradicated, as a dysfunctional element of organizational life. However Box 6.3 below highlights a number of other metaphors for management which Alvesson and Willmott (1996) have argued to be appropriate from a critical theory perspective.

Box 6.3   Alternative metaphors of management

Management as distorted communication
This relates to the ways in which management privileges instrumental rationality, in other words, the ways in which debate is focused on the means of achieving goals rather than upon what those goals should be. The goals of management are thus deemed to be so commonsensical as to be beyond debate. Instead of enabling communicative interaction and encouraging more differentiated world views, modern corporations tend to require and preserve communications that are systematically distorted.

Management as mystification
This metaphor draws attention to the ways in which managers contrive to shape the ways people make sense of the world, for example by constructing a favourable image of themselves and/or their organization through the careful arrangement of symbols and ceremonies.

Management as cultural doping
This metaphor highlights the ways in which organizations socialize their employees. Cultural doping could be argued to be a major aspect of many HRM and TQM programmes which try to influence workers' attitudes, values and expectations (Willmott, 1993; Legge, 1995).

Management as colonizing power
This metaphor highlights the way in which a particular set of practices and understandings comes to dominate. Each new philosophy can be seen to address aspects of the contradiction as managers strive to extend their control from control over behaviour to control over values through socialization and other cultural control mechanisms. (Alvesson and Willmott, 1996: 96–108)

These metaphors of management highlight more controversial and often undiscussed (or seemingly undiscussable) aspects of the management process and suggest that researchers should not view management as a neutral activity. This is not to say that critical theory is always anti-management. Rather, it is concerned with exposing the underlying values associated with knowledge and particular modes of operating. Its thrust 'is pro-liberation and anti-closure rather than pro-worker and anti-management' (Deetz and Kersten, 1983: 166). According to Grice and Humphries (1997), this means to adopt a position that explicitly attempts to move outside institutionalized managerial values.

There remains a good deal of debate about the role of managers from a critical perspective and whether they themselves should be considered as oppressed groups upon which research should focus. As mentioned previously, there has been a tendency to view management as a homogeneous group by some critical theorists, particularly those inspired by Marx. The focus has been on the fundamental conflict between groups within organizations (management and workers) and insufficient attention has been given to differences and conflicts within groups. Hence writers such as LaNuez and Jermier (1992) argue the need to recognize that managers differ on a number of dimensions. For example, they focus on social and political dimensions in differentiating between five distinct orientations of managers. It is argued that these, along with other factors such as function and hierarchical level, mean that all managers should not be viewed equally and some managers may themselves feel oppressed.

In addition, if we go back to early critical theory, all human beings were viewed as candidates for enlightenment and emancipation (Horkheimer and Adorno, 1947). Indeed Horkheimer (1989) identified white collar employees, including managers, as the social group that merited most urgent critical examination. Hence Braverman in *Labour and Monopoly Capital* (1974) contends that managers and 'mental workers' are both targets and agents of capitalist control. Others have also shown how managers, rather than being unthinking functionaries, often experience moral and ethical dilemmas and could easily be perceived as victims (Alvesson and Willmott, 1992a; 1996; Jackall, 1988). Middle managers, in particular, have been picked out as a group who often suffer in modern work organizations (Scarborough and Burrell, 1996).

Fay (cited in Nord and Jermier, 1992: 202) argues that instead of hierarchical position, it is the feeling of being oppressed by others that is necessary for one to be a fit subject for critical social science:

> it is the experience of unhappiness which is the wedge a critical theory uses to justify its entrance into the lives of those it seeks to enlighten and emancipate . . . If they are happy before it approaches them, they are not a fit subject for a critical theory.

Others are far more sceptical of this approach, asking

what happens to the disenfranchised when the privileged are recast as victims? . . . Managers are the victims of their own privileges and oppressive practices. But this gives an odd twist to the poststructuralist dismantling of the subject as agent because it seems to condemn us all as victims, although we clearly live out dramatic differences. (Sotorin and Tyrell, 1998: 322)

Sotorin and Tyrell (*ibid.*) also express concern regarding Alvesson and Willmott's micro-emancipatory projects. Essentially these are humanistic approaches towards management and, whilst Alvesson and Willmott accept that proponents of critical theory would generally consider humanistic management theory to be at best fatally flawed and at worst a cynical attempt to extract more from workers, they also suggest that a cautious welcome could be given to approaches recognizing higher order needs. This leads Sotorin and Tyrell to question whether critical management studies risk an unintended capitulation to the temptations of managerial endorsement, adapting critique and reflection to managerial demands for pragmatic effectiveness. On the other hand, of course, it could be argued that managers are precisely the people who must be reached if the conditions of the workplace are to be transformed. Sotorin and Tyrell extend their critique of critical theorists in their review of Clegg and Palmer's (1996) edited book *The Politics of Management Knowledge*. They suggest that certain authors compromise their critiques of ideologies by complementing dominant rationalities. For example they suggest that, in an effort to assess contemporary management strategy, Hansen (1996) implicitly promotes a more rational–functional model of leadership; that Child and Rodrigues (1996) create new typologies for managerial strategies focused on effectiveness and efficiencies in international knowledge transfers; and that Ramsay (1996) proposes analytic schemes designed to manage new organizational techniques more effectively.

Thus debates continue as to the way in which critical theory can be used in management studies and whether there are risks that it could be used to reinforce rather than challenge the dominant elite. Alvesson and Willmott (1996) suggest the following research agenda:

1 developing a non-objective view of management techniques and organizational processes;
2 exposing asymmetrical power relations;
3 counteracting discursive closure;
4 revealing the partiality of shared interests;
5 appreciating the centrality of language and communicative action.

Fundamental to the approach is that management is seen as a social and political phenomenon rather than a technical function and it is this, coupled with the emancipatory ideal, which clearly impacts upon the approach towards research methodology and the relationship between researcher and researched.

Research methodology

the seeming avoidance of values is the strongest value commitment of all.

(Agger, 1991: 11, cited in Jermier, 1998: 238)

Critical theorists have been criticized for failing to provide a clear exposition of the impact of their approach upon research methods, hence creating a gap between an extensive tradition of critical empirical research on the one hand and guidelines for how to conceptualize and conduct such research on the other (Morrow and Brown, 1994: 39).

As discussed earlier, critical methodology is concerned with an analysis of the current situation which enables us to understand how this has developed and liberates us from seeing this as the natural order of things. Gebhart argues that within a critical approach we consider what could be and that 'as against the current scientific fatalism, motives like dreaming, hope . . . assume a cognitive function in a less zealously restrictive science' (cited in Morrow and Brown, 1994: 320). Moon, on the other hand, highlights the role of critique arguing that:

> critical theory seeks to provide an interpretation of social conditions which begins with self understandings of the social actors, but . . . subjects them to sustained criticism with the objective of uncovering their basic contradictions, incoherences and ideological distortions. Further critical theory seeks to explain the power and persistence of such ideological distortions by showing how systematically distorted ideas and belief systems arise and the role they play in maintaining a system of social interaction. Moreover it also provides an analysis of the workings of the social system showing the ways in which a crisis could arise, thereby providing for the possibility of critical theory becoming itself a material force leading to a system change. (Moon, 1983: 175, cited in Hammersley, 1992: 101)

It should not be assumed, however, that the methodological approach of all critical theorists is necessarily the same. A reading of the works in critical theory reveals a good deal of diversity and tension. Thus writers like Kincheloe and McLaren (1998) argue that critical theory should be treated as a broad church, stressing underlying commonality rather than difference. Following on from this, they define a criticalist as a researcher or theorist who attempts to use her or his work as a form of social or cultural criticism and who accepts certain basic assumptions, explained in Box 6.4 below.

An attempt to articulate the methodological foundations of critical theory through interpretative structuralism (or hermeneutic structuralism) has been put forward by Morrow and Brown. They identify several central principles:

- social relations and social analysis always have an interpretative (hermeneutic) dimension;

- meaning and language (hence discourses) are the basis of forms of reality construction that both reveal and conceal the experiences of subjects;
- structures may be species-specific or historically constituted and sometimes consciously transformed even if they have a kind of objective facticity that appears independent of immediate actors;
- that social and cultural structures constrain human action as does a grammar language, hence not the way implied by variables as probablistic determinants;
- that meaning and structures constantly are reproduced (statically) and produced (dynamically) across space and time. (1994: 24)

Box 6.4   Basic assumptions of a critical researcher

- that all thought is fundamentally mediated by power relations that are socially and historically constituted;
- that facts can never be isolated from the domain of values or removed from some form of ideological inscription;
- that the relationships between concept and object and between signifier and signified are never stable or fixed and are often mediated by the social relations of capitalist production and consumption;
- that language is central to the formation of subjectivity (conscious and unconscious awareness);
- that certain groups in any society are privileged over others and although the reasons for this privileging may vary widely, the oppression that characterizes contemporary societies is most forcefully reproduced when subordinates accept their social status as natural, necessary or inevitable;
- that oppression has many faces and that focusing on only one at the expense of others (e.g. class oppression as opposed to racism) often elides the interconnectedness among them;
- that mainstream research practices are generally, although most often unwittingly, implicated in the reproduction of systems of class, race and gender oppression. (Kincheloe and McLaren, 1998: 263)

From this perspective, research strategies need to take account of both phenomenological and structural issues; phenomenological in that they are sensitive to the understandings of those being researched and structural in the sense that consideration is given to the economic, political and social contexts in which actions take place. This opens the door for a wide variety of data collection and analysis techniques:

> critical social research is clearly not constrained by its data collection techniques . . . empirical studies . . . include the whole gamut of research tools: observations both participant and non participant; formal interviews with random samples; semi structures, unstructured and in-depth interviewing; key informants testimonies, analysis of personal and institutional documents; mass media analysis; archive searching; examination of official statistics; and reviews of published literature. Furthermore critical social research also uses a wide

variety of analytic techniques: ethnographic interpretation, historical recon-struction, action research, multi-variate analysis, structuralist deconstruction and semiological analysis. (Harvey, 1990: 196)

However, whilst the quote above shows the possibility for a certain amount of methodological pragmatism, this is combined with a critical realist ontology which sets an agenda and priorities with respect to research problems that tends to privilege some methods over others as part of research designs. In general the stance taken is an interpretative one which attempts to construct a sense of situations from personal and institutional standpoints through participation, observation and analysis of contextual data.

In delineating between different research approaches used we are going to focus on three aspects. The first will be a general discussion of critical ethnography. We will then move on to discuss the work of two writers who have sought to utilize what they have termed a Habermasian approach to ethnography and finally we will consider some of the more participatory approaches towards research. It is important to recognize that these three groupings are not necessarily distinct and that particular works may fit (albeit not very neatly) in all of these categories. The aim here is to give some brief examples before going on to look at some of the issues which face those undertaking research from this perspective.

Critical ethnography

Whilst a good deal of work from a critical theory perspective adopts an ethnographic approach, there remains some ambiguity regarding what distinguishes critical from conventional ethnography. Conventional ethno-graphy is necessarily conservative in nature. It seeks to describe the situation as it is, with no standpoint from which to critique it or consider alternatives. There is also a tendency for conventional ethnographers to hold on to the positivist notions of value neutrality and a correspondence theory of truth. (For discussion of this see Hammersley, 1992.)

Critical ethnography is oriented towards exposing oppressive practices in organizations and critical ethnographers are up-front about their emancipatory values. Whilst impact on practice seems fundamental, much of what is taken to be critical ethnography is not praxis-oriented in the immediate sense of impacting directly on social practice. This is not necessarily problematic as it could be argued that the impact on practice takes place through a more indirect route, for example education. Ethno-graphy is appealing from a critical perspective because 'letting people in organizations speak for themselves by conducting ethnographic studies is a vital means of moderating totalizing accounts of management and organization' (Alvesson and Willmott, 1992b: 437). Critical ethnogra-phers thus accept the complexity and ambiguity of people's discourses and recognize that the current situation does not necessarily reflect a natural order. Hence one of their key tasks is to be aware of the historical context in which research takes place and to reflect this critically on to the research process itself (Harvey and Myers, 1995).

An important challenge for the critical ethnographer therefore is to take account of the meanings that local actors ascribe to situations and explain them in a wider context. Harvey (1990) discusses three possible ways to link the detailed analysis of ethnography to wider social structures and systems of power relations:

1 consider the subject group in a wider context (weakest form);
2 focus on the wider structural relations and examine the ways in which the social processes that are evident in the subject group are mediated by structural relations;
3 incorporate ethnography directly into a dialectical analysis where the understanding developed from the ethnographic study is integrally related to the deconstruction of social structures: 'ethnographic techniques are thus used to elaborate an understanding that goes beyond surface appearance and thereby specifies the nature of the essential relationship of the structure under analysis'. (Harvey, 1990: 12)

Hence, in addition to portraying the individual's world view, critical ethnographers also aim to reveal socio-economic conditions that produce and reinforce asymmetrical structures of control. Interviewees may not articulate these. Therefore the most controversial aspect of critical theory is to 'go beyond informants reports to articulate socio-economic context that envelops their informants world without relying exclusively on either pre-existing theory or mere speculation' (Jermier, 1998: 241).

Morrow and Brown highlight two overlapping contributions of critical ethnography beyond its descriptive and explanatory value: cultural critique as defamiliarization and cultural critique as ideology critique. The contribution of ethnography to ideology critique, as discussed earlier, focuses on the demystification of hidden power relations. The more general strategy of defamiliarization is less well known and has been reconstructed from recent work on ethnographic writing (Marcus and Fisher, 1986). Such work uses poststructuralist themes for critical purposes and focuses on challenging ethnographers' ways of thinking about and conceptualizing the situation they are addressing. This can be done by becoming aware of alternative ways of thinking about reality and also by using cross-cultural juxtaposition which involves direct comparisons between similar situations in very different contexts to highlight critical issues (Marcus and Fisher, 1986; Morrow and Brown, 1994).

Morrow and Brown argue that defining critical ethnography in these terms helps to make sense of a series of misunderstandings. The first misunderstanding they argue derives from those who stress that critical theory's distinctiveness comes from focusing on political practice and breaking down the gap between the researcher and researched. One clear example of this comes from Hammersley (1992) who argues that critical ethnography 'is always necessarily political in the sense of serving someone's interests, wittingly or unwittingly; and that only by consciously linking it to the right sort of politics can we ensure it will serve the right interests' (Hammersley, 1992: 104). They suggest that the second misunderstanding relates to the focus on practice, which whilst it may be applicable to some forms of action research scarcely touches on the deeper issues involving the intensive analysis concerned with combining interpretive understanding, causal analysis and critique. We will return to this issue later. For now we move on to examine writers who have classified their research approach as Habermasian and have attempted to use Habermas' ideas of the ideal speech situation and the consensus theory of truth in different ways.

The Habermasian approach

John Forrester's work utilizing a Habermasian framework to examine decision making in the context of a planning department is much cited. He argues that an empirically oriented critical theory should be '1) empirically sound and descriptively meaningful and 2) interpretively plausible and phenomenologically meaningful and 3) critically pitched and ethically insightful as well' (Forrester, 1993: 2). He suggests (1989; 1991; 1992) that in the past Habermas has been too often pigeonholed as meta-theoretical and insufficient attention has been given to the important ways in which Habermas' work can be used empirically. Challenging this, Forrester uses Habermas' theory of communicative action as the basis for analysing text from a municipal staff meeting to show the impact of power relations on the planning process.

Forrester examines how the four 'validity claims' actually work in practice. He argues that doing fieldwork in a Habermasian way enables researchers to examine the processes and the outcomes of relations of power:

> quite contrary to prevailing misinterpretations of Habermas, we come not to expect any idealized truth-telling; instead we look closely at the ways in which appeals to truth (and quite differently truthfulness) serve varied and significantly contingent, variable ends. We presume neither that truth always serves the powerful nor that truth shall necessarily set anyone free; instead we look at concrete communicative practices to see what differences they can and do make. (Forrester, 1992: 62)

Forrester is concerned thus to examine the ways in which people interact and the production and reproduction of social organization. Whilst he uses Habermas' work to examine communicative practices, his approach has far less to say about the implications of the consensus theory of truth for the relationship between the researcher and the researched than that proposed by writers such as Laughlin and Broadbent (Broadbent and Laughlin, 1997; Laughlin, 1987; Power and Laughlin, 1992) discussed below.

Broadbent and Laughlin (1997) have conducted studies on accounting in GP practices and schools following a three-stage process, as discussed by Laughlin (1987). Central to the approach is the role of the researcher and the researched. In the first stage the researchers are the prime focus as they enter the organizational arena and aim to utilize qualitative research methods to generate insights which will form the basis of 'critical theorems'. These insights or theorems are then subjected to debate utilizing Habermas' idea of the ideal speech situation. Essentially this is a process where the aim is to 'come to some agreement (which may be an agreement to differ and does not have to be a positive consensus) allowing the force of the better argument to prevail' (Broadbent and Laughlin, 1997: 4). The next stage is called the stage of enlightenment as the critical theorems are used as the basis for further discourse between the researchers and the researched. Both parties thus become enlightened about each other's perceptions of the situation. In the final stage of the research the focus moves to the selection of strategies for intervention. This stage is led by the researched, the aim being to allow organizational members, on the basis of the understandings generated, to select the strategies which they feel are appropriate.

Whilst this research provides a powerful illustration of research in a Habermasian tradition, it also highlights problematic issues in the notion of the ideal speech situation as it is very difficult to accept that it is possible to achieve consensus regarding the core issues of the research which is not influenced by the respective power and interests of the individuals who constitute the researchers and researched. Hence while the authors discuss the discourse between different members of the researcher group, there is little information regarding how contradictory perceptions were dealt with. Similarly in some cases it was assumed that consensus had been achieved between those conducting the research and those under study because the researched had not sent negative comments on a report of the critical theorems handed to them. We will return to these issues at the end of the chapter when we examine problematic issues in undertaking research from a critical theory perspective.

Participation and critical theory

The constructivist stance of critical theory and the importance given to processes of self-reflection and emancipation have naturally led some writers to focus on approaches which encourage participation from those being researched. Kincheloe and McLaren (1998) discuss the benefits of worker-led research which has been conducted in Sweden involving 150,000 study circles and 1.4 million participants:

1 production of more useful and relevant research on work – critical theory provides an account of the world of work from the marginal perspective of the workers;

2 legitimation of worker knowledge – those engaged in the work are involved in the research;

3 empowerment of workers – worker researchers produce a provisional vision of empowerment as part of a larger critical project;

4 forced reorganization of the workplace – challenges the assumptions upon which the cult of the expert and scientific management are based;

5 inspiration of the democratization of science – when workers take part in research and legitimate their own knowledge then scientific research will be better able to serve progressive democratic goals;

6 undermining of technical rationality – a critical workplace would instead start with research by workers themselves on the conditions of their labour;

7 promotion of an awareness of worker cognition – 'highlights an awareness of reality by both logic and emotion'. (Kincheloe and McLaren, 1998: 286)

Similarly Sayer (1992) discusses a major piece of research informed by a critical approach (Institute for Workers Control Committee of Enquiry into the Motor Industry, 1977). This was a piece of research where academics, unions and workers co-operated to investigate workers' circumstances in a way which could simultaneously gather information and raise consciousness so they could better defend their interests. Although divisions between the groups could not be completely removed, they were softened. For example, interviews and questionnaires were organized so that workers would not simply give information to external researchers who offered nothing in return and who retreated to ivory towers once the data had been collected. Rather, the research process was kept interactive and open-ended so that workers could pose and discuss questions and hence reconsider their position. Sayer raises doubts about the efficacy of this approach to bring about change, however, commenting 'That objective conditions did not change much as a result should not surprise us: education is not a sufficient condition for social change and actions which attempt to change practice are constrained by existing structures' (1992: 255). Again this raises a problematic issue for critical theory research to which we will return at the end of the chapter.

   Reason (1998) discusses three approaches towards participative research – co-operative inquiry, participatory action research and action inquiry, each of which he argues could be seen to be informed by a critical theoretic approach. While writers may not come in with a straight Marxist line, the impact of critical philosophy can be seen and historical materialist language and thinking occur at a number of points (Reason and Rowan, 1981).

Co-operative inquiry directly involves the researched in undertaking the research process. Reason identifies four key stages of action and reflection central to the process. First, co-researchers agree an area for inquiry and identify some initial research propositions. This may involve an examination of a particular aspect of their experience or seeking to change some aspect of their world. They also agree some procedures by which they will observe and record their own and each other's experience. In the second phase the group then applies these ideas and procedures in everyday life and work. Phase three involves what Reason calls 'full immersion', as the co-researchers become fully engaged with their experience and may develop an openness to what is going on for them and their environment that allows them to bracket off their prior beliefs and preconceptions and to see the experience in a new way. Finally in Phase four the co-researchers return to consider their original propositions and hypotheses in the light of experience, modifying, reformulating, rejecting and so on.

Participatory action research follows a similar participatory process to co-operative inquiry. It originated in studies of the Third World and focuses much more explicitly on the emancipation of disadvantaged and oppressed groups. The primary task has been defined as 'enlightenment and awakening of common peoples' (Fals-Borda and Rahman, 1991: vi). This primary concern for the powerless means that concerns for epistemology and methodology appear secondary (Reason, 1998: 269). Participatory action research has two objectives: one is to produce knowledge and action directly useful to a group and the second is to empower people through raising consciousness. Whilst some researchers have applied the term to their work in Western organizations, others claim that the origins of participatory action research in under-privileged parts of the world make it inappropriate for Western organizations and societies (for example, Hall, 1991, quoted in Park, 1999).

Finally, Kemmis and McTaggart define action research as 'a form of collective self reflective inquiry undertaken by participants in social situations in order to improve the rationality and justice of their own social or educational practices, as well as their understanding of these practices and the situations in which these practices are carried out' (1988: 3). The link between action research and critical theory is also argued by Argyris et al. who demonstrate how critical theory proceeds by making explicit the epistemic principles that agents already use but of which they are unaware and by showing that the agents' world view may be false by the criteria of these epistemic principles (Argyris et al., 1985: 73–4). They go on to argue that to be effective action science must devise a process 'that will allow participants to make explicit the data they select and the meanings they impose and that will enable them to negotiate the differences in meaning that arise so that they might reach agreement' (*ibid.*: 239). Action science utilizes a range of qualitative methods designed to collect data on how individuals interact and the meanings they ascribe to those interactions. Common to each method is that first the data are generated in a way that makes participants feel causally responsible for them. This seeks to minimize researcher control over what problems are studied, what data are selected and the means by which they are selected or generated. Secondly, each method is designed to elicit data on how individuals actually act and on what they are thinking or feeling at the time.

Fundamental to these three approaches is that the research makes a difference to individuals' experience and that those who are being researched play an active role in the process, rather than being passive subjects. Whilst this commitment to participation may be the ideal in critical theory research, it is not always possible and it does not necessarily negate a commitment to emancipation and praxis. For example Jermier (1998) makes the point that often critical researchers do not give feedback to those involved in the research. He argues that this does not negate the critical potential of the work as it can be put to use in the service of oppressed groups in indirect ways, for example through teaching and research. Morrow and Brown (1994) also warn that we need to be wary of the leap from general epistemological claims about the ultimate grounding of inquiry in knowledge interests in Habermas to a conception of the immediate transformative effects of the practice of such research. That said, the aim of critical theory as a liberating force clearly has major implications for the role of the researcher and the relationship between the researcher and the researched. It is this to which we now turn.

The role of the researcher and their relationship with the researched

by recognizing the link between studying others and discovering about self as learner and change agent researchers 'bring the place of epistemology, the place of the meaning of data and enquiry to the forefront of activity'.

(Rosen, 1991: 2)

Harvey (1990) has argued that the conventional relationship between the researcher and researched assumed by a positivist stance is contrary to the aims of critical theory because:

1 it subverts the critical process, presupposing the primacy of the researcher's frame of reference;
2 it presupposes a one-way flow of information which leaves the respondent in exactly the same position after having shared knowledge and ignores the self-reflexive process that imparting the information involves;

3 the direct corollary of the self-reflection is the inevitable engagement in dialogue where information is required or perspectives need to be discussed. The involvement of the researcher in this real dialogue involves them in the critical process;

4 the critical ethnographic interview (in whatever its form) is not neutral but directs attention at oppressive social structures and informs both researcher and respondent. Thus, digging down to reveal the respondent's frame of reference is not meant to be an oppressive hierarchical process but a liberating dialogical one. (Harvey, 1990: 12–13)

This raises two fundamental issues to address in terms of the role of the researcher. The first relates to the values of the researcher and how these impinge on the research process and findings. The second relates to the consensus theory of truth which underpins Habermasian approaches to research and the ways in which researchers from this perspective judge the veracity of their own truth claims.

Emancipatory values

As discussed earlier in this chapter, the idea of value-free knowledge is questionable because it deflects attention from how in practice what counts as scientific knowledge is the product of value judgements that are conditioned by historical and cultural contexts. Whatever claims to objectivity are made, knowledge remains a product of particular values that give it meaning and direction (Alvesson and Willmott, 1996). Thus 'critical researchers maintain that the meaning of an experience or observation is not self evident. The meaning of any experience will depend on the struggle over the interpretation and definition of that experience (Giroux 1983; Mclaren 1986; Weiler 1988)' (Kincheloe and McLaren, 1998: 273). In other words, the ways in which we analyse and interpret empirical data are conditioned by the way they are theoretically framed and the researchers' ideological assumptions. It cannot be treated as indisputable fact.

Therefore research in the critical tradition takes the form of 'self conscious criticism' (Kincheloe and McLaren, 1998), in the sense that researchers try to become aware of the ideological imperatives and epistemological presuppositions that inform their sense-making: 'no one is confused concerning the epistemological and political baggage they bring with them to the research site' (*ibid.*: 265). Thus it is not just postmodernists who are humble about the grounds for their analysis. This approach requires 'a deflation of pretensions, including the (self) deceptions of those who occupy positions of relative power and advantage' (Marcus and Fisher, 1986: 25). But Marcus and Fisher also point out that users of critical theory should be sensitive to the accomplishments of those in power and in particular relate such pretensions to the historical and existential conditions within which their subjectivity is constituted.

According to Putnam et al. (1993: 227), the quality of research from a critical theory standpoint is not based on the ability to tell a good story but 'on the ability to participate in a human struggle – a struggle that is not always vicious or visible but a struggle that is always present. Research should be part of a larger human struggle rooted in the right to participate in the construction of meanings that affect our lives'. A critical text is judged by its ability reflexively to reveal hidden structures of oppression as they operate and impact upon individuals' experience. It should create a space where many voices can speak – in particular, those who have little power are asked to articulate their definitions of their situations. Thus a good critical text is one which is 'multivocal, collaborative, naturalistically grounded in the worlds of lived experience, and organised by a critical interpretive theory' (Denzin, 1998: 332).

Given the acceptance that knowledge is not independent of interests and value, some analysts argue that 'validity' may be an inappropriate term in a critical research context as it reflects a concern for acceptance within a positivist concept of research rigour. Kincheloe and McLaren (1998) argue instead for trustworthiness as a more appropriate word to use in the context of critical research. It is helpful because it signifies a different set of assumptions about research purposes. The identified criteria by which critical trustworthiness could be assessed, according to Kincheloe and McLaren (1998), are shown in Box 6.5 below.

Box 6.5   Validity in critical theory

1   *Credibility of portrayals of constructed realities* – Critical researchers reject the notion of a cause–effect reality, there to be measured and portrayed accurately in research descriptions. Credibility from this perspective comes when constructions are plausible to those who constructed them. Controversially, the researched may disagree as they may not see the effects of oppression which the researcher can. Thus it would be very difficult to measure a trustworthiness quotient.

2   *Anticipatory accommodation* – Kinchloe and McLaren reject traditional notions of external validity and transferability. Instead they utilize the Piagetian notion of accommodation whereby researchers use their knowledge of a variety of comparable contexts to begin to assess their similarities and differences. Hence they try to accommodate unique aspects of what they perceive in new contexts.

3   *Catalytic validity* – Kincheloe and McLaren utilize Lather's notion of catalytic validity. This considers the degree to which research moves those it studies to understand the world and the way it is shaped in order for them to transform it (Lather, 1991). In other words, it is the emancipatory impact of the research upon those being researched.

Judging the veracity of truth-claims

> for those new to critical theory perhaps the most difficult issue to
> comprehend is how a critical researcher can reject the claim that
> objectivity results from scientific detachment and still aspire to express
> more than a speculative opinion.
>
> (Jermier, 1998: 239)

As a researcher from a critical theory perspective it is important to consider
what constitutes warranted knowledge. Following Habermas, some
researchers have adopted a consensus approach towards truth whereby the
emphasis is upon socio-rational decision-making processes and the
development of knowledge through debate engendered in an ideal speech
situation. Thus, for example, Broadbent and Laughlin (1997), discussed
earlier, utilized a participative research design where attempts were made to
generate conditions under which genuine discourse, unpolluted by issues of
power, could develop between researchers and researched and within the
group of researchers. Jermier sees this as one key way of enhancing objectivity
by conducting debates within communities of researchers seeking mutual
understanding. This debate is at its most rational, according to Habermas,
when validity claims are examined and critiqued by self-reflective
participants.

The second method of strengthening objectivity, according to Jermier,
comes from standpoint critique. Thus:

> although all theoretical perspectives and empirical studies are inevitably situated
> in a limited point of view (Haraway 1988) and although it is impossible to take
> a disinterested 'view for nowhere' (Calhoun 1995: 11), studying some groups
> and individuals in certain social situations tends to generate the most objective
> knowledge claims. As Harding (1991: 150) so aptly puts it, research should
> being with the concrete circumstances and lived experiences of 'the system-
> atically oppressed, exploited and dominated, those who have fewer interests in
> ignorance about how the social order actually works . . . Thus rather than
> surrendering objectivity contemporary critical theorists push for more self
> conscious forms of objectivity by working to explain how values and interests
> affect the research process and by focussing attention on the strengths and
> limitations of various standpoints. (1998: 239)

As we will move on to discuss, whilst the notion that free debate can
generate a picture of reality has enabled Habermas to avoid the relativism
inherent in postmodernism, this has also created a number of problematic
issues for researchers following his approach. First, however, we will
examine the difficulties raised by the emancipatory values which are such
an important part of critical theory.

Problematic issues

A number of problematic issues arise when trying to assess the impact of
researcher values. Not least these arise because rarely is there in-depth

discussion of how these have influenced the interpretative process. Denzin argues that critical theory approaches 'with their action criteria, politicize qualitative research. They foreground praxis, yet leave unclear the methodological side of the interpretive process that is so central to the grounded theory and constructionist approaches' (1998: 332).

There are other more fundamental issues to be addressed, however. The rejection of value neutrality is central to critical theory and is a powerful critique of positivism and some other interpretative approaches. Whilst this has been criticized as an over-simplistic reading of critical theory (Morrow and Brown, 1994), in its crudest form there seems to be a suggestion that researchers are either in favour of emancipation or against it. Hammersley (1992) criticizes this as an extremely naïve view of politics 'in which the only roles are the good the bad and the naïve' (1992: 104).

There are also difficulties associated with the concept of oppression. It is questionable whether the oppressor/oppressed model reflects the complexities of organizational life. For example, is there only one source of oppression? Can individuals (managers) be oppressors and oppressed? Furthermore the notion of oppression suggests that we can identify what are 'real' needs and that these will be homogeneous. Hence Geuss (1982: 58) argues that critical theory 'doesn't merely give information about how it would be rational for agents to act if they had certain interests; it claims to inform them about what interests it is rational for them to have'. Thus the views and values of the researcher may come to be privileged over the 'false consciousness' of the researched. The question remains as to how the researcher is able to stand outside that false consciousness. Hence critical theorists have been criticized for their tendency to impose their voices and values on the groups studied (Quantz, 1992: 471) and for being too preoccupied with theory verification (Roman, 1992). This also relates to the essentialist critique of critical theory – that it attempts to reduce or totalize all phenomena so that they fit within a single integrated framework (Alvesson and Willmott, 1992a).

Critical theory has also been criticized for its intellectualism. For example Fay (1987) questioned whether the sequence: suffering – critical reflection – emancipation is as unproblematic as Habermas has suggested. Without denying that reason is a potent emancipatory force, Fay argues that the powers of reason are inherently limited by our experiences and our understandings of the present.

Some writers have argued that the success or otherwise of a critical theory in bringing about enlightenment or emancipation is a crucial, if not the crucial, aspect of any assessment of its validity (Geuss, 1982; Hammersley, 1992; Lather, 1991). However Geuss (1982) questions whether there are any clear public criteria for success and failure of emancipation, making the point that

> emancipation can miscarry: the agents may steadfastly refuse to accept the views about freedom embodied in critical theory or they may recognise that they acquired certain beliefs or traits under conditions of coercion but maintain they

would have acquired them anyway, even if they had been in circumstances of complete freedom; finally when they have experienced the state of freedom the critical theory proposes they may discover that it imposes unexpected and intolerable burdens on them and must be abandoned. (1982: 89)

From a poststructuralist/postmodern perspective this poses fundamental problems for critical theory. Doubts are raised as to whether the truths assumed by critical theory's critique of ideology can be separated from relations of power – in other words, can critical theorists step outside hegemonic power relations to assess reality? In addition the question is raised whether the ideal of the autonomous subject who, having become more reflexively aware, is able to overcome the consciousness-distorting effects of power is actually attainable. Critical theorists also have to address the issue that all forms of knowledge are interest-based and that all (including critical theory) have the potential to become new sources of domination.

This clearly contrasts with a postmodern approach where writers would argue that to enter research with the view to explore relationships between pre-identified groups such as managers and workers imposes untenable boundaries that dominate the researchers' findings. Thus, the metanarratives of the critical theorists are said to 'assume the validity of their own truth claims' (Rosenau, 1992: xii). This is argued to be paradoxical as any such claim to truth represents an arbitrary privileging inconsistent with the emancipatory pursuit of critical theory (Grice and Humphries, 1997).

Further critique develops from Habermas' epistemological attachment to the consensus theory of truth and the ideal speech situation as a vehicle for achieving consensus. First, presumably for Habermas we do not yet live in societies free from domination and therefore ideal speech situations are not yet possible. If so what is the epistemological status of Habermas' own work – is it too just another example of systematically distorted communication or is he somehow exempt from such processes? Of course, is any claim to such an exemption itself based upon the exercise of epistemic authority and hence power?

Secondly, if rational consensus is only possible in the ideal speech situation, how far are we from such a situation in any communication, or conversely how would we know if we have actually achieved it? For instance, one could be misled into believing that an ideal situation existed since we have no criteria to give us an indication of its existence that are in themselves known to be uncontaminateable by the exercise of power. Therefore how could we ever know that we know the truth?

Thirdly, Habermas' own notion of rational consensus in conditions of communicative competence invokes values that are derived from the Enlightenment tradition which he calls 'Old European Dignity' (1971: 143). Given his own critique of Gadamer's uncritical acceptance of 'tradition' and hence repressive power and authority relations referred to earlier, Habermas appears to be contradicting himself. As Arbib and Hesse point out with regard to the Enlightenment:

the liberal values of freedom and equal rights are derived from this tradition, as are the norms of participatory democracy and the search for truth by means of rational argument. Ideal speech resting on Enlightenment values is not too far from Gadamer's grounding in tradition with some Western Ethnocentrism thrown in. (1986: 198)

Fourthly, perhaps the most important criticism of Habermas relates to the claim that any consensus must arise out of discourse, for this implies the possibility of the neutral adjudication of knowledge claims by rational investigators. As Fay comments:

theoreticians cannot know for certain whether they have provided the best interpretation of their experience – indeed they cannot even be certain what their experience is. There is nothing given to them, neither the meaning of their experience, nor what is to count as evidence, nor the relations of this evidence to their theories. In a situation of this sort, it is folly to think that all competent rational participants will ultimately agree on a particular theory as uniquely the best. (1987: 178)

As Fay proceeds to observe, without the prior assumption of the possibility of a theory-neutral observational language, rational analysis will not dictate to them 'the single answer to which any rational agent must adhere' (1987: 179). This is a significant problem for Habermas – his attempt to avoid relativism by developing a regulative ideal based upon unconstrained consensus cannot be sustained without some recourse to the contradictory presupposition of the availability and use of a theory-neutral observational language to resolve disputes. Indeed Habermas' epistemological position seems to restore inadvertently the epistemic privilege embraced by empiricists through a critique aimed at repudiating all forms of epistemic privilege based upon empiricism.

This raises a number of questions for researchers who are embarking upon a study using Habermas' framework:

1   Is it possible to reach an ideal speech situation? Hammersley (1992) raises the point that the notion of an ideal speech situation is based on a circular argument in the sense that it is defined in terms of freedom from the effects of ideology yet presumably we need to be free from ideology to recognize the situation.

2   Is agreement being achieved because of underlying power issues? Even though agreement has been achieved does this necessarily mean we have accessed 'the truth'? What role does false consciousness play? Deetz (cited in Payne, 1996) acknowledges that the goal of interpretation is a deeper understanding of events but questions how such knowledge is gained and used. Does it try to produce a sense of coherence out of what may just as likely be seen as contradictions or paradoxes and does it reinforce existing relations of domination? Focusing on how consensual realities may de-emphasize or unfairly represent different competing interests and their efforts to produce meaning, Deetz argues for organizational research to include a critique

in terms of how conditions of consensus serve or disserve organizational interests.

3   Could the researchers have indulged in 'consensus collusion' where co-researchers 'band together as a group in defense of their anxieties, so that areas of their experience that challenge their worldview are ignored or not properly explored' (Reason, 1998: 268).

4   Will communication necessarily lead to consensus? Layder argues that 'in his drive for a "formal" model of interaction he [Habermas] confuses understanding with agreement and does not sufficiently attend to the fact that often communication leads nowhere in particular. In fact it may lead to a profound lack of substantive agreement rather than to shared understanding' (1994: 199). What do researchers do if consensus is not reached? As we suggested earlier, it is clearly problematic to rely on empirical observation to provide the 'facts of the situation'.

Thus the achievement of the ideal speech situation where rationality can be attained has been used by Habermas to rescue critical theory from the perils of relativism. However, as can be seen above, it raises many questions which critical researchers need to address.

Conclusions

Critical theory provides a powerful critique of positivism and some neopositivist interpretative approaches. Critical theorists reject the idea of theory-neutral observational language, showing how knowledge is underpinned by values and interests. Therefore a key issue in critical theory relates to the need for researchers and the researched to be reflexively aware of their own presuppositions and values. This reflexive awareness, it has been argued, is best achieved in open, undistorted communication. Thus Habermas provides a new communication-based model for epistemic evaluation where inquiry occurs in an intersubjective context in which the goal is better understood as mutual agreement rather than knowledge of an object. Critical theorists argue that our current institutions are the result of a particular historical context and that communication within these institutions is systematically distorted. Once we achieve the ideal speech act where communicative distortions are removed, however, we are able to assess the validity of particular claims to truth in open and honest debate.

It is important to remember that Habermas has a fear of relativism, and this approach does not assume that all points of view are equally defensible or equally illuminating. Rather there is a focus on the oppressed as these people have less to gain from maintaining the *status quo*. As we have already discussed, there are a number of problematic issues here, but critical theory is an interesting approach towards management research as it provides a framework through which it is possible to examine the political nature of management and organizations and it also provides a standpoint from which to critique these processes and institutions. Whilst many of the techniques of critical theory and postmodernism are similar and there are obvious areas of overlap, critical theory's rejection of relativism and attachment to the goal of emancipation provide a distinctive ethical position and writers have produced a good deal of instructive work in the area of management. The next chapter, on critical realism, shows some similarity with critical theory but offers an alternative approach to avoiding relativism.

Further reading

Partially due to the problems of translation, Habermas' work is very difficult to read therefore we advise the interested reader to start with Held's (1989) *An Introduction to Critical Theory* or Pusey's (1987) *Jurgen Habermas*. Thorough reviews of the issues posed by relativism are to be found in either Siegel (1987) or in Hollis and Lukes (1982). Calhoun's (1995) *Critical Social Theory* also provides an excellent overview. For discussion of critical theory and management Alvesson and Willmott's 1992 text *Critical Management Studies* and their 1996 text *Making Sense of Management* both provide excellent starting points. If you are interested in the link between critical theory and empirical research, it is worth looking at Kincheloe and McLaren (1998) 'Rethinking Critical Theory and Qualitative Research' in Denzin and Lincoln's book *The Landscape of Qualitative Research*, and Morrow and Brown's (1994) *Critical Theory and Methodology*.

7

Pragmatism and Critical Realism – Transcending Descartes' Either/Or?

> If science is to be possible the world must be one of enduring and transfactually active mechanisms; and society must be a structure (or ensemble of powers) irreducible to but present only in the action of men [*sic*]. Science must be conceived as an ongoing social activity; and knowledge as a product which individuals must reproduce or transform, and which individuals must draw on to use in their own critical explorations of nature.
>
> (Bhaskar, 1978: 248)

In the previous chapter we have shown how at first sight critical theory, through its commitment to a consensus theory of truth, attempts to occupy some intellectual space between foundationalism and relativism. In contrast to the 'legitimation crisis' created by postmodernists' 'linguistic turn', we can infer from critical theory's 'intersubjective turn' that for knowledge to be legitimate it must be located in the rational consensus thought to be achievable in Habermas' ideal speech situation. Therefore the space occupied by critical theory entails a modified form of rationalism: a socio-rationalist (Gergen, 1982) epistemology where legitimate knowledge is not located in the privileged reasoning of the individual mind but is the outcome of negotiated consensus embedded in democratic social relationships. However, as we have shown, such an epistemological niche is difficult to sustain and, in practice, critical theorists are inadvertently drawn towards what amounts to a foundationalist position.

The same search attempted by critical theorists, for an 'intermediate niche' (Harvey, 1989: 52) that spurns the totalizing grand narratives of positivism yet serves as an antidote to the nihilism of relativism, now leads us to what we will present as the interrelated philosophical terrains of pragmatism and critical realism. As we shall show, the use and meaning of 'pragmatism' and 'realism' varies in the philosophical literature. Therefore having clarified what we mean by each of the two terms, we shall illustrate how they have been tacitly combined to provide a distinctive epistemological position. This epistemology, which we call pragmatic–critical realism, may be understood as a synthesis which emerges from, and attempts to transcend, positivism's thesis of a foundational–absolute stance and postmodernism's antithesis of chaotic relativism. To paraphrase

Bernstein (1983: 18), by fighting a war on two fronts, such a synthesis tries to avoid what Descartes construed as an ineluctable either/or dichotomy – either foundationalism or relativism. By eschewing this dichotomy and the Cartesian anxiety it provokes, we shall outline the implications of pragmatic–critical realism for management and organizational research.

Realism

At first sight the impact of realism upon debates within the social sciences generally, and within management theory in particular, seems to have been limited when compared to that of the competing philosophical tendencies we have reviewed so far. This may be because, as Haack (1987) has demonstrated, the term 'realism' has a variety of different meanings and therefore it is difficult to identify an agreed and coherent realist position or contribution. For instance realism is usually defined as a rejection of the subjectivist ontologies currently put forward by postmodernists and in the past by idealists. Hence realists are united by a rejection of the view that the world is created by the minds of human observers. Moreover, as Trigg (1980: vii) observes, a key characteristic of realism is 'the notion of objectivity – of things being the case whether people recognize them or not'. When left at this definition it is evident that realism could be embraced by a variety of different positions including positivism and some conventionalists. However causing much of the confusion that surrounds realism is that some commentators go so far as to see no difference between realism and positivism – that they are one and the same philosophy.

Here, if we take Rorty's work as an example, it is evident that, like other postmodernists, he attempts to demolish the notion that it is possible for any knowledge, scientific or otherwise, to be an accurate representation of the external world. However Rorty associates the demise of such positivistic notions with the necessary demise of realism (see Callinicos, 1983: 119–26). But such a claim depends upon what is meant by 'realism' in the first place and Rorty associates realism exclusively with positivist notions (for example, 1979: 7). Through this discursive ploy, Rorty limits realism to what is often called 'empirical realism' (for example, Schlick, 1981) where what is real is only that which may be observed and measured – in other words, the objects of direct sensory experience. By what amounts to a definitional legerdemain alternative renditions of realism are in effect silenced. For Beck (1996: 7) the unfortunate result is the mistaken, yet only too common, view that realism and social constructivism have to be mutually exclusive. Another example of such a mistake is provided by Hammersley who defines realism as

> the idea that there is a reality independent of the researcher whose nature can be known, and that the aim of research is to produce accounts that correspond to that reality. (1992: 43)

Likewise, Keat and Urry seem to argue that realism shares with positivism a general conception of science as an

> objective, rational enquiry which aims at true explanatory and predictive knowledge of an external reality . . . by reference to empirical evidence. (1982: 44)

From the above statements it is evident that many commentators (others making this mistake would include Burrell and Morgan, 1979) conflate an objectivist epistemological stance with a realist ontological element in such a manner that they ignore the possibility of combining alternative epistemologies with a realist ontology. Here, in understanding the role of such alternatives, it is initially necessary to realize that agreement with the idea that all knowledge is the outcome of social construction does not necessarily lead to a subjectivist ontology and the consequent notion that transactions between people (i.e. subjects) and reality (i.e. objects) have no role to play in the development of knowledge. It is in these transactions where lies a potential escape route from the relativistic snares articulated by postmodernists via which they entrap themselves within the legitimation crisis of their linguistic turn. Obviously such an escape route would be dismissed by postmodernists as some attempt at restoring the grand narratives of modernism – even though, as we have shown, their radical scepticism undermines their own ability to make such claims.

It is from the position that knowledge entails *both* social construction and the transactions of human knowers with an independent reality where it is possible to discern a very different understanding of realism: an ontological and epistemological position dismissed by postmodernists and treated with equivocation by many of those we have classified as either conventionalists or critical theorists. Several writers explore expressions of this position under the rubrics of realism (for example, Sayer, 1981, 1992; Trigg, 1980), or pragmatism (for example, Hesse, 1980; Margolis, 1986), or critical realism (for example, Bhaskar, 1978; Collier, 1994). As a way into these debates, we shall start with critical realism.

Critical realism

Critical realists reject 'empirical realism' as an example of the 'epistemic fallacy' that lets the question 'what can we know?' determine our notions of what exists (Bhaskar, 1978: 36). Simultaneously, critical realism is allied to the post-Kuhnian attack upon positivism which, nevertheless, also distances itself from what is seen as Kuhn's relativism through repudiating the idea 'that we create and change the world, along with our theories' (Bhaskar, 1986: 2). Relativism may well have the laudable aim of opposing positivist's naïvely objectivist epistemology, but the resultant sceptical alternative is devoid of any possible grounds for critique or intervention. Hence critical realism eschews any attempt at collapsing ontology and epistemology into one another regardless of how this is done. The philosophical imperative for the critical realist is that truth must be more than the outputs of a language game yet it cannot be absolute. It follows that critical realism is unlike many popular characterizations of realism (for example, Burrell and Morgan, 1979; Hammersley, 1992; Keat and Urry, 1982; Rorty, 1979) since its adherents aim to be both anti-positivist and anti-relativist at once – a position hinted at by the writers quoted in Box 7.1.

Box 7.1

As we have seen in Chapter 5, it is precisely ontological realism that postmodernists such as Baudrillard (1983) overtly reject. Meanwhile in Chapter 4 we have shown how key conventionalists (for example, Kuhn, 1970 and Morgan, 1986) have oscillated between subjectivist and realist ontological positions. In a similarly equivocal manner, several management and organization theorists have tacitly sought to rescue postmodernism from its relativistic trajectory by tacitly attempting to combine its social constructivism with a largely unrecognized ontological realism. For instance Alvesson and Deetz argue

> since *any something in the world* may be constructed/expressed as many different objects, limited only by human creativity and readers of traces of past understandings, meaning can never be final but is always incomplete and indeterminate . . . Any attempt at representation is thus always partial. (our emphasis) (1996: 208)

Likewise, Kilduff and Mehra agree with the notion that

> the material world imposes constraints on the multiplicity of meanings that can be attributed to signifiers. (1997: 461)

A similar point is made by Parker who seeks to re-establish the capacity for critique by distancing himself from postmodernism:

> unlike postmodernists I believe that there are limits to human action . . . I do not believe that the world is infinitely pliable and would want to assert that physical, biological and social constraints exist in a real sense . . . Language may be the medium for all forms of inquiry . . . but it does not follow from that premise that language is all there is. (1993: 207–8)

While Parker proposes that the term 'reflective' or 'critical' modernism may capture this stance, he does not proceed to outline fully the implications of this stance for subject–object transactions.

A particularly helpful starting point for understanding this epistemological and ontological position is provided by Margolis (1986: 283) where he argues that there is a clear connection between what he calls metaphysical (i.e. ontological) realism – that the structures of the world do not depend upon the cognitive structures of human investigators – and what he calls epistemological realism – the view that such structures are cognitively accessible to those investigators. For Margolis much of 'realism' embraces

both aspects (see also Putnam, 1981). Yet despite this norm for inter-
weaving metaphysical and epistemological realism, and although the
epistemological necessitates prior acceptance of the metaphysical, the
acceptance of the metaphysical does not necessarily entail the acceptance
of the epistemological. In a similar manner Trigg (1980: 55–9) argues
that what reality is and how we have conceived it are different questions
since many things are beyond our conceptual and linguistic capacities.
Hence for both Margolis and Trigg a key realist orientation is a metaphysical commitment to unobservable entities – to put it bluntly, things
that cannot be measured or observed via our senses may be still real.
Naturally this orientation immediately begs the question – how then can
we know something to be real if we haven't observed it or cannot observe
it? These are questions to which we shall return later.

The position of Margolis and Trigg is similar to Bhaskar's (1978; 1986;
1989a; 1989b; 1993) differentiation between the 'intransitive objects of
scientific inquiry' that exist and act independently of their identification in
human knowledge and the 'transitive', socially constructed, dimension
(i.e. epistemology) that allows us to make sense of our world(s). According to Bhaskar, the products of science are always transitive, but they are
about an intransitive object because

> if changing experience of object is to be possible, objects must have a distinct
> being in space and time from the experience of which they are the objects. For
> Kepler to see the rim of the earth drop away, while Tycho Brahe watches the
> sun rise, must presuppose that there is something that they both see (in
> different ways). Similarly when modern sailors refer to what ancient mariners
> called a sea-serpent as a school of porpoises, we must suppose that there is
> something which they are describing in different ways. (1978: 31)

Later in the same work he claims that whenever

> we speak of things or of events etc. in science we must always speak of them
> and know of them under particular descriptions, descriptions which will always
> be to a greater or lesser extent theoretically determined, which are not neutral
> reflections of a given world. Epistemological relativism, in this sense, is the
> handmaiden of ontological realism and must be accepted. (1978: 249)

So while Bhaskar accepts what he defines as 'epistemic relativism' – that
knowledge is always socially constructed – he claims that this does not
entail 'judgemental relativism' – that there are no grounds for preferring
one knowledge claim to another. In Bhaskar's terms postmodernism
would entail *both* epistemic and judgemental relativism – a 'superidealism'
which conflates the transitive and intransitive so that reality becomes an
outcome of our variable epistemological engagements and allows the
propagation of certain variants of the incommensurability thesis.

In developing the synthesis illustrated by Figure 7.1 Bhaskar (1986:
72–5) differentiates the 'sense' or meaning of a theory from the objects to
which the theory refers – its 'referent'. He argues that where 'incommensurability of sense' occurs between two competing theories, it is still
possible to make a rational choice between them through an appeal to the

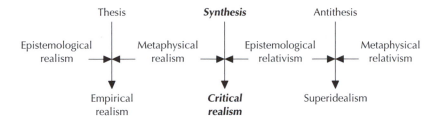

Figure 7.1 Bhaskar's synthesis

intransitive dimensions – their 'common referent' – the common aspects of reality over which they compete. This adjudication is in terms of how much of the common referent each theory is able to explain under their competing descriptions. However it is precisely the destruction of the common referent which is accomplished by postmodernism's subjectivist ontology which in turn enables a full-blown version of the incommensurability thesis – that incommensurability of sense, due to epistemic relativism, is thought to entail the creation of different realities which necessarily leads to incommensurability of referents and hence entails judgemental relativism since there are no common grounds for adjudication between the theories.

While Bhaskar's opposition to judgemental relativism through his appeal to a common referent is pivotal to critical realism it also poses a key problem: how can we judge the explanatory power of a theory? Such a judgement must be problematic since our apprehension of the reality the theory purports to explain is, simultaneously, on Bhaskar's (1978: 249) own admission, 'to a greater or lesser extent theoretically determined'. We shall return to this problem and the role of pragmatism once we have more fully developed Bhaskar's position.

For Bhaskar it is evident that judgemental relativism deprives us of any basis for an informed evaluation of science since it reduces science to a self-referential exercise. A purpose of Bhaskar's realist stance is to restore such a capacity for critique – hence the term 'critical realism'. Nevertheless he also uses the term 'critical' to differentiate this version of realism from what he sees as the naïveté of 'empirical' realism – where the facts of a cognitively accessible reality speak for themselves. As we have indicated above, Bhaskar acknowledges the role of discourse in influencing how we apprehend reality and by implication in how we think and behave. Therefore a central issue in critical realism is the active role of the human agent, but this is with reference to their interaction with an independent external reality which can constrain or facilitate human action. So while our transitive explanations of events change according to socio-historical variations in human understanding, intransitive causal mechanisms located in external reality do not change unless they are themselves dependent upon human action and intent – an important difference between the objects of social science and those of the natural sciences. Key aspects of Bhaskar's critical realism are summarized by Box 7.2 below.

Box 7.2 The six key commitments of critical realism

1 As the term implies, critical realists emphasize a metaphysical ontology which states that social and natural reality consist of intransitive entities which exist independently of our human knowledge.

2 Those entities may not be observable and different people may apprehend different (i.e. transitive) realities according to the varying paradigmatic, metaphorical or discursive conventions deployed through their human agency.

3 The perceived epistemic role of human agency means that critical realism rejects the possibility of a theory-neutral observational language and a correspondence theory of truth.

4 Critical realists do not see science as being merely a prestigious artefact of conventionally derived self-directed and self-deferential paradigms, or discourses, or language games and so on – instead and despite the pivotal role of its 'collective unconscious' science is construed as being about something other than science itself.

5 The model of science propagated by positivism has little bearing upon actual scientific practice save for the manner in which scientists will often explain themselves and their activities to each other.

6 Critical realism entails an epistemological defence of causal explanation – causation is not solely expressed through a constant conjunction of events as in positivism. Rather critical realists identify causation by also exploring the mechanisms of cause and effect which underlie regular events, mechanisms which Hume (see Chapter 2) claimed were unobservable but which critical realists claim can be shown to be real through their deployment of what Bhaskar calls 'retroductive' argument.

Critical realists consider that the observable behaviour of people and objects ('appearances') is not explicable unless located in the causal context of non-empirical structures, or intrinsic natures ('essences') and their interactions. Therefore, observed constant conjunctions may be explained as being connected by an underlying necessity which derives from the essential structure of the observations in question. For instance Bhaskar (1989a: 16) presents a stratified ontology where reality is comprised of causal 'generative mechanisms' – 'real' non-empirical 'deep' structures which can produce 'actual' events some of which are conceptually mediated in 'empirical' experience, impression and observation. So for critical realists causation is not merely about the regular empirical appearance of a Humean constant conjunction which positivists take either as a deductive test or as necessary and sufficient proof of causation thereby construing prediction and explanation as symmetrical. Instead, according to critical realists, causation is identifiable by exploring the underlying generative mechanisms, or powers, which produce events. Central to critical realism's project is the abstract identification of the structures and mechanisms which, although not directly observable, underlie and govern the events of experience and hence explain *why* regularities occur.

Bhaskar calls the manner in which we can delve into apparent regularities so as to postulate underlying causal powers 'retroduction' (see Box 7.2). Retroduction moves from a description of some given phenomenon to a description of a different type of thing – a mechanism or structure which either produces the given phenomenon or is a condition for it. So once some regularity is identified, a scheme is then postulated which would explain it and then the scheme is somehow tested to see if it matches some real structure. But, as we have indicated earlier, the ambiguity in critical realism relates to how this last step can be accomplished. It would seem that such retroduction entails movement from 'surface' appearances to a knowledge of 'deep' structures which cannot be obtained through sense experience. Bhaskar styles this 'movement of thought' as involving

> the construction of an explanation for, that is, the production of the knowledge of the mechanism of, some identified phenomenon . . . [which involves] . . . the building of a model, utilizing such cognitive materials and operating under the control of something like a logic of analogy and metaphor, of a mechanism, which *if* it were to exist and act in the postulated way would account for the phenomenon in question. (1989a: 12) (emphasis in the original)

So for Bhaskar, the objective of a critical realist science is metaphorically to 'dig deeper' so as to identify these 'real' 'intransitive' essences, or 'causal powers', which lie behind conceptually mediated (i.e. transitive) empirical patterns. Evidently he holds that although our knowledge of real underlying causal mechanisms and their empirical manifestation is inevitably socially constructed through our prior cultural preconceptions, they can be reliable and improved. In contrast, Keat and Urry ambiguously play down Bhaskar's epistemological relativism by presenting an essentialist aim for realism – to represent the 'unobservable' 'structures and mechanisms' or 'essences' 'correctly' so that the 'phenomena could be causally explained' (1982: 35). However either agenda for critical realism begs several questions.

A key question must be: how can we ever know whether the intransitive essences (socially) constructed by scientists are mere fictions of their imagination or are real 'non-empirical' structures or 'generative' mechanisms? Surely the metaphysical dimension to critical realism makes it difficult to substantiate knowledge-claims about processes which are simultaneously thought to be unobservable save for their testing through empirical examination of their effects in observable events. For instance, the desire to represent essentials correctly implies an advocacy of epistemic privilege which might only be sustained through a contradictory appeal to what critical realists would simultaneously regard as an unsustainable epistemological objectivism grounded in a theory-neutral observational language. Even any conclusions about the effects of those structures through empirical examination of their 'surface' event-effects must be equally questionable if critical realism's own attacks upon empiricism are to be maintained. To be blunt, in order for critical realism to avoid internal self-contradiction, it has to deal with two interrelated epistemological problems:

First, because critical realists reject the possibility of a theory-neutral observational language how can they then establish the veracity of, by their own admission, epistemically transitive constructions yet simultaneously avoid the articulation of the very 'superidealism' which Bhaskar so vehemently decries?

Secondly, if traditional forms of empiricism are untenable since experience cannot provide us with knowledge of intransitive reality, and if science is not to be exclusively self-referential as in postmodernism, how does science involve socially mediated transitive transactions with the 'common referent' – an intransitive reality?

These problems seem to create a new set of options. The first option is for the critical realist to invoke the possibility of privileged knowledge, through some epistemological back door, albeit no longer grounded in a neutral observational language but in some contemplative or intuitive act of metaphysical revelation retroductively accomplished by critical realists. However such a tactic would also entail repudiating epistemic relativism and the tacit assertion of a rationalist epistemology whereby the critical realist studies what is construed as unobservable social structures through positing theories which are logically coherent, rather than empirically grounded. It is almost as if they are appealing to Mannheim's view that a sociologically clarified intellect allows (in this case) the critical realist to transcend their own culture and ideology so as to operate 'with situationally congruous ideas and motives' (1960: 175). As Halfpenny wryly observes, this choice is not viable since 'what restrictions are there upon the mechanisms which can be invoked as causal explanation . . . why not demons or witches' spells?' (1994: 65). To put it another way – whose socially constructed criteria of logic etc. are going to be invoked so as to evaluate the revelations? Or alternatively, are there any checks upon the critical realist's imagination? The result is a conundrum composed of two equally unpalatable and unsustainable alternatives for critical realists – either a departure into a fully fledged superidealism or some form of rationalistic contemplation of reality's essences.

However there is another option. This entails the search for a means of establishing subject–object transactions which explore causality in a non-foundational manner. It is precisely the problem of establishing our descriptions and causal explanations by accessing the real social and natural world that lies beyond our discourses while avoiding the various pitfalls of empiricism, rationalism and superidealism, that Andrew Sayer (1981; 1992) addresses. For sake of a better term, we shall call this departure 'pragmatism'.

Pragmatism

Nowhere does Sayer use the term 'pragmatism' to categorize his position. Nevertheless this semantic oversight does not stop him from in effect practising pragmatism. Through an alternative synthesis of social constructivism and ontological realism, Sayer tries to deal with the epistemological conundrums encountered by Bhaskar's critical realism. This is attempted by providing critical realism with a non-foundational means of understanding and establishing socially mediated transactions between human agents and an ontologically prior intransitive reality.

Sayer begins by mounting a thorough attack upon correspondence theory. Here, just like postmodernists, he emphasizes the socially constructed character of any science. However he moderates this position by his argument that our social constructions are bounded by the tolerance of an external reality which exists independently of our cognitive processes. Sayer would therefore agree with Bhaskar's view that ontologically, things 'exist and act independently of human activity' (Bhaskar, 1989a: 13) and therefore they are not infinitely pliable according to the vicarious play of the transitive language-games, metaphors and paradigms etc. deployed by human agents.

So while Sayer adopts an ontological position which others have hinted at and which critical realists overtly adopt, what is crucial in Sayer's work is the manner in which he establishes how non-foundational epistemological transactions take place between people and an ontologically prior reality. These concerns of Sayer lead him to what amount to pragmatist ideas – however, again, some terminological ambiguity needs to be resolved initially.

According to Rescher (1977) pragmatist thought can be traced back to ancient Greece and the criticisms by the sceptics of Plato's distinction between '*episteme*' (genuine knowledge) and '*doxa*' (knowledge only suitable for the conduct of everyday affairs). Particularly Carneades (213–129 B.C.) argued that Plato's quest for a foundationalist *episteme* was an unrealizable *chimera* because of the inherent fallibility of sense-experience. For Carneades all that could be achieved was knowledge that might guide human practice and purposes. Hence the derivation of the term 'pragmatism' – the Greek word '*pragma*' – which means 'deed' or 'action'. Despite this archaic beginning, today's pragmatism is primarily North American in origin and character. Its origins lie in the posthumously published work of Peirce (1931–58) in which he adapted the term 'pragmatism' from Kant. Kant had used the term when distinguishing the practical, that related to the will and action, from the pragmatic which related to the consequences of action. Other important pragmatists included James (1909), Schiller (1907) and Dewey (1929a; 1929b; 1938).

Pragmatism's North American character is expressed through its sceptical anti-authoritarian stance towards all claims for knowledge save those that demonstrate the utility of knowledge in advancing 'human happiness'. Nevertheless it is difficult to describe pragmatism as a 'school' of philosophy since the term is used to refer to a variety of different epistemological positions. This lack of unity has led some self-styled pragmatists (for example, Schiller, 1907) to admit that there are as many pragmatisms as there are pragmatists. While this may be an exaggeration, it is important to realize that the key ambiguity about the term 'pragmatism' is that it can be used to invoke two distinct philosophical positions which tend to be united only by their rejection of positivism.

The first of the above pragmatisms is closely associated with the work of Richard Rorty (1979, 1982, 1998) – which Haack (1995: 182) has dubbed 'vulgar pragmatism'. As we have seen in Chapter 5, Rorty insists that knowledge is not, and cannot be, the result of the 'mind's eye' looking at a reflection of the 'world' in a mirror located in the mind. By this objection to the 'ocular' or 'mirror' metaphor, he abandons any objectivist claims for science grounded in the possibility of a subject–object dualism. Instead he advances the idea that knowledge will be socially justified if it is supported by the *pragmatic consensus* of people in mutually intelligible linguistic communication within a specific community (1979: 357–61). Hence Rorty associates pragmatism exclusively with social construction where knowledge arises out of the language-games of a community of people which is incommensurable with that of other communities and which cannot be judged by the standards of another community (1982: 188–9). The result is that there is nothing which can be said about epistemology which is over and above the incommensurable cognitive practices embedded in community language-games.

This attack upon 'representationism' leads Rorty to a position where truth is a changeable artefact (1982: 92) according to the variable culturally prescribed language-games of different communities. But, as we have demonstrated, to deny the possibility of some degree of grounding knowledge in our transactions with the 'world' invites the problem which Bhaskar calls judgemental relativism. As we have noted with regard to other postmodernists, such relativism sanctions an uncritical disinterestedness in the guise of pluralism. Indeed Rorty certifies his position by equating it with 'anti-authoritarian Deweyan Pragmatism' and 'Bourgeois Liberalism' (1982: 207). For Rorty it was Dewey's opposition to authoritarianism which motivated his opposition to all forms of 'otherworldly' or 'external reality' based thought (1998: 29–31). However Rorty's ploy of invoking John Dewey as an ally in his rejection of epistemology, and hence his adoption of the term 'pragmatism' to describe his position, derives from a long-standing misinterpretation of Dewey's work.

To some extent Dewey is himself to blame for Rorty's misinterpretation and misappropriation of the term 'pragmatism'. This is because of Dewey's own lapses as he attempts to navigate a course between what he called a 'spectator theory of knowledge' (i.e. positivism's theory-neutral observational language) and 'idealism' (i.e. relativism). For example

Dewey (1929a: 19) sometimes failed to distinguish between saying that a scientific inquiry socially constructs non-foundational *knowledge of reality* and that scientific inquiry *produces reality*. As we have seen, the former assertion is consistent with a realist ontology while the latter is consistent with a subjectivist ontology. Evidently Rorty has pounced upon the latter assertion so as to legitimate his 'vulgar' reading of Dewey's pragmatism. However Rorty's interpretation ignores how Dewey's aim was to navigate a middle way through an articulation of reality's contribution to our knowledge which also eschewed the 'spectator theory of knowledge'. This is an aim supported implicitly by James where he observes that when 'we give up the doctrine of objective certitude, we do not thereby give up the quest or hope of truth itself' (1897: 17). His pursuit of this middle way leads Dewey to propose a pragmatism located in subject–object trans-actions, and commensurable with today's critical realism: a pragmatism which argues that to have knowledge is the ability to anticipate the consequences of manipulating things in the world.

Dewey (1929a) thought that the notion that knowledge could be absolutely true, whether it was substantiated by an empirical claim or by religious fervour, was a fictional product of humanity's quest for certainty – a quest which had dominated philosophy since the time of the Ancient Greeks. Rorty similarly dismisses this quest as an 'infantile need for security' which lacks 'intellectual courage' (1998: 34). For Dewey this quest served to divert attention from the kind of understanding necessary for dealing with practical problems as they arise and the daily task of improving the human condition by making our interactions with nature and other people more viable. So for Dewey humans are not passive receivers or spectators of sense-data. Rather we are primarily active agents whose critical reflection upon the effectiveness of our practical problem-solving, in terms of what we accomplish, could make the world less insecure – a world that 'will do'. Thus Dewey defined truth as 'processes of change so directed so that they achieve an intended consummation' (1929b: iii) where justified knowledge was a socially constructed artefact created so as to aid humans in their practical endeavours of 'settling problematic situations' (*ibid.*). Hence as with James' (1909) pragmatic criterion, truth was not a question of empirical verifiability or testing; rather an assertion is true, or in Dewey's terms possessed 'warranted assertability', if it works by helping people to deal with the(ir) worlds. Hence the goal of inquiry may be a transformed situation rather than some correspondence with an inaccessible reality where

> the only guarantee we have against licentious thinking is the circumpressure of reality itself, which gets us sick of concrete errors, whether there be a trans-empirical reality or not. (James, 1909: 72)

Despite James' circumpressure of reality, since knowledge cannot be created which mirrors reality the possibility of error can *never* be ruled out. Hence the resultant pragmatist view of truth, which challenges any quest for certainty, has to be fallibilistic to its core – any knowledge claims, at any given time, may be wrong and all beliefs are thus revisable.

So while the pragmatism of James and Dewey may well express what is often described as a North American ethos, it is interesting to note that Remmling has argued that Marx was much closer to American Pragmatist thinkers than his European predecessors, for 'what he represented may be described as a political pragmatism – in order to discover whether our ideas are true, we must act upon them' (1973: 143). Some support for this view derives from Marx's critique of Feuerbach:

> The question whether objective truth can be attributed to human thinking is not a question of theory but is a practical question. Man must prove the truth, i.e. the reality and power, the this-sideness of his thinking in practice [*sic*]. The dispute over the reality or non-reality of thinking that is isolated from practice is purely a scholastic question. (1975: 3)

As we have already indicated, although he doesn't use the term, it is the second set of meanings that are associated with the term 'pragmatism', which are also directly relevant to the aim of establishing non-foundational transactions between subject and object, which are drawn upon by Sayer (1992). Like Dewey, Sayer admits to the significance of social construction and how this also entails transactions between subject and object. Relativism is thereby avoided as extra-discursive criteria of truth are incorporated. These extra-discursive criteria are in the form of what Sayer calls the 'actual realization of expectations' through practical interventions which enable contact with the 'tolerance of reality' (Collier, 1979) – something which they cannot ignore or erase (see Box 7.3).

Box 7.3

The postmodernists' free-play of signifiers destroys Bhaskar's common referent – Kant's noumenal world. Hence it would encourage us to argue the following: observe the glass in the window in a room . . . while the terms such as 'glass', 'window' and 'room' are commonly used linguistic resources, they refer to nothing beyond themselves. What we take to be external reality – the glass in the window of our room – is merely the product of our discursive practice. Presumably, by changing our discursive practices, we could deny the existence of glass in the window and the window would cease to contain that discursive product. While pragmatists would argue that how we construe the world is an outcome of social construction, they would also point to how an ontologically real external reality intervenes and imposes pragmatic limits upon our discursive analyses . . . if you wanted to test this in relation to window glass, and we strongly advise you *not* to do this, you could try stepping through a window without opening it first and see if the postmodernist free-play of signifiers allows you to remain unharmed!

Like pragmatists and critical realists, Sayer is, in effect, adopting what amounts to a Kantian position as he differentiates between 'thought objects'

(Kant's *phenomena*) and 'real objects' (Kant's *noumena*) by suggesting that there is an external reality, independent of, and resistant to, human activity. External reality is a 'thing in itself' which remains unknowable. As Kolakowski argues, such 'things in themselves' do not have conceptual counterparts, rather our objects of knowledge – 'things for us' – are constituted by 'active contact with the resistance of nature . . . (that) . . . creates knowing man and nature at one and the same time [*sic*]' (1969: 75). In this manner external reality imposes pragmatic limits upon what postmodernists assume to be a free-play of signifiers (see Box 7.3 above).

It is evident that this pragmatist orientation is by no means alien to Bhaskar's own stance. As we illustrated earlier, Bhaskar's view of causality is to do with the properties of things-in-themselves (e.g. structures, mechanisms and so on). It follows that it is in practice where these unobservable yet 'transfactually efficacious powers' will be realized. In Bhaskar's own terms 'if there is a real reason, located in the nature of stuff, such as molecular or atomic structure, then water must tend to boil when it is heated' (1993: 35). For Bhaskar (1986) we can act on the physical relationships which exist in the natural world and learn how to manipulate them. Nevertheless we cannot create new relationships in the natural world. In contrast, the social world is an outcome of human action and therefore there is always the potential for changing existing relationships through action. If social reality consists of causal structures it must be possible to intervene and manipulate that structure. As Bhaskar indicates elsewhere, although

> social theory and social reality are causally interdependent . . . this is not to say that the social theorist 'constructs' social reality. But it is to say that social theory is practically conditioned by, and potentially has practical consequences in society. (1989b: 5)

This implies a pragmatic solution to the problems noted earlier regarding the retroductive development and evaluation of critical realist theories. It follows that anything does not go in the sense that the enactment of some language-games is impossible. So while the pragmatist dimension remains immanent within Bhaskar's work, it is emphasized by Andrew Sayer when he summarizes this position as

> the world can only be understood in terms of the available conceptual resources, but the latter do not determine the structure of the world itself. And despite our entrapment within our conceptual schemes, it is still possible to differentiate between more and less practically-adequate beliefs about the material world. Observation is neither theory-neutral nor theory-determined but theory-laden. Truth is neither absolute nor purely conventional and relative. (1992: 83)

In a similar vein Arbib and Hesse (1986) argue that the constraints of spatio-temporal reality provide a feedback mechanism that enables the evaluation of the practical efficacy of our 'cognitive systems' and 'networks of schemas'. As Sayer emphasizes, although an intersubjective and conventional dimension exists 'not just any conventions will do: they must be usable in practice' (1992: 69). This pragmatic criterion prevents 'science' becoming purely an intersubjective representation of, and consensus about, reality. While these schemas allow people to make sense of the world (a world so complex that it is amenable to many interpretations) they are neither individualistic nor socially determined. Rather they are socially shaped and constructed guides for human action. In Murphy's (1994) terms social factors mediate between the dynamics of spatio-temporal reality and science. Thus science is seen as the result of 'both social action and nature's dynamics' (*ibid.*: 971). The pragmatic criterion operates as people adjust and reject schemas when the practical ends and expectations they support are perceived as having been violated. As Law and Lodge put it (1984: 125), if a theory allows people to interact satisfactorily with their social or natural environments then it is reinforced, but if from the stance of the theory, those environments become unpredictable then the theory is undermined and is likely to change (see also Barnes, 1977; Knorr-Cetina, 1984).

Therefore central to the pragmatic–critical realist position is the notion that although language shapes all forms of science this does not mean that nothing exists beyond language. Reality intervenes and puts limits upon the viability of our descriptions and explanations. Here a means of evaluating the veracity of cognitive systems and theories, that avoids the final totalizing grand narratives of both relativism and objectivism, is through their practical success or failure. This is derived from the view that our everyday practical actions as human agents tacitly presume that external causal regularities exist which we may act upon. Even though our conceptualization and explanation of such regularities are always open to question (due to our lack of a theory-neutral observational language), our ability to undertake practical actions that are successful and our ability to reflect upon and correct actions that seem unsuccessful implies that we have feedback from an independent 'reality' which constrains and enables practices that would otherwise be inconceivable.

So without assuming epistemic privilege, this pragmatic–critical realist position allows for adjudication through the corrective feedback that derives from the tolerance of that mind-independent spatio-temporal reality – that is their 'practical adequacy'

> to be practically adequate knowledge must generate expectations about the world and about the results of our actions that are *actually realised* . . . [These expectations] . . . in turn are realised because of the nature of the associated material interventions . . . and of their material contents. In other words, although the nature of objects and processes . . . does not uniquely determine the content of human knowledge, it does determine their cognitive and practical possibilities for us. (our emphasis) (Sayer, 1992: 69–70)

In sum, this pragmatic–critical realist position asserts that there is a transcendental reality beyond our discursive productions. So while the truth may well be 'out there' we may never know it in an absolute sense

because we lack the necessary cognitive and linguistic means of apprehending it. This is not to say that anything goes according to whatever
language we adopt. For instance such a postmodernist position would be
anathema since it would treat phrenology, demonology and homeopathy
as epistemic equals – regardless of their evidently variable practical adequacy. Hence from the pragmatic–critical realist stance we can develop,
and indeed identify, in a fallible manner, more adequate social constructions of reality by demonstrating their variable ability to realize our
goals, ends or expectations since our practical activities allow transactions
between subject and object.

Thus science is neither self-referential nor objective. Rather, science is
construed as a social activity where people intervene and manipulate an
intransitive reality which they confront and change on the basis of socially
constructed transitive theory through practice. The underlying theoretical
schema is principally assessed through evaluating the efficacy of an
intervention in achieving particular ends – outcomes which inevitably
express underlying partisan values and interests. We can therefore infer
that to adjudicate the veracity of knowledge claims from this pragmatic–
critical realist stance could for instance entail: defining the practical
intervention and expected outcomes which the claim articulates through a
causal association; implementing the practical intervention; and assessing
how efficacious the intervention is at achieving the expected outcomes.
However there may be some dislocation between theoretical explanation
and practice. For instance practice may demonstrate that a particular
intervention is efficacious with regard to particular ends even though the
causal mechanism by which the intervention works is as yet unclear since
a fully fledged theoretical explanation is yet to be socially constructed.
Further dislocation may occur because practice inevitably occurs in
conditions where the efficacy of an intervention may be either counter-
vailed or dependent upon the operation of extraneous factors excluded
from the theory guiding the interventions. Hence the need to recognize
that science deals with tendencies (and not with certainties) which problematize the apparent results of our practical activities – as we have said,
pragmatism must be fallibilistic to its core.

The implications for management research

Bhaskar (1986; 1989a) argues that, apart from in astronomy, constant
conjunctions in the natural sciences occur only in the artificially enclosed
environments created by experimental control, even though the resultant
experimentally determined knowledge is often successfully applied outside
those experimental contexts.

According to Bhaskar, the purpose of an experiment is to isolate one
mechanism, which normally operates alongside others, so as to create a

Box 7.4   Closed and open systems

A closed system is a condition where a causal sequence, such as the action of gravity upon an object, may be observed without the interference of other (i.e. extraneous) causal forces (such as wind, air density etc.) upon the object. So for example gravity may be described as the regularity with which a lead weight accelerates towards the ground when released from a specific height. However if we were to choose the fall of an autumn leaf so as to observe the operation of gravity, the actions of the leaf would not be as regular as those of the lead weight since they would be not merely governed by gravitational pull but also more open to the vicissitudes of wind, air density, aerodynamics etc. than the lead weight. However if either the lead weight or the leaf were dropped in a completely closed system, such as a vacuum, their behaviour would be exactly the same because all extraneous forces to that of gravity have been held at bay through the creation of a closed system. Hence Bhaskar defines an experiment, in terms of the creation of closed systems, as

> an attempt to trigger or unleash a single kind of mechanism or process in relative isolation, free from the interfering flux of the open world, so as to observe its detailed workings or record its characteristic mode of effect and/or to test some hypothesis about them. (1986: 35)

closed system where a given cause will always produce the same effect (see Box 7.4). However such closure is rarely spontaneous and seldom occurs without strenuous human intervention since most natural open systems are composed of a multiplicity of mechanisms which combine to produce events. For Bhaskar the ability to extrapolate from such experimental contexts cannot be explained by positivism's empirical realism. Empirical realism depends upon a misidentification of causal laws with a constant conjunction. If we were to follow empirical realism we would end up 'logically committed to the absurdities that scientists, in their experimental activity, cause and even change the laws of nature' (1989b: 15–16). Therefore extrapolation in the natural sciences can only be explained by invoking a critical realist ontology of real, but unmanifest, generative mechanisms that underlie the appearance of events in the 'open' natural world which lies beyond the confines of experimental protocols.

For Bhaskar it follows that the experiment can be seen as an intervention that enables the artificial isolation of a generative mechanism, and thereby empirical identification of the way it acts, by closing off, or controlling, all other extraneous mechanisms which are normally in operation in the 'open' world. Hence experiments gain access to causation by creating conditions of closure. This is not to suggest that the mechanism doesn't normally operate in open systems, rather its effects may be disguised by nature's diverse openness and the subsequent operation of other countervailing extraneous mechanisms. Hence in the open systems of both the natural and social worlds, constant conjunctions do not pertain. Therefore positivist prescriptions and claims for science cannot be possible. Instead science in both the natural and the social domain is united by attempts at identifying real structures which exist and operate independently of the patterns of events they generate. Causal claims are not about actual outcomes rather causation:

> must be analysed as the tendencies of things, which may be possessed unexercised and exercised unrealised, just as they may of course be realized unperceived. (Bhaskar, 1989a: 9)

For Bhaskar this has significant implications for the social sciences. Since human behaviour arises out of the exercise of our interpretative faculties, which entail the exercise of knowledgeable choice and intentionality, experiments in the social sciences can never approximate the conditions of closure which are possible in the natural sciences. Human agency cannot happen without our knowledge of the resources available and the material social conditions we act upon, sustain and transform through our interventions. While our knowledge of these structures is always interpretative, human agency draws upon extant structures as a condition of action. Moreover it is through human agency that social structures come about, are reproduced and transformed – regardless of our intentions or awareness that this is so.

So while human behaviour in, for instance, organizations may often lie in and be caused by the inner interpretative reasoning of actors: for the critical realist there may be causes that are not recognized by, nor accessible to, those actors. Hence Bhaskar asserts an analytical distinction between agency and structure which is denied by postmodernists through their decentring of the subject where agency is lost to the discursive determination of behaviour and a subjectivist ontology. For the critical realist the enduring structures of social reality and human agency reciprocally presuppose each other, but they cannot be reduced to, nor reconstructed from, nor explained in terms of each other. For Bhaskar

> the existence of social structure is a necessary condition for any human activity . . . it is the unmotivated condition for all our motivated productions. We do not create society – the error of voluntarism. But these structures which pre-exist us are only reproduced or transformed in our everyday activities; thus society does not exist independently of human agency – the error of reification. The social world is reproduced and transformed in daily life. (1989b: 3–4)

From this critical realist stance the aim of social science is the identification of the structures which generate behavioural tendencies through the examination of social phenomena. So for critical realism, rather than rejecting experience and observation in order to delve 'deeper' and beyond the conceptual limitations they impose, any analysis should include *both* the unobservable structures and subjectively experienced social phenomena.

Therefore explanation of organizational behaviour entails:

1   providing a hermeneutic understanding of the interpretations and intentions that consciously motivate members' behaviour;

2   identifying the unacknowledged yet causal structural conditions which
    impinge upon these social activities which agents skilfully sustain and
    transform through those intentionally motivated activities yet which
    remain opaque to individuals involved.

Central to this analysis is the location of micro-level ethnographic
descriptions of members' activities within the explanatory context of the
complex interplay of macro-level structures which constrain and enable
members' activities (see Tsoukas, 1989). As Reed observes, organizational
forms

> consist of relational structures into which people enter and pre-exist the people
> who enter into them and whose activity reproduces or transforms them. They
> are structures by virtue of the fact that they have spatially, temporally and
> socially enduring institutional properties that are irreducible to the activities of
> contemporary agents. Yet these same structures derive from the historical
> actions which generated them and which establish a structured context for
> current action . . . These structures possess certain 'causal powers' or capabili-
> ties that explain their 'ways of acting' on social practices. (1997: 33)

Therefore the causal powers above cannot be observed directly; rather
they can only be theoretically inferred through examination of their relational effects in human agency. So just as the attraction of a lead weight to
the ground may be abstractly conceived in terms of the power of gravity
(see Box 7.4), relations between shareholders and managers express the
power deriving from the ownership of private property. However this
poses the problem of how to legitimate those inferences epistemically
since the danger is that critical realism could insulate its explanations of
organization from any relationship with members' experiences as human
agents.

   Here pragmatic–critical realism would argue that while agents socially
construct versions of reality through language (interpretative processes
from which there is no immunity), the structures of social reality constitute a practical order which acts independently of these constructions
so as to constrain or enable our practical actions and interventions. Hence
it is only in and through practice that we confront the tolerance of
Bhaskar's generative mechanisms which may otherwise remain unmanifest, and upon which we can only ever have a transient and partial
understanding rather than the factual status Reed seems to accord in the
quotation above. This is a position, at least in the social sciences, which
seems to be supported by Collier (1994) in his evaluation of critical
realism.

   The diagram in Figure 7.2 is adapted from that used by Collier to
represent the situation in the natural sciences. He argues that practical
experience

> leads to a degree of concrete knowledge of the object . . .; this suggests
> explanatory conjectures which produce abstract models which can then be
> tested by experiments; the results of experiments lead to confirmation,
> refutation or revision . . . the resulting body of tested abstract knowledge can be

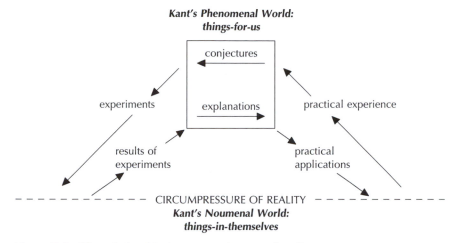

Figure 7.2   The relationship between science and reality

(Adapted from Collier (1994) *Critical Realism: An Introduction to Roy Bhaskar's Philosophy*, Verso, p. 249)

> used to explain the concrete object more accurately and this explanation used to generate new and more effective kinds of practical interaction with the object which in turn will yield new practical experience of it, and so on. (Collier, 1994: 249–50)

Although the pragmatic–critical realist position would question both the possibility of experiments allowing such testing and notions such as the 'more accurate' representation of things-in-themselves (Collier's concrete objects), it would agree with Collier's subsequent observation that, due to the open nature of the social sciences, the processes 'represented by the arrows at the left of the figure are absent' and that 'abstract models that are conjectured cannot be tested before the explanations they generate are used in practice' (1994: 250).

This pragmatic–critical realist position has important implications for the status of the various research methodologies available to management research. In Chapter 3 we showed how management research is currently dominated by a particular form of positivist epistemology, which encourages an exclusive focus upon deductive and often quantitative methodologies. This dominance has been confronted by a neopositivist interpretative challenge which shifts the methodological focus to the inductive and qualitative (see Gill and Johnson, 1997). In contrast the pragmatic–critical realist position would thrive on multi-methodological approaches where there is room to utilize the full range of methodological techniques that are available to management researchers. In effect a form of methodological pluralism (see McLennan, 1995: 57–75) would be the norm based upon two arguments.

The first of these arguments would allude to analysis involving what Keat and Urry call a unification of interpretative and explanatory understanding 'in the analysis of structural relations, and the ways in which they affect and are affected by, the subjective meanings of human beings' (1982: 174). The result would be the deployment of particular methods for exploring structural relations and others for capturing members' subjective meanings (see also: Fielding, 1988; Fielding and Fielding, 1986).

The second argument derives from epistemological subjectivism where no methodology can be construed as epistemically superior to any other – all are partial and fallible modes of engagement which simultaneously socially construct and occlude different possible renditions of an onto-logically prior social-organizational reality. With this methodological focus, the blind men in the Indian tale referred to in the discussion of Morgan's work in Chapter 4 (1986: 341), now acquires more relevance. According to Smith, different methods may illuminate different aspects of a phenomenon, therefore

> we are really like blind men led into an arena and asked to identify an entity (say an elephant) by touching one part of that entity (say a leg). Certainly we might make better guesses if we could pool the information of all the blind men, each of whom has touched a different part of the elephant. (Smith, 1975: 273)

However within the pragmatic–critical realist position pluralism is not based upon an egalitarian ambivalence; rather the various methods avail-able to the management researcher are redirected and/or re-assessed through the lens of practical adequacy. For instance, *verstehen* through ethnographic research is not about the researcher gaining privileged access to members' subjectivity by somehow intuiting and re-stating their cul-turally derived preferences and dispositions etc. Because of the lack of a theory-neutral observational language, the possibility of such an immacu-late perception is dismissed – it is impossible to experience the experience of another no matter how sophisticated our ethnographic techniques. So an ethnographic account of members' cultural dispositions is attained through the ethnographer's systematization and analysis of their imputa-tions and reconstructions rather than being the result of an act of dis-covery through their hermeneutic penetration of members' culture(s). Here the practical adequacy of any ethnograher's 'picturing' of an organ-izational culture could be assessed, for instance, by examining the extent to which they are able to pass themselves off as a member of that parti-cular culture. That is, their cultural knowledge would be practically ade-quate if it generated expectations about the norms and values shared by members of the research setting which enabled the researcher to behave in a socially approved manner.

In a similar fashion, methodologies which rely upon some degree of quantification are reassessed through practical adequacy. For instance, for many positivists, the point of selecting and operationalizing theoretical concepts is to enable the hypothetico-deductive testing of the causal imputations in the theory through confrontation with what are taken to be empirical facts. Usually this process will entail some form of measurement of the relevant theoretical concepts during the operationalization process. This mathematization enables the assessment of statistical covariance between dependent and independent variables as well as the statistical control of extraneous variables. The pragmatic–critical realist position would not rule out such endeavours – rather it would ask, as Sayer (1992: 176) demands: what must objects and processes be like for mathematical representations of them to be practically adequate? For Sayer meaningful measures can only be developed for objects and processes which are 'qualitatively invariant', that is

> they can be split up and combined without changing their nature. We can measure them at different times or places in different conditions and know that we are not measuring different things. (1992: 177)

According to Sayer (*ibid.*), whether or not a process can adequately be represented mathematically depends upon the type of change involved. Here he differentiates three types of change: the purely quantitative, that reducible to the movement of qualitatively unchanging entities, and finally that which is irreducibly qualitative. For Sayer the first and second types of change may be mathematicized since the changes involved affects only external relations between objects. However in the case of the third type quantitative measurement would not be practically adequate because mathematical operations such as addition or subtraction might destroy or create emergent powers in the processes: powers which have practical implications and which cannot be reduced to the constituent elements in a phenomenon such as the ability of water to put out a fire even though its constituent elements are both flammable (*ibid.*: 118).

However even if it were possible to assume that quantification of our objects of interest were possible there are other issues which problematize quantification from Sayer's point of view. In order for theories to be practically adequate they must be guides for action, and in order to be guides for action they must explicate causal relations. But statistical modelling is acausal in that it can only identify measurable change and not causation. It can only identify covariances between variables – necessary but not sufficient grounds for assigning a causal relationship. In order to avoid the possibility of a spurious correlation and thus provide descriptive meaning so as to explain causal mechanisms as well as to allocate direction to the causation, qualitative analysis is necessary. For Sayer it would seem that statistical models are tacitly based upon a Humean theory of causation, which focuses only upon regular sequences of events (i.e. constant conjunctions). Hence the use of statistical techniques will not expose underlying generative causal mechanisms – a key epistemological commitment of the critical–realist position where prediction and explanation do not possess the symmetry assumed in statistical analysis.

If such depth causal inference is beyond the domain of statistical or mathematical technique, research methodologies reliant upon mere quantification provide no means of rejecting, including or explaining correlated variables in a causal model without tacit recourse to much sense-making through appeal to theory and logic. Ultimately they depend upon what amounts to a qualitative analysis through the act of interpretation that involves sense-making on the part of the researcher – sense-making which cannot be included in orthodox positivist empirical testing formats. So as to meet the demands of *practical adequacy* any resultant theoretical account must provide a guide to practical action that enables the pursuit of particular interest-laden human purposes through active intervention in the social world.

Pragmatic interventions and management knowledge

For the pragmatic–critical realist it is through human practical interventions that causal tendencies and potentialities may become activated through our intentional and unintentional manipulation of ambient conditions which contingently lead to the attainment of particular results. However the openness of the social world will mean that there can always be a lack of symmetry between our theoretical explanations and predictive attainment through practice – hence the importance of fallibilism to the pragmatic–critical realist stance. From such a stance it is evident that reality might sustain a variety of different descriptive and explanatory schema that are produced from specific socio-historical standpoints and which articulate different interests. Hence alternative theoretical frameworks may be compared in terms of their success in achieving their varying pragmatic goals and realizing the interests those goals express. So, as Knorr-Cetina observes, any knowledge claim cannot be understood adequately without analysis of its social construction since the

> products of science are contextually specific constructions which bear the mark of their situational contingency and interest structure of the processes by which they are generated. (1984: 227)

Therefore the adjudication of the veracity of *any* knowledge-claim can only occur through reference to the pursuit of the interests encoded, by epistemic subjects, during social construction. Such interests are pursued through goal-directed human actions and interventions which, through practical activities, confront the tolerance of a mind-independent reality. For Barnes (1977: 29), such interests act as a filter upon experience as they intensify the investigation of some aspects of 'reality' and cause others to be ignored. Veracity might only be judged from within a specific context through reference to the efficacious practical realization, or violation, of the expectations generated by that knowledge-claim. Therefore in considering management knowledge, it is necessary to stimulate debate about the socio-historical processes that have led to its development, thereby problematizing extant disciplinary knowledge-claims.

The context-dependence of management knowledge necessitates the investigation of the socio-historical development of management recipes through a focus upon how they enable the interest-laden, but fallible, interaction of humans with aspects of their 'external' worlds. Therefore management knowledge must be conceptualized as a mutable cultural resource that influences, constrains and legitimizes particular social and organizational arrangements, relationships and practices. Hence there would be a focus upon management knowledge as a social artefact which serves to reflect, change or exclude differing interests and concerns along with their attendant renditions of reality in different socio-historical contexts.

From this position, an 'internalist' (Barnes, 1977) view of management knowledge, which understands its historical development in terms of an unproblematic and progressive accumulation of privileged knowledge, must be rejected. Similarly, the positivistic pretensions of much management discourse would be seen as generating

an ideology of technocratic expertise and managerial authority as well as, and perhaps to go with, its quasi-egalitarian mystique of commonsense and everyman. (Bhaskar, 1986: 272)

But equally it would not be possible to claim that management knowledge is fundamentally wrong. Instead it would be important to consider the ways in which different resources have been historically used, by active human agents, to favour particular schemes that are practically adequate for the pursuit, by particular socio-economic interest groups, of their perceived interests in a fallible manner. This will reveal how such bodies of knowledge have been established and the coalitions of interest they appear to serve. Weber's notion of 'elective affinity' (1968: 90–2) is helpful here, since it focuses upon the processes whereby 'ideas' are selected by people (elective) that are compatible with their perceived material interests (affinity).

Unlike a postmodern concern to de-centre subjects, elective affinity entails both the consideration of the social conditions that enable the articulation of certain recipes of knowledge and the analysis of the proactive and serendipitous efforts of various 'carrier groups' (Law and Lodge, 1984) of knowledge to secure and aggrandize their authority in the cognition of potential clients and patrons. For Bourdieu (1975) such appeals to legitimacy may be greatly influenced by the relative strengths of carrier groups who calculatively use a variety of cognitive and social resources to both advance their ideas and, according to Shapin (1984), eventually to ensure the closure of debate. For management, such processes may have been bolstered by a growing objectification and abstraction of management knowledge that entailed its characterization as neutral. Latour (1987) demonstrates how such knowledge claims are constituted as factual by carrier groups through their establishment of networks of association and alliances with supportive significant others, as well as their success in overcoming opposition and resistance. As Rouse (1987) has pointed out, epistemic power derives, in part, from the ability to silence opposing accounts of the same phenomena. To borrow Tinker's terminology, in the 'horse race of ideas' some horses 'never reach the starting gate, others are excessively handicapped, and still others may be nobbled . . . before the race' (1986: 377). But for Latour the paradox of this process is that a carrier group may have to simultaneously

> increase the number of people taking part in the action – so that the claim spreads, and to decrease the number of people taking part in the action – so that the claim spreads as it is. (1987: 207)

The resolution of this paradox in management may be mediated by a carrier group's ability persuasively to 'manage the meanings' (Clark and Salaman, 1996a; 1996b) of managerial communities. Central to such practices is the manipulation of 'the mutually acceptable symbols of knowledge in the course of convincing performances' (Clark and Salaman, 1998: 147) so as to instil or enhance a positive self-image in the perceptions of senior managers by discursively establishing a heroic sense of order and moral worth. Effective manipulation of these domains can temporarily mitigate the evident fallibility of many in vogue ideas by ensuring that they appeal to, and are harmonious with, the expectations and values of their managerial audiences (see Grint, 1994). However from their analysis of the activities of 'management gurus', Clark and Salaman (1998) argue that management audiences are not passive receptors of knowledge disseminated by gurus and that such knowledge is more an outcome of the parties' interactions where a sense of mutual gain and perceived coincidence of interest are crucial.

An alternative example of these social processes is provided by Armstrong (1985; 1987) where he has drawn attention to the 'fate' of the 'carrier group' of particular recipes of knowledge in explaining the ascendancy of accountancy in British and North American enterprises. Implicitly he points to the pre-emptive activities of carrier groups in propagandizing and aggrandizing their knowledge and practices. This facilitated the adoption, by entrepreneurial elites, of that knowledge which was practically adequate for their pursuit of their perceived interests and for the resolution of their perceived problems which had arisen from the exigencies created by their organization and control of enterprises. For instance he traces the increasing representation of accountants in British and North American managerial hierarchies. He has emphasized that this process was not an automatic consequence of the 'objective needs' of capitalism. Rather this phenomenon was the result

> of efforts by the profession to develop their original techniques into a system of managerial control in competition with other methods . . . as a means of achieving managerial ascendancy. (1985: 145)

In support of Armstrong, it is important to note that many of the cost accounting and internal reporting techniques employed by modern enterprises were known by 1925 (Johnson, 1978; Kaplan, 1984) yet their utilization as a means of regulating business was slow and sporadic (de Roover, 1974; Yamey, 1977). This temporal disparity emphasizes the need for closer inspection of the socio-historical contexts that confront 'carrier groups' and the influences upon how potential patrons constructed their 'problems'. As Delanty has observed about social science generally, it is

> shaped in the definition of problems. To that extent it is itself constructed in the process of problem definition . . . The professionalized culture of social science does not itself construct social problems from its own discourse but does so in response to public and media agenda setting. Problem construction is a dynamic process involving many social actors who define, negotiate and thereby construct problems. In this way social science enters social scientific discourse as a constructed reality and one which is the product of contentious action. (1997: 140)

It may be that social science and its disciplinary off-shoots that coalesce under the nomenclature 'management' are both discursively shaped by, and discursively shape, the identification and fallibilistic resolution of 'problems'.

This leads us to a critical element of the pragmatic–critical realist perspective – as epistemic subjects we are *all* complicit in the processes through which we socially construct versions of reality. Our lack of a theory-neutral observational language means that there is no Archimedian fixed position from which we can objectively assess veracity in a correspondence sense. It suggests a '*nouvelle alliance*' where the unity of the natural and social sciences is based upon their constitution by social context rather than by a shared methodology or subject matter (Zolo, 1990: 165). From this perspective, if we are to avoid the quagmire of relativism, 'truthfulness' is ultimately only assessable through the success or failure of our interest-laden practices since it is in practice where ontologically prior realities, social constructions and social constructors interact together.

Two points arise here: first, it is incumbent upon commentators to reflect critically upon their own intellectual assumptions in their social construction of any discourse and to provide a clear guide to its practical ramifications – choices that have overt political, moral and evaluative elements (Fay, 1975: 94–5); secondly, it must entail acceptance by management researchers of their (albeit fallible) role as partisan participants in interest-laden discourse thereby divesting themselves of allusions to the role of detached observer occupying a neutral position (see Carchedi, 1983; Chubin and Restivo, 1983; Tinker, 1991). If all management knowledge is the result of social construction, it is not sufficient to deconstruct only hegemonic constructions; it behoves deconstructors reflexively to 'open' their own 'black box' and apply to themselves their own epistemic commitments (see Beck, 1996). For Zolo (1990: 163) it is through such a epistemically reflexive feedback loop that any social science can establish what amounts to a sociology of itself.

Conclusions

Pragmatic–critical realism articulates an overt recognition of the active and projective role of the epistemic subject whose engagements are bounded by the tolerance of reality. *Any* knowledge is thus evaluated in the context of how successfully it may guide action towards the realization of particular objectives which express particular interests: that is in terms of what it does for, and to, various groups of human actors. This leads to an explicit consideration of how different bodies of socially constructed knowledge are practically adequate in terms of varying ethical, moral, ideological and political purposes. If knowledge is evaluated in terms of how successfully it may guide action towards the realization of particular interest-laden objectives, this will necessarily entail those conducting such critique reflecting upon the partisan nature of their own constructs and thereby make the implicit explicit. Research and discourse embracing such a position must entail epistemic reflexivity on the part of participants. This behoves the subject to reflect upon, address and reshape their conceptual choice in terms of the values, mores and goals which they are projecting on to the phenomenon of interest by engaging with it. It would support the notion that there is no pre-ordained route along which any knowledge unfolds since any outcome is influenced by the action of social and political processes.

Accordingly there must develop a political debate that eschews epistemic privilege and examines the justifications of existing gazes, the relevance of their approaches to different audiences, and the sources and forms of support they receive. This suggests the possibility of a rapprochement between the political economy and the social constructivist views of science (see Lawson, 1994; Yearley, 1988). However the pragmatic–critical realist ontological and epistemological position would demand a consideration of how such a critique might be translated into practical action – the latter constituting not only the ultimate source of arbitration for 'truth claims', but also a conduit for both epistemically reflexive research initiatives and political practices that aid the development of alternative gazes. Here, as in critical theory, an important project would be the development of modes of engagement that articulate interests currently excluded or neglected by extant management knowledge and its theoretical categories. This will entail political dialogue with extant management discourses and, by revealing their hidden prejudices, serve to counter their hegemony. In preparing for such a political dialogue the pragmatic–critical realist perspective raises a variety of questions regarding management knowledge: Who were (are) the carrier groups of management knowledge? How did (do) those carrier groups gain and maintain a position that enables them to authoritatively present to practitioner significant others their particular interpretations of, and solutions to, their problems? What were (are) those problems and what were (are) the motivations of those practitioner significant others? What were (are) the outcomes of these social processes? How might (is) management knowledge develop(ing) as it both caters for and constructs the concerns of practitioner significant others?

In sum, from the epistemological and ontological stance of pragmatic–critical realism, five key insights arise:

1   This combination of pragmatism and critical realism supports the view that a correspondence theory of truth is ultimately unattainable because of the projective role of the epistemic subject. This inevitably leads to an anti-positivist conception of knowledge – that all knowledge is socially constructed. But if we completely divorce epistemology from ontology, and thereby do not allow for human contact with external reality, there is the danger that we follow postmodernists into a relativism which states that what is 'real' is a matter internal to a community's language-games. As we saw in Chapter 5, critique is thereby undermined since there appears to be no good reason for preferring one theory to another.

2   All human behaviour and all human knowledge occurs within and simultaneously reconstructs culturally derived meanings.

3   The purpose of social scientific inquiry into management or whatever is to produce causal explanations which can guide, and may be evaluated through, efficacious human interventions into our social worlds.

4   Pragmatic–critical realism demands a reflexive political praxis. As we have emphasized, for the pragmatic–critical realist the adjudication of *any* knowledge-claim does not relate to some quest for foundational knowledge. Instead adjudication would focus upon evaluating the ways in which knowledge serves to guide and shape human activities, that is, its practical and political consequences.

5   As Bhaskar (1989b) argues, the role of philosophy becomes that of 'underlabourer', illuminating the epistemological and ontological conditions for human inquiry rather than certifying particular theoretical or substantive claims.

Further reading

Trigg (1980) provides an accessible introduction to realism and its variants – including pragmatism. Nevertheless it is the work of Roy

Bhaskar which is of central importance to critical realism. However it is extraordinarily difficult to read and understand. Hence we would advise anyone interested in Bhaskar's work to first read Collier's (1994) introduction to Bhaskar's philosophy since it is helpful for making sense of Bhaskar's often idiosyncratic idiom. The application of critical realism in management and organizational research is relatively rare. Notable exceptions include Whittington's (1989) analysis of strategic choice; Tsoukas' (1989) review of case study research; Marsden's (1993) consideration of power; Lawson's (1994) critique of economic theory; and Reed's (1997) deliberations about agency and structure. Obviously Sayer's work (1992) covers realism, and by implication pragmatism, in much depth as do Rescher (1977) and Margolis (1986).

8
Conclusions – A More Reflexive Approach towards Management Research

Scientists, in order to understand themselves as scientists, first have to become anthropologists, sociologists, psychologists, and historians of themselves.

(Zolo, 1990: 162)

By now it is probably only too evident to the reader that a chapter proposing to 'conclude' a book on epistemology is difficult to write since to conclude about epistemology is surely impossible as there can be no final, incontrovertible, end-point better than what has gone before. Therefore our aim in this chapter is modest as all we can do is to emphasize that there are no definite answers to epistemological issues. The possibility of coming to a foundational set of epistemological standards whose insights allow us to appraise all other disciplines, management or otherwise, must remain a forlorn hope due to the inevitable circularity of epistemological issues – that any theory of knowledge presupposes knowledge of the conditions in which knowledge takes place. However what we can say is that there are a variety of different epistemological positions which legitimize their own distinctive ways of engaging with management and doing management research. So the aim for management researchers should be that they maintain consistency with regard to the epistemological assumptions they do deploy – something which would be enhanced by them being more aware of, and indeed more critical of, the substance, origins and ramifications of those assumptions. In such respects management researchers must heed the advice of Zolo quoted above, albeit originally aimed at natural scientists. Of course this raises issues about reflexivity on the part of the management researcher.

In the introduction to this book we wrote that we hoped to encourage the new spirit of reflexivity which seemed to be developing in management research. Here we must proceed with some caution since social scientists' variable deployment of the notion of reflexivity is nothing new as it may be traced back to before World War II. However it is only with the comparatively recent realization by some researchers that social construction must embrace *both* the lay and the scholarly domains, that the importance of reflexivity has been extended and brought to the fore in social science epistemology (e.g. Beck, 1992; Bourdieu, 1990; Holland, 1999; Pollner, 1991; Sandywell, 1996; Steier, 1991). These developments are seen to be so important by some scholars that, for instance, Holland goes as far as to claim that reflexivity is an inalienable 'human capacity which defines our existence' (*ibid.*: 482) while Sandywell (*ibid.*) argues that a failure to engage in reflexivity amounts to an abdication of intellectual responsibility which results in poor research practices. However placing such demands upon a management researcher raises a significant ambiguity since the form that reflexivity takes, not to mention whether or not it is perceived to be possible in the first place, are outcomes of *a priori* philosophical assumptions.

For instance, it is initially possible to differentiate two forms of reflexivity. These are indicated by Harding (1987) where she discusses the importance of reflexivity:

> The *beliefs* and the *behaviours* of the researcher are part of the empirical evidence for (or against) the claims advanced in the results of the research . . . [which] . . . must be open to critical scrutiny no less than what is traditionally defined as relevant evidence . . . This kind of relationship between the researcher and the object of research is usually discussed under the heading of the 'reflexivity of social science'. (*ibid.*: 9) (our emphasis)

Harding's definition implies that one form of reflexivity is concerned with the monitoring by the researcher of their *behavioural* impact upon the social settings under investigation which is created by their deployment of particular research protocols and associated field roles. This may be called '*methodological reflexivity*' where the aim is to improve research practice through the facilitation of a more accurate representation of reality via the eradication of methodological lapses. Methodological reflexivity may be contrasted with a second form of reflexivity implicit in Harding's definition. Here systematic attempts are made to relate research outcomes to the knowledge-constraining and -constituting impact of the researcher's own beliefs which derive from their own socio-historical location or 'habitus' (Bourdieu, 1990). We shall call this alternative '*epistemic reflexivity*'.

Epistemic reflexivity entails the researcher attempting to think about their own thinking by excavating, articulating, evaluating and in some cases transforming the metatheoretical assumptions they deploy in structuring research activities as well as in apprehending and interpreting what is observed. Here, the implication is that researchers must hold their own 'research structures and logics as themselves researchable and not immutable, and by examining how we are part of our own data, our research becomes a reciprocal process' (Steier, 1991: 7). But as Fay (1987) has pointed out, because epistemic reflexivity insists that researchers must confront and question the taken-for-granted assumptions which traditionally inform our knowledge-claims and ultimately give meaning to our lives, then resistance to epistemic reflexivity is only to be expected. For instance, researchers committed to epistemic reflexivity would see those who focus purely upon methodological reflexivity as being fatally limited, as dogmatic, since they exclude from scrutiny their own taken-for-granted views. The probable riposte to such accusations from those engaging solely in methodological reflexivity would be the counter-accusation that epistemic reflexivity inevitably leads to an incipient and debilitating relativism.

Bourdieu (*ibid.*) attempts to cast some light upon how what we have called epistemic reflexivity might be accomplished. He argues that any science is embedded in, and conditioned by, an underlying socially derived collective unconsciousness that conditions what is taken to be warranted knowledge. For Bourdieu epistemic reflexivity entails systematic reflection by the social scientist aimed at making the unconscious conscious and the tacit explicit so as to reveal how the social scientist's social location forms a sub-text of research which conditions any account – an analysis of analysis. This must entail some form of metatheoretical examination of the presuppositions which researchers have internalized and will inevitably deploy in understanding any organizational experiences. It follows that management research cannot be carried out in some intellectual space which is autonomous from the researcher's own biography. Indeed it would seem that epistemic reflexivity must relate to how a researcher's own biography affects the forms and outcomes of research (Ashmore, 1989) as well as entailing acceptance of the conviction that there will always be more than one valid account of any research.

Paradoxically, both forms of epistemic reflexivity would seem to share the epistemological assumption that it is possible for the researcher autonomously and *rationally* to reflect upon and engage with their own mode of engagement at either a metatheoretical or a methodological level – something which is contested by some of the epistemological positions reviewed in this book. Hence our aim in this chapter is to summarize the various orientations we have considered and give an overview of the patterns which emerge with regard to how they construe reflexivity in management research.

Reflexivity and management research

One way of understanding the various approaches to undertaking management research and their interrelationships is illustrated by the matrix in Figure 8.1 above. The two axes of the matrix are constituted by objectivist and subjectivist assumptions about epistemology and ontology. Obviously one has to be cautious about using such binary models in that they set up dualisms which may occlude some of the subtle similarities

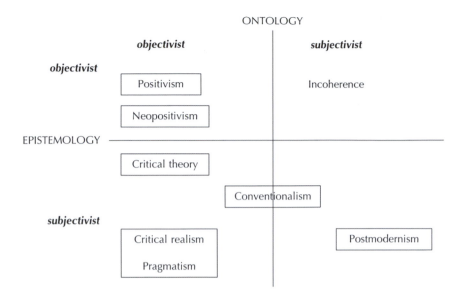

Figure 8.1   Reflexivity and management research

and distinctions which exist between various schools of thought – issues which we will deal with in the text since they cannot be represented in terms of the binary dimensions in Figure 8.1. Hence Figure 8.1 must be treated with caution since it can provide only an initial orientation for the various perspectives represented.

To remind the reader, an objectivist view of epistemology presupposes the possibility of a theory-neutral observational language – in other words, it is possible to access the external world objectively. A subjectivist view of epistemology denies, for various reasons, the possibility of such an epistemological foundation. Meanwhile an objectivist view of ontology assumes that social and natural reality have an independent existence prior to human cognition whereas a subjectivist ontology assumes that what we take to be reality is an output of human cognitive processes. As is shown above, an objectivist epistemology is necessarily dependent on objectivist ontological assumptions – to say that one can have an objective view of realities which don't exist independently of the act of cognition would seem incoherent. On the other hand a subjectivist epistemology can be combined with either a subjectivist or an objectivist ontology. The result is a matrix in which only the north-west, south-east and south-west quadrants are occupied by distinctive positions. Within each quadrant positions are differentiated according to particular local disputes. We shall now review each of our three quadrants in turn so as to give a summary and overview of the book. Simultaneously we shall explore the implications of each occupied quadrant for epistemic and methodological reflexivity(ies).

The north-west quadrant: objectivist ontology, objectivist epistemology

Within this quadrant two approaches to management research are evident – positivism and neopositivism. Both forms of positivism share the empiricist commitment that our sensory experience of the objects of reality provides the only secure foundation for social scientific knowledge. Through the assumed availability of a theory-neutral observational language located in a Cartesian dualism, observers can 'picture' an *a priori* external world objectively and thereby deductively test, or inductively generate, theory. Thus truth, as correspondence, is to be found in the observer's passive registration of the facts that constitute reality. Where these two approaches part company is over what they understand to be observable as opposed to metaphysical. Unlike what we have termed positivism, neopositivists argue that in order to understand human behaviour in organizations we must gain access to those actors' subjective interpretations of reality – to access and describe their cultures through '*verstehen*' and the deployment of reputedly qualitative methods of data collection. So as to legitimate this interpretative methodological imperative neopositivism questions the methodological unity of the sciences, grounded in '*erklaren*', as proposed by positivists. Positivists reciprocate by denying the possibility of '*verstehen*', thereby restoring the methodological unity of natural and social sciences. Nevertheless neopositivists retain what many philosophers define as positivism's key epistemic characteristic – the presupposition of a theory-neutral observational language. In positivism this act of passive registration would be construed as a subject–object dualism – a differentiation of the knower-researcher from the known-observed. In neopositivism this same dualism would be combined with a subject–subject dualism – a differentiation of the knower-researcher from their descriptions of what other knowers know so as to enable the researcher's ability to experience neutrally, and provide an account of, the other's organizational experience.

Since each of the dualisms noted above rests on a rhetoric of epistemic objectivity, which privileges the consciousness of the researcher who is deemed capable of discovering the 'truth' about the world in a correspondence sense, the reflexivity which is deployed is limited to that of methodological reflexivity. Here the researcher's reflexivity entails a localized critique and evaluation of the technical aspects of their own deployment of a particular methodology from within the positivist or neopositivist epistemological commitments the methodology deploys. So, for instance, organizational ethnographers may consider the variable impact upon the research setting of the various field roles (Gold, 1958) they might adopt during data collection so as to ensure a 'necessary' balance between 'outsider' and 'insider' (Horowitz, 1986), between 'distance' and 'inclusion' (Pollner and Emerson, 1983) and between 'detachment' and 'involvement' (Shalin, 1986) so as to facilitate access to uncensored organizational 'backstages' (Goffman, 1969) while avoiding 'overrapport' by retaining 'social and intellectual distance' and 'analytical space' (Hammersley and Atkinson, 1995: 115). Alternatively, survey researchers might evaluate the adequacy of the operationalization processes through which they have translated the abstract concepts they need to measure into a set of indicators in the form of questions on their questionnaires (Reeves and Harper, 1981). Meanwhile experimenters may be concerned with ensuring that every respondent had experienced the same experimental treatment within an experimental group as far as is possible in the quasi-experimental conditions which usually apply in organizations (Campbell and Stanley, 1963).

The point is that reflexivity in this quadrant is limited to a critical evaluation of the methodology deployed rather than the underlying meta-theoretical assumptions that justify the methodology in the first place. It is rather like Kuhn's chess player analogy referred to in Chapter 3 – the chess player *qua* researcher evaluates their own style of play, its strengths and weaknesses etc. without any concern about, or questioning of, the rules of the game. It is our second type of reflexivity, the epistemic, which entails thinking about the rules and the possibilities of different rules and different possible games. To extend this analogy, sports like football and Rugby Union could be seen as becoming increasingly concerned with epistemic reflexivity as illustrated by recent campaigns to adjust their rules so as to make their games more of a media spectacle or in some instances safer for the players. Hence more fundamental questions are being posed, such as: who is the game for? And what should the rules be?

It follows that Habermas (1972: 67) was largely correct when he accused positivist epistemology of serving to immunize positivism from epistemological self-reflection since one outcome of positivism's commitment to a theory-neutral observational language is to protect its adherents from epistemic reflexivity. The assumption that due to their methodological training etc. they are able passively to accumulate facts from an ontologically prior world so as objectively to test any knowledge-claim renders their own involvement in the research process unproblematic, beyond ostensibly technical methodological issues. In the case of neo-positivists, one effect of such closure is that what they have learned about human behaviour in organizations or elsewhere – that it is interpretative and based upon members' social construction – is not recursively applied to their own working. Of course epistemic reflexivity entails a denial of the possibility of any neutral vantage point, thereby forestalling any such internal immunization from the effects of the researcher's own learning. However in doing so epistemic reflexivity can be taken to be an unending process as its own products must in turn become open to further iterations of epistemic reflexivity. This process of endless reflexive loops is often called 'hyper-reflexivity' and is most evident in our next quadrant where ontological and epistemological subjectivism meet – the south-east.

The south-east quadrant: subjectivist ontology, subjectivist epistemology

In the south-east quadrant of Figure 8.1 we have located postmodernism and much of conventionalism. If we take conventionalists first, it is evident that their ontological oscillation means that at times they adopt a relativistic position which justifies the incommensurability thesis. At other times they drift to an objectivist ontology, support a commensurable view of paradigms and seem to have more in common with critical realists except that they usually fail to articulate how non-foundational transactions may take place between human knowers and reality. The result is that epistemic reflexivity is treated variably, depending upon where the conventionalist stands upon the incommensurability thesis.

As Holland (1999) points out, conventionalists will either have an emphasis upon comparing incommensurable paradigms with each other so as to reflexively highlight their contradictions and conflicts, or they will have an emphasis upon a commensurable view of paradigms – as clusters of disciplinary alternatives which may be drawn upon in an eclectic manner so as to give different socially constructed snapshots of the same reality. The point is that the common ontological referent allows commensurability and the notion that we can advance our understandings of that reality through both methodological and epistemic reflexivity. So, for instance, Burrell and Morgan's (1979) brand of conventionalism would support an epistemic reflexivity driven by incommensurability whereas a commensurability emphasis would be more evident in some of Morgan's later work on metaphors (e.g. 1986). Intriguingly, following the more subjectivist voice of Kuhn (1970a), both types of reflexivity within conventionalism may be dismissed as rationalistic and hence even epistemic reflexivity is of limited utility since our embedded paradigmatic assumptions cannot easily be subjected to rational evaluation or testing.

If we turn to postmodernism it is evident that the subjectivist themes of conventionalist incommensurability are replicated. As we have shown, the postmodernist's epistemological and ontological subjectivism is based upon the denial of the possibility of a theory-neutral observational language – far from language allowing access to and representation of reality, language creates reality. Any science is seen as a 'language game' – part of a 'form of life' into which the individual has been socialized. For the postmodernist, notions of truth and objectivity are merely the outcomes of prestigious discursive practices which sublimate partiality by masking how the scientist, the processes of observation and scientific knowledge, are all inextricably intertwined. One of the benefits of the arrival of postmodernism in the management field has been its focus on the multiple versions of reality which means that researchers (or anyone else) have to be humble about any claims they make to represent reality. This, it could be argued, encourages reflexivity on the part of the researcher. On the other hand, postmodernism's epistemological and ontological position problematizes epistemic reflexivity in two quite different ways driven by the same relativistic arguments – silence and hyper-reflexivity.

First by decentring the subject, the possibility to reflect rationally upon and develop self-knowledge by interrogating one's own metatheoretical assumptions is dismissed since people can neither possess such agency and independent volition nor autonomously choose their discursive communities. Some of those who deny that any form of epistemic reflexivity is possible could, presumably, go so far as to foresake any act of representation – including their own presentation of such arguments in any form. If everything is relative, what is the point in saying anything? Indeed is there a danger that by saying or writing something you privilege it? Hence people who adopt such an extreme interpretation of postmodernism's relativism would remain silent, unpublished and hence unreportable other than in a hypothetical manner. While such a tactic would seem consistent with postmodernist attacks upon representationism, they would remain unknown to others by definition. For postmodern scholars, pressing the 'self-destruct button' in this way, thereby ending their academic careers, is probably most unappealing – hence the use of alternative tactics by most postmodern academics.

Thus some postmodernists are keen to demonstrate the implications of their relativism for epistemic reflexivity. This reported/reportable postmodern approach to reflexivity takes the relativistic notion that the world is the result of representational practices as justifying the demand that management researchers must reflexively deconstruct their own representational practices. However, where can this process end? Surely relativism must mean that such reflexivity must be an endless process where postmodernists continuously deconstruct their own deconstructions of themselves? For example Ashmore (1989) and Woolgar (1988a; 1988b) advocate the use of what they call 'hyper-reflexivity', the 'deconstruction of deconstruction' and the development of 'new literary forms'. Released 'from the constraints of representational realism' (Ashmore, *ibid*.: xxix) their project abandons the conventional mode of writing exemplified by the authoritative monologue of a single official writer. Instead a number of voices appear, disappear and reappear throughout the self-referential text, interrupting and disrupting each other where any 'author' is debated by 'meta-authors' who in turn are debated by their own 'meta-authors', and so on, in a potentially endless spiral of introspective reflexive iterations.

So for some postmodernists if there can be no external independent ontological referent epistemic reflexivity becomes an autopoietic (i.e. self-generating) process within a recursively closed cognitive system. As we have shown in Chapter 5, the result can be a conservative inactivity with regard to organizational practices. In contrast the occupants of our south-west quadrant see epistemic reflexivity as involving a hermeneutic relationship with reality which entails a commitment to societal change through the transformation of knowledge. Such realism is illustrated by

Latour's (1988) critique of hyper-reflexivity in which he argues for 'infra-reflexivity' which is of the 'world not the word' and therefore entails a 'multiplicity of genres . . . not . . . the tedious presence of "reflexive loops" . . . genres which appertain to different interpretations of a world "still unknown and despised"' (*ibid.*: 173). Elsewhere Beck (1996: 7) describes this position as 'reflexive realism' where reality, social construction and the interpreter interact together so that the reflexive realist has to be committed to investigation of how 'self evidence is produced, how questions are curtailed, how alternative interpretations are shut up in black boxes and so on'. For Beck the result of our south-west quadrant must be a discursive democratization of social science through public critique. Such a debate pervades critical theory, critical realism and pragmatism. We will now turn to consider how and why this particular view of epistemic reflexivity arises.

The south-west quadrant: objectivist ontology, subjectivist epistemology

Occupants of the south-west quadrant regard epistemic reflexivity as emancipatory by both sanctioning and enabling the investigation and problematization of the taken-for-granted social constructions of reality which are located in the varying practices, interests and motives which constitute different communities' sense-making. In doing so they attempt to establish the conditions necessary for the development of differential constructions of reality and to show the possibility of alternative accounts. This enables people to

> alter their lives by fostering in them the sort of self-knowledge and understanding of their social conditions which serve as a basis for such an alteration. (Fay, 1987: 23)

For instance in Chapter 6 the point of departure for understanding the constitution of critical theory was the work of Jurgen Habermas. As we tried to show, this entails both constructivist and socio-rationalist epistemological commitments located in an objectivist (i.e. realist) ontology. The main target for Habermas is positivist epistemology whose 'objectivist illusions' are dismissed by drawing attention to the socio-cultural factors that influence sensory experience. From Habermas' standpoint it is necessary to treat all management theory as serving particular sectional interests and view all claims to neutrality or common sense as a masquerade that hides partiality. In this manner Habermas articulates a constructivism based upon the object-constituting activities of epistemic human beings. However by dismissing notions of objectivity through tying all forms of knowledge to the imperatives of human life, Habermas becomes haunted by relativism. In particular, he has to rescue the status of his own critique by finding some epistemological refuge from which that very critique might be defended.

Habermas' solution is the 'ideal-speech situation' in which discursively produced socio-rational consensus is induced when that consensus derives from argument and analysis without resort to coercion, distortion or duplicity. In contrast to the 'legitimation crisis' created by postmodernists' 'linguistic turn', we might infer from Habermas' 'intersubjective turn' that for knowledge to be legitimate it must be grounded in the relational intersubjective consensus achievable in an ideal-speech situation. This communal consensus implies agreement not only regarding the outcomes of discourse but also upon the rules and logics of reasoning that lead to them. This gives epistemic reflexivity a pivotal role in critical theory: knowledge cannot and should not be the outcome of privileged access and dissemination by the authoritative few; rather legitimate knowledge must be the outcome of unconstrained public debate and agreement. Here Habermas relies upon a modified rationalism where rationality is not conceived as the egocentric reasoning of an epistemically privileged individual. Rather (socio-)rational knowledge occurs in social relations that are established among people when they democratically negotiate their socially constructed definitions of reality.

However it is evident to Habermas that such a consensus is not attained in everyday social interaction due to the asymmetrical operation of power and domination which systematically distorts communication. Therefore it must remain a regulative ideal. Hence one important focus for epistemic reflexivity would be consideration of the extent to which social constructions in use have been democratically arrived at. As far as management research is concerned this raises two important questions for critical theory. First, who are the potential communicants in any discourse about knowledge, and secondly, how could communicants ever be certain that systematic distortions were not taking place, given the insidious nature of power and domination?

Identification and involvement of all potential communicants presumably must start with the mobilization of every organizational stakeholder. While this in itself is highly problematic, the subsequent power relations between communicants could pose insurmountable problems. The danger is that notionally democratic communication may be a facade in which the more powerful deploy a rhetoric of democracy to impose their own knowledgeable preferences upon, and silence or marginalize, the less powerful. Moreover where Habermas argues that any consensus must arise out of discourse, he seems to imply the possibility of the neutral adjudication of knowledge-claims by rational investigators. But without the prior assumption of the possibility of a theory-neutral observational language, rational analysis will not indicate the answer to which any rational agent would adhere. This is a significant problem for critical theorists as their attempts to avoid relativism could propel them towards the very objectivist epistemologies which they vehemently decry elsewhere.

Although there are many similarities between critical theorists and pragmatic–critical realists, there are some significant differences. For instance pragmatic–critical realists would agree that a correspondence theory of truth is ultimately unattainable because of the projective role of the epistemic subject. This inevitably leads to an anti-objectivist conception of knowledge – that all knowledge is socially constructed. Simultaneously pragmatic–critical realists would argue that if we completely divorce epistemology from ontology, and thereby do not allow for human contact with external reality, there is the danger that we retreat into a relativism which states that what is 'real' is a matter of consensus, democratic or otherwise.

Of course the problem which pragmatic–critical realists would have with Habermas is that his approach, while ostensibly retaining a realist ontology, does not indicate how this external referent will play a regulative role upon our social constructions. There appears to be no good reason, besides democratic consensus, for preferring one theory to another. For the pragmatic–critical realist a viable means of evaluating the veracity of cognitive systems and theories, that avoids both relativism and objectivism, is through their practical success or failure. This is derived from the view that our everyday practical actions as human agents tacitly presume that external causal regularities exist which we may act upon. As Zolo has argued (1990: 155–7), even though our conceptualization and explanation of such regularities must always be open to question (due to our lack of a theory-neutral observational language), our ability to undertake practical actions that are successful and our ability to reflect upon and correct actions that seem unsuccessful, imply that we have feedback from an independent 'reality' which constrains and enables practices that would otherwise be inconceivable. In other words, practical activity demands and enables processes of adjudication through the feedback that derives from the tolerance of that mind-independent spatio-temporal reality – that is their 'practical adequacy'.

Hence the differences between critical theory and pragmatic–critical realism seem differences of emphasis rather than irresolvable dispute. Both would eschew the hyper-reflexivity of some postmodernists while simultaneously denying that epistemic reflexivity can enable some form of neutral self-evaluation. Instead they would affirm that epistemic reflexivity is a process that entails thinking about thinking, which can only employ the limited thought processes available to us, and hence is itself socially and historically conditioned. This reminder serves as an antidote to any construal which infers that any form of reflexivity allows us to get outside constructivist processes and attain some position of disinterested objectivity. Hence a key point for critical theorists and pragmatic–critical realists is that epistemic reflexivity reframes the management researcher's self-knowledge but does not lead to a 'better' and more 'accurate' account. Rather, by engendering the possibility of conscious variation of our metatheoretical assumptions epistemic reflexivity can create *different* accounts of the same phenomenon which thereby become available to transformation.

So through a critical interrogation and reassessment of the researcher's own analysis, the meanings that have been attached to experience may be reformulated to create what amount to rereadings and rewritings of the 'text'. Here, due to their socio-rationalism, critical theorists will emphasize the role of epistemic reflexivity in enabling both the construction of new interpretations and the achievement of consensus. Meanwhile pragmatic–critical realists, because of their commitment to concepts like practical adequacy, will emphasize epistemic reflexivity's role in engendering new forms of practice located in new versions of reality. For both there can be no final account since any reflexive output and the practices it sanctions can in turn become new objects for reflexive investigation.

For all occupants of this quadrant, because our variable knowledge products have different practical interest-laden implications, it follows that our knowing selection of one knowledge system as opposed to an alternative becomes a question of ethical priority. Therefore epistemic reflexivity is seen as a resource which helps researchers recognize their own creative inputs and surfaces the ethical priorities which construct what we know about management. So all occupants recognize that they must reflexively interrogate and deconstruct their own representational practices; in doing so pragmatic–critical realists emphasize how they can elucidate, and *must* act upon, the practical and interest-laden ramifications of their knowledge products in the light of competing ethical concerns. This coincides with what Holland describes as the highest level of reflexive analysis which is

> not so much a fixed location as a method of evaluating existing systems of knowledge, tied in as they are to sectional interests and constellations of power. It invites re-entry into the epistemological and sectional complexities of our human condition to intervene, 'knowingly' according to our ethical priorities. (1999: 476)

This self-comprehension demands a genealogy of pragmatic–critical realist discursive practices by researchers reflexively including themselves in any analysis so as to engender a consciousness of their own history, philosophy, aims, ethical priorities and practical implications. From the above it follows that a further key implication is that any researcher

> has no new truths to bring to the world; these are all deeply embedded in people's own experiences and ways of defining their own worlds. The social scientist among them can only aid the actors in releasing the suppressed contents constituting their self-understandings. (Melucci, 1996: 224, quoted in Delanty, 1997: 142)

For both critical theorists and pragmatic–critical realists Melucci's observation poses questions regarding how alternative modes of apprehending the world, constituted by those interests currently excluded by the engagements of much management theory, might be democratically socially constructed and thereby fulfil an emancipatory potential. Here the educational work of Friere (1972a; 1972b) which questions received knowledge as a means of creating a more democratic society, is relevant to all occupants of the south-west quadrant.

Friere argues that in order for education to be 'liberating' it must eschew the traditional passivity that is assigned to the learner when a pedagogue assumes and imposes epistemic privilege. In the traditional context the teacher is the subject of the learning process and the students the object: teachers decide what will be taught and how it will be taught – the students thereby become passive assimilators. Such educational practices are underpinned by what Friere considers to be a 'digestive' concept of knowledge in which the 'undernourished' are 'fed' as if their consciousnesses were 'empty space' (Friere, 1972b: 23–6). For Friere, the passivity engendered by such 'education for domestication' entails the 'introjection by the dominated of the cultural myths of the dominator' (1972a: 59) and fails to enable the development of a critical consciousness (1972b: 46). In contrast, Friere argues that the necessary prerequisites for the development of a 'critical consciousness', that dismantles the current hegemonic constructions of vested interest, are the recognition by actors of their present oppression through that hegemony and the understanding that a liberating education programme must eschew a pre-processed and prescriptive character. A 'critical consciousness' is only constitutable through an authentic dialogue with the educator, in which both educators and learners are 'equally knowing subjects' (Friere, 1972b: 31). Here Friere is asserting agency in the subject by stressing the possibility of learner empowerment as well as resistance to the extant hegemonic social order.

In following the implications of these prerequisites, Friere develops his 'problem-posing' model of pedagogy for the 'oppressed' in which the educator's role 'is to propose problems about the codified existential situations in order to help the learners arrive at an increasingly critical view of their reality' (1972b: 36). Friere's 'educative' programme conceives relations between 'teacher' and 'student' as dialogic in the sense that the content of the programme is based upon the student's own experience. Such a programme is an educative and therapeutic catalyst because the intent is to engender, through epistemic reflexivity, new (socially constituted) self-understandings and simultaneously expose the interests which produce and disseminate management knowledge which was taken to be authoritative and hence unchallengeable. Therefore the educative experience should enable people to attach new meanings to the social practices that they encounter in organizations, or elsewhere, and thereby begin to understand those practices as interest-laden social constructions located in Bourdieu's 'habitus', and hence to be mutable rather than inevitable.

Through such a de-reification of social practices, Friere argues that a liberated phenomenological world might arise which could be utilized to identify and pursue alternative practices, dispositions and ends that result in 'socially transformative' actions which are commensurable with subjects' interests. In other words, de-reification is an essential step in developing reflexive knowledge that is practically adequate for achieving the interests apprehended through the lens of a liberated phenomenological world (see Beck, 1992; Unger, 1987). Thus it is inappropriate for a pedagogue to attempt to deposit putatively privileged recipes of knowledge into a learner. Education must develop those subjects' ability to assess their own circumstances through developing a self-conception in which they are epistemic subjects who are able to determine and change their collective situation, as opposed to powerless objects determined by an immutable situation.

So, from the viewpoints of both critical theory and pragmatic–critical realism, management researchers should be concerned to develop new modes of engagement that allow subjects to pursue interests and objectives which are currently excluded by the dominant management discourses. Therefore it follows that those subjects must democratically co-determine and co-develop the substantive basis of that knowledge so that their interests and objectives become metaphorically permitted and encoded into its 'gaze'. Facilitated by epistemic reflexivity, the management researcher's contribution must therefore focus upon the *processes* of de-reification and knowledge development rather than upon any subsequent *content*: the role must be one of facilitating subjects' ability to comprehend themselves and their problems in new ways; to read and express their own organizational realities in new ways through their creation of their own texts; those texts would become the basis for reflexive transformative action by enabling the development of knowledge and strategies that are practically adequate for coping with and resolving subjects' problems.

Conclusions

As the preceding sections show, each of the different epistemological approaches encourages different kinds of reflexivity. Table 8.1 below provides a brief summary of the main focus of each approach.

Returning to our earlier analogy of a football match, it is possible to highlight the different foci upon which each approach towards reflexivity would centre. Within this analogy, positivists would be busy implementing the rules and finding new ways to ensure that the existing rules are implemented fairly. Their focus thus may be on the capabilities of the referee or any observer, making sure that they know the rules and have the skills and support needed to implement them effectively. More reflective positivists may take this a stage further and consider the link between the rules and the objectives of the game – thus they may recommend that

Table 8.1   The various epistemological approaches and their implications

Epistemological approach	Approach towards reflexivity	Focus/Issues
Positivism and neopositivism	Methodological reflexivity	Improving methods and their application
Critical theory/critical realism	Epistemic reflexivity	Exposing interests Enabling emancipation through self-reflexivity Participation of those being researched Importance of praxis
Postmodernism (1)	Hyper-reflexivity	Reflexive deconstruction of own practices Danger of relativism
Postmodernism (2)	Impossibility of reflexivity	Recognition of the impossibility of 'pure' knowledge Conservatism/silence?

certain rules be changed to meet the existing objectives better. Post-modernists recognize that it is impossible for anyone to be a neutral observer – thus they might argue that there are many different games going on at the same time and question whether it is worth playing the game at all, given the partial nature of our knowledge and the impossibility of neutral arbitration. Critical theorists and critical realists would also recognize the importance of values and interests in shaping the game. They would perhaps stand back and question the fundamental underlying structures, posing questions such as: Who is the game for? What do the various stakeholders think it should look like? In particular, what do those stakeholders who have little say in the operation of the game feel about how it is organized?

Clearly, both epistemic and methodological reflexivity have value and are perhaps at their most powerful when used in conjunction. There should be no reason why those with a focus upon epistemic reflexivity should ignore their methods and the ways in which these methods can be improved. Obviously, though, from a constructivist perspective, method is not all and it is also necessary to address the impact of the researcher's 'self' upon the research process. As we have indicated earlier, this is by no means easy. It is an incomplete and perhaps messy process which recognizes that in undertaking epistemic reflexivity we do not arrive at 'the answer'. Rather, researchers gain more (but not complete!) understanding of the complex and ongoing interrelationship which exists between themselves and their research.

Finally, having talked about reflexivity, it is incumbent upon us to explain where we stand in relation to epistemological issues. Like most of our colleagues, we do not feel particularly comfortable being pigeonholed into one category. However, having done precisely this to others, it would seem somewhat hypocritical to consider ourselves above such boundaries. Thus whilst we do not share identical views, we would both fall broadly within a critical realist approach. And, while we have attempted to be even-handed in our discussion, obviously our own views and preferences will have impacted upon our assessment of each approach – such is the circularity of epistemological debate.

References

Abbott, A. (1988) 'Transcending general linear reality', *Sociological Theory*, 6: 169–86.

Abel, T. (1958) 'The operation called Verstehen', *American Journal of Sociology*, 54: 211–18.

Adorno, T. and Horkheimer, M. (1987) *Dialectic of Enlightenment*. New York: Continuum.

Alcoff, L. (1997) 'Continental Epistemology', in J. Dancy and E. Sosa, *A Companion to Epistemology*. Oxford: Blackwell. pp. 76–81.

Alvesson, M. (1995) 'The Meaning and Meaninglessness of Postmodernism: Some Ironic Remarks', *Organization Studies*, 16 (6): 1047–75.

Alvesson, M. and Deetz, S. (1996) 'Critical Theory and Postmodernism Approaches to Organization Studies', in S.R. Clegg, C. Hardy and W.R. Nord (eds), *Handbook of Organization Studies*. London: Sage.

Alvesson, M. and Willmott, H. (1988) *Critical Theory and the Sciences of Management. The Frankfurt School: How Relevant is it Today?* Rotterdam: Erasmus University.

Alvesson, M. and Willmott, H. (1992a) 'Critical Theory and Management Studies: an Introduction', in M. Alvesson and H. Willmott, *Critical Management Studies*. London: Sage. pp. 1–20.

Alvesson, M. and Willmott, H. (1992b) 'On the Idea of Emancipation in Management and Organisation Studies', *Academy of Management Review*, 17 (3): 432–49.

Alvesson, M. and Willmott, H. (1996) *Making Sense of Management: A Critical Introduction*. London: Sage.

Andreski, S. (1974) *The Essential Comte* (translated by Margaret Clarke). London: Croom Helm.

Anthony, P. (1977) *The Ideology of Work*. London: Tavistock.

Arbib, M.A. and Hesse, M. (1986) *The Construction of Reality*. Cambridge: Cambridge University Press.

Argyris, C., Putnam, R. and Smith, D.M. (1985) *Action Science: Concepts, Methods and Skills for Research and Intervention*. San Francisco: Jossey Bass.

Armstrong, P. (1985) 'Changing Management Control Strategies: The Role of Competition between Accountancy and other Organizational Professions', *Accounting, Organizations and Society*, 10 (2): 129–48.

Armstrong, P. (1987) 'The Rise of Accounting Controls in British Capitalist Enterprises', *Accounting, Organizations and Society*, 12 (5): 415–36.

Arndt, J. (1985) 'On making marketing science more scientific: the role of observations, paradigms, metaphors and puzzle solving', *Journal of Marketing*, 49: 11–23.

Aronson, E. and Carlsmith, J.M. (1986) 'Experimentation in social psychology', in G. Lindzey and E. Aronson (eds), *Handbook of Social Psychology*. Reading, MA.: Addison Wesley.

Ashmore, M. (1989) *The Reflexive Thesis: Wrighting the Sociology of Scientific Knowledge*. Chicago: University of Chicago Press.

Ayer, A.J. (1971) *Language, Truth and Logic*. Harmondsworth: Penguin.

Bacon, F. (1620/1960) 'Novum Organum' in F.H. Anderson (ed.), *The New Organon and Related Writings.* New York: Liberal Arts Press.

Baker, T. (1988) *Doing Social Research.* New York: McGraw-Hill.

Barnes, B. (1977) *Interests and the Growth of Knowledge.* London: Routledge and Kegan Paul.

Baudrillard, J. (1983) *Simulations.* New York: Semiotext(e).

Bauman, Z. (1988) 'Viewpoint: sociology and postmodernity', *Sociological Review,* 36 (4): 790–813.

Bauman, Z. (1989) *Modernity and the Holocaust.* Oxford: Polity Press.

Bauman, Z. (1995) *Life in Fragments: Essays in Postmodern Morality.* Oxford: Basil Blackwell.

Beck, U. (1992) *The Risk Society: Towards a New Modernity.* Cambridge: Polity Press.

Beck, U. (1996) 'World risk society as cosmopolitan society? Ecological questions in a framework of manufactured uncertainties', *Theory, Culture & Society,* 13 (4): 1–32.

Behling, O. (1980) 'The case for the natural science model for research in organisational behaviour and organisation theory', *Academy of Management Review,* 5 (4): 483–90.

Bell, D. (1973) *The Coming Post-Industrial Society.* New York: Basic Books.

Berg, P.O. (1989) 'Postmodern management? From facts to fiction in theory and practice', *Scandinavian Journal of Management,* 5 (3): 201–17.

Berger, P.L. and Luckmann, T. (1971) *The Social Construction of Reality.* Harmondsworth: Penguin University Books.

Berger, P.L., Berger, B. and Kellner, H. (1973) *The Homeless Mind: Modernization and Consciousness.* Harmondsworth: Penguin Books.

Bernstein, R.J. (1983) *Beyond Objectivism and Relativism: Science, Hermeneutics and Praxis.* Philadelphia: University of Pennsylvania.

Bessant, J. (1991) *Managing Advanced Manufacturing Technology.* Oxford: Blackwell.

Best, S. and Kellner, D. (1991) *Postmodern Theory: Critical Interrogations.* London: Macmillan.

Bharadwaj, A. (1998) 'Integrating Positivist and Interpretative Approaches to Information Systems Research: A Lakatosian Model'. http://hsb.baylor.edu/ramsower/ais.ac.96/papers (electronic document).

Bhaskar, R. (1975) *A Realist Theory of Science.* London: Leeds Books.

Bhaskar, R. (1978) *A Realist Theory of Science* (2nd edn). Brighton: Harvester.

Bhaskar, R. (1986) *Scientific Realism and Human Emancipation.* London: Verso.

Bhaskar, R. (1989a) *The Possibility of Naturalism* (2nd edn). Brighton: Harvester.

Bhaskar, R. (1989b) *Reclaiming Reality: A Critical Introduction to Contemporary Philosophy.* London: Verso.

Bhaskar, R. (1993) *Dialectic: the Pulse of Freedom.* London: Verso.

Blau, P.M. (1955) *The Dynamics of Bureaucracy.* Chicago: University of Chicago Press.

Blau, P.M. and Scott, W. (1963) *Formal Organizations: A Comparative Approach.* London: Routledge and Kegan Paul.

Bloor, D. (1976) *Knowledge and Social Imagery.* London: Routledge and Kegan Paul.

Bluestone, B. and Harrison, H. (1988) *The Great U-Turn.* New York: Basic Books.

Boje, D. (1994) 'Organizational storytelling: The struggles of premodern, modern and postmodern organisational learning discourses', *Management Learning,* 25 (3): 433–61.

Bourdieu, P. (1975) 'The Specificity of the Scientific Field and the Social Conditions of the Progress of Reason', *Social Science Information,* 14 (1): 9–47.

Bourdieu, P. (1990) *The Logic of Practice.* Cambridge: Polity Press.

Bourgeois, V.W. and Pinder, C.C. (1983) 'Contrasting philosophical perspectives in administrative science: a reply to Morgan', *Administrative Science Quarterly,* 28 (4): 608–13.

Braverman, H. (1974) *Labor and Monopoly Capital.* New York: Monthly Review Press.

Broad, C.D. (1978) *Kant: An Introduction*. Cambridge: Cambridge University Press.

Broadbent, J. and Laughlin, R. (1997) 'Developing empirical research: an example informed by a Habermasian approach', *Accounting, Auditing and Accountability*, 10 (5): 622–48.

Brown, S. (1993) 'Postmodern Marketing', *European Journal of Marketing*, 27 (4): 19–34.

Brownell, P. and Trotman, K. (1988) 'Research methods in behavioural accounting', in K. Ferris, *Behavioural Accounting Research: A Critical Analysis*. Columbus: Century.

Bryman, A. (1992) *Research Methods and Organisational Studies*. London: Routledge.

Bryman, A. (1993) *Quantity and Quality in Social Research*. London: Routledge.

Bulmer, M. (1984) 'Facts, concepts, theories and problems', in M. Bulmer, *Sociological Research Methods: An Introduction*. London: Macmillan.

Burawoy, M. (1979) *Manufacturing Consent*. Chicago: University of Chicago Press.

Burnes, B. (1992) *Managing Change*. London: Pitman.

Burrell, G. (1993) 'Eco and the Bunnymen', in J. Hassard and M. Parker (eds), *Postmodernism and Organizations*. London: Sage.

Burrell, G. (1997) *Pandemonium*. London: Sage.

Burrell, G. and Morgan, G. (1979) *Sociological Paradigms and Organizational Analysis*. London: Heinemann.

Calhoun, C. (1995) *Critical Social Theory*. London: Blackwell.

Callinicos, A. (1983) *Marxism and Philosophy*. Oxford: Oxford University Press.

Callinicos, A. (1989) *Against Postmodernism: A Marxist Critique*. Cambridge: Polity Press.

Campbell, D.T. (1957) 'Factors relevant to the validity of experiments in social settings', *Psychological Bulletin*, 54: 297–312.

Campbell, D.T. (1969) 'Reforms as experiments', *American Psychologist*, 24: 409–29.

Campbell, D.T. and Stanley, J.C. (1963) *Experimental and Quasi-Experimental Designs for Research*. Chicago: Rand McNally.

Carchedi, G. (1983) 'Class analysis and the study of social forms', in G. Morgan (ed.), *Beyond Method*. London: Sage.

Carter, P. and Jackson, N. (1993) 'Modernism, postmodernism and motivation, or why expectancy theory failed to come up to expectations', in J. Hassard and M. Parker (eds), *Postmodernism and Organizations*. London: Sage. pp. 84–100.

Cassell, J. (1996) 'The woman in the surgeon's body: understanding the difference', *American Anthropologist*, 98: 41–53.

Chia, R. (1995) 'From modern to postmodern organizational analysis', *Organization Studies*, 16 (4): 579–604.

Chia, R. (1996a) 'Metaphors and metaphorization in organizational analysis: thinking beyond the thinkable', in D. Grant and C. Oswick (eds), *Metaphors and Organizations*. London: Sage. pp. 127–46.

Chia, R. (1996b) *Organizational Analysis as Deconstructive Practice*. Berlin: De Gruyer.

Child, J. (1972) 'Organisation structure, environment and performance: the role of strategic choice', *Sociology*, 6: 1–22.

Child, J. (1977) 'Organisation design and performance: Contingency theory and beyond', *Organisational and Administrative Sciences*, 8: 169–83.

Child, J. (1984) *Organisation: A Guide to Problems and Practice*. London: Harper and Row.

Child, J. and Rodrigues, S. (1996) 'The role of social identity in the international transfer of knowledge through joint ventures', in S.R. Clegg and G. Palmer, *The Politics of Management Knowledge*. London: Sage. pp. 46–68.

Chua, W.F. (1986) 'Theoretical constructions of and by the real', *Accounting Organizations and Society*, 11 (6): 583–98.

Chubin, D.E. and Restivo, S. (1983) 'The "mooting" of social studies: research programmes and science policy', in K.D. Knorr-Cetina and M. Mulkay (eds), *Science Observed; Perspectives on the Study of Science*. London: Sage.

Clark, T. and Salaman, G. (1996a) 'The use of metaphor in the client–consultant relationship: a study of management consultants', in D. Grant and C. Oswick (eds), *Metaphors and Organizations*. London: Sage. pp. 154–71.

Clark, T. and Salaman, G. (1996b) 'Telling tales: management consultancy as the art of story telling', in D. Grant and C. Oswick (eds), *Metaphors and Organizations*. London: Sage. pp. 166–84.

Clark, T. and Salaman, G. (1998) 'Telling tales: management gurus' narratives and the construction of managerial identity', *Journal of Management Studies*, 35 (2): 137–61.

Clegg, S. (1990) *Modern organizations: Organization studies in the postmodern world*. London: Sage.

Clegg, S. and Dunkerley, D. (1980) *Organisation Class and Control*. London: Routledge and Kegan Paul.

Clegg, S. and Hardy, C. (1996) 'Conclusion: representations', in S. Clegg, C. Hardy and W. Nord, *Handbook of Organization Studies*. London: Sage. pp. 676–708.

Clegg, S.R. and Palmer, G. (eds) (1996) *The Politics of Management Knowledge*. London: Sage.

Cobley, P. and Jansz, L. (1997) *Semiotics for Beginners*. Cambridge: Icon Books.

Cohen, L., Duberley, J. and Mcauley, J. (1999a) 'Fuelling discovery or monitoring productivity: research scientists' changing perceptions of management', *Organization*, 6 (3): 473–98.

Cohen, L., Mcauley, J. and Duberley, J. (1999b) 'The purpose and process of science: contrasting understandings in UK research establishments', *R&D Management*, 29 (3): 233–45.

Cohen, S. and Bailey, D. (1997) 'What makes teams work: group effectiveness research from the shopfloor to the executive suite', *Journal of Management*, 23 (3): 239–90.

Cohen, S. and Ledgford, G. (1994) 'The effectiveness of self managing teams: a quasi experiment', *Human Relations*, 47 (1): 13–43.

Collier, A. (1979) 'In defence of epistemology', *Radical Philosophy*, 20: 8–21.

Collier, A. (1994) *Critical Realism: An Introduction to Roy Bhaskar's Philosophy*. London: Verso.

Collins, D. (1998) *Organizational Change: Sociological Perspectives*. London: Routledge.

Comte, A. (1853) *The Positive Philosophy of Auguste Comte*. London: Chapman.

Cook, T.D. and Campbell, D.T. (1979) *Quasi-Experimentation: Design and Analysis for Field Settings*. Chicago: Rand McNally.

Cooper, R. (1989) 'Modernism, postmodernism and organizational analysis 3: the contribution of Jacques Derrida', *Organization Studies*, 10 (4): 479–502.

Cooper, R. and Burrell, G. (1988) 'Modernism, postmodernism and organisational analysis: an introduction', *Organization Studies*, 9: 91–112.

Coser, L. (1975) 'Presidential address: two methods in search of substance', *American Sociological Review*, 40: 691–700.

Czarniawska-Joerges, B. (1988) *Ideological Control in Nonideological Organizations*. New York: Praeger.

Daft, R.L. (1980) 'The evolution of organisational analysis in ASQ 1959–1979', *Administrative Science Quarterly*, 26 (2): 207–24.

Daudi, P. (1990) 'Con-versing in management's public place', *Scandinavian Journal of Management*, 6: 285–307.

Davis, J. (1985) *The Logic of Causal Order*. Beverly Hills, CA: Sage.

de Roover, R. (1974) *Business, Banking and Economic Thought*. Chicago: University of Chicago Press.

DeCock, C. (1998) 'It seems to fill my head with ideas: A Few thoughts on postmodernism, TQM and BPR', *Journal of Management Inquiry*, 7 (2): 144–53.

Deetz, S. and Kersten, S. (1983) 'Critical models of interpretive research', in L. Putnam and M. Pacanowsky, *Communication and Organisations*. Beverly Hills, CA: Sage.

Delanty, G. (1997) *Social Science: Beyond Constructivism and Relativism*. Buckingham: Open University Press.

Denzin, N. (1978) *The Research Act: A Theoretical Introduction to Sociological Methods* (2nd edn). London: McGraw-Hill.

Denzin, N. (1998) 'The art and politics of interpretation', in N.K. Denzin and Y.S. Lincoln, *Collecting and Interpreting Qualitative Materials*. Thousand Oaks, CA: Sage.

Derrida, J. (1973) *Speech and Phenomena*. Evanston, IL: Northwestern University Press.

Descartes, R. (1637/1968) *Discourse on Method*. Penguin: Harmondsworth.

Descartes, R. (1641/1968) *Meditations on Philosophy*. Penguin: Harmondsworth.

Dewey, J. (1929a) *The Quest for Certainty*. New York: Milton Bach.

Dewey, J. (1929b) *Experience and Nature*. Chicago: Open Court.

Dewey, J. (1938) *Logic: The Theory of Inquiry*. New York: Henry Holt.

Di Maggio, P. (1995) 'Comments on an article entitled What Theory is Not', *Administrative Science Quarterly*, 40: 391–7.

Donaldson, L. (1995) *American AntiManagement Theories of Organization: A Critique of Paradigm Proliferation*. Cambridge: Cambridge University Press.

Donaldson, L. (1996) *For Positivist Organization Theory*. London: Sage.

Donaldson, L. (1997) 'A Positivist Alternative to the structure action approach', *Organisation Studies*, 18 (1): 77–92.

Downey, H.K. and Ireland, R.D. (1979) 'Quantitative vs qualitative: Environmental assessments in organisation studies', *Administrative Science Quarterly*, 24: 630–7.

Drucker, P.F. (1993) *Post-Capitalist Society*. New York: Harper and Row.

Duhem, P. (1962) *The Aim and Structure of Physical Theory*. New York: Atheneum.

Easterby Smith, M., Thorpe, R. and Lowe, A. (1992) *Management Research: An Introduction*. London: Sage.

Eilon, S. (1980) 'The role of management science', *Journal of the Operational Research Society*, 31: 17–28.

Ely, R.J. (1995) 'The power in demography: women's social construction of gender identity at work', *Academy of Management Journal*, 38: 589–634.

Fals-Borda, O. and Rahman, M.A. (1991) *Action and Knowledge: Breaking the Monopoly with Participatory Action Research*. New York: Apex.

Fay, B. (1975) *Social Theory and Political Practice*. London: Allen and Unwin.

Fay, B. (1987) *Critical Social Science*. Cambridge: Polity Press.

Feldman, S. (1998) 'Playing with the pieces: deconstruction and the loss of moral culture', *Journal of Management Studies*, 35 (1): 59–79.

Feyerabend, P. (1978) *Against Method*. London: Verso.

Feyerabend, P. (1987) *Farewell to Reason*. London: Verso.

Fielding, N.G. (1988) 'Between micro and macro', in N.G. Fielding (ed.), *Action and Structure*. London: Sage.

Fielding, N.G. and Fielding, J.L. (1986) *Linking Data*. London: Sage.

Filstead, W. (1979) 'Qualitative methods: a needed perspective in evaluation research', in T. Cook and C. Reichardt, *Qualitative and Quantitative Methods in Evaluation Research*. Beverly Hills, CA: Sage. pp. 33–48.

Flek, L. (1935–79) *Genesis and Development of a Scientific Fact.* Chicago: University of Chicago Press.

Forrester, J. (1983) 'Critical theory and organisational analysis', in G. Morgan (ed.), *Beyond Method.* Beverly Hills, CA: Sage. pp. 234–46.

Forrester, J. (1989) *Planning in the Face of Power.* Berkeley, CA: University of California Press.

Forrester, J. (1991) 'Questioning and organizing attention: toward a critical theory of planning and administrative practice', *Administration and Society*, 13 (2): 161–205.

Forrester, J. (1992) 'Critical ethnography: on fieldwork in a Habermasian way', in M. Alvesson and H. Willmott, *Critical Management Studies.* London: Sage. pp. 46–65.

Forrester, J. (1993) *Critical Theory, Public Policy and Planning Practice.* Albany, NY: University of New York Press.

Foucault, M. (1977) *Discipline and Punish: The Birth of the Prison.* Harmondsworth: Penguin.

Foucault, M. (1980) *Power/Knowledge.* Brighton: Harvester.

Friere, P. (1972a) *Pedagogy of the Oppressed.* Harmondsworth: Penguin.

Friere, P. (1972b) *Cultural Action for Freedom.* Harmondsworth: Penguin.

Gaarder, J. (1995) *Sophie's World: A Novel About the History of Philosophy.* London: Phoenix House.

Gadamer, H. (1975) *Truth and Method.* London: Sheed and Ward.

Geertz, C. (1973) *The Interpretation of Cultures.* New York: Basic Books.

Gephart, R.J. (1993) 'Review of critical management studies by Alvesson and Willmott', *Academy of Management Review*, 18 (4): 798–804.

Gephart, R., Thatchenkerry, T. and Boje, D. (1996) 'Conclusion: restructuring organizations for future survival', in D. Boje, R. Gephart and T. Thatchenkerry (eds), *Postmodern Management and Organisation Theory.* Thousand Oaks: Sage.

Gergen, K. (1990) 'Social understanding and the inscription of self in cultural psychology', in J. Stigler, R.A. Shweder and G. Herd (eds), *Essays on Comparative Human Development.* Cambridge: Cambridge University Press.

Gergen, K. (1992) 'Organization theory in the postmodern era', in M. Reed and M. Hughes (eds), *Rethinking Organization.* London: Sage. pp. 207–26.

Gergen, K. and Thatchenkerry, T.J. (1996) 'Organization science as social construction: postmodern potentials', *The Journal of Applied Behavioural Science*, 32 (4): 356–77.

Geuss, R. (1982) *The Idea of a Critical Theory: Habermas and the Frankfurt School.* Cambridge: Cambridge University Press.

Giddens, A. (1976) *New Rules of Sociological Method.* London: Hutchinson.

Giddens, A. (1984) *The Construction of Society.* London: Polity Press.

Giddens, A. (1991) *Modernity and Self-identity: Self and Society in the Late Modern Age.* Cambridge: Polity Press.

Gill, J. and Johnson, P. (1997) *Research Methods for Managers.* London: Paul Chapman.

Gioia, D.A. and Pitre, E. (1989) 'Multi-paradigm perspectives on theory building', *Academy of Management Review*, 5 (4): 584–602.

Giroux, H.A. (1992) *Border Crossings: Cultural Workers and the Politics of Education.* New York: Routledge.

Glaser, B.G. and Strauss, A.L. (1967) *The Discover of Grounded Theory.* Chicago, IL: Aldine.

Goffman, E. (1969) *The Presentation of Self in Everyday Life.* Harmondsworth: Penguin.

Gold, R.L. (1958) 'Roles in sociological fieldwork', *Social Forces*, 36 (3): 217–23.

Goldthorpe, J., Lockwood, D., Bechhofer, F. and Platt, J. (1968) *The Affluent Worker: Industrial Attitudes and Behaviour.* Cambridge: Cambridge University Press.

Gouldner, A. (1976) *The Dialectic of Ideology and Technology.* New York: Seabury Press.

Gowler, D. and Legge, K. (1986) 'Personnel paradigms: four perspectives on Utopia', *Industrial Relations Journal*, 17: 225–35.

Grant, D. and Oswick, C. (eds) (1996) *Metaphor and Organizations*. London: Sage.

Gray, J. (1995) *Isaiah Berlin*. London: Harper Collins.

Gribbin, J. (1985) *In Search of Schrodinger's Cat: Quantum Physics and Reality*. London: Corgi.

Grice, S. and Humphries, M. (1997) 'Critical management studies in postmodernity: oxymorons in outer space?', *Journal of Organisational Change Management*, 10 (5): 412–15.

Grint, K. (1994) 'Reengineering history: social resonances and business process reengineering', *Organization*, 1 (1): 179–201.

Grint, K. and Willcocks, L. (1995) 'Business process reengineering in theory and in practice: business paradise regained?', *New Technology Work and Organization*, 10 (2): 286–310.

Guba, E. and Lincoln, Y.S. (1994) 'Competing paradigms in qualitative research', in N. Denzin and Y. Lincoln (eds), *Handbook of Qualitative Research*. Newbury Park, CA: Sage.

Haack, S. (1987) 'Realism', *Synthese*, 17 (2): 275–99.

Haack, S. (1995) *Evidence and Inquiry: Towards Reconstruction in Epistemology*. Oxford: Blackwell.

Habermas, J. (1970a) 'On systematically distorted communication', *Inquiry*, 13: 205–18.

Habermas, J. (1970b) 'Towards a theory of communicative competence', *Inquiry*, 13: 360–75.

Habermas, J. (1971) *Towards a Rational Society*. London: Heinemann Educational Books.

Habermas, J. (1972) *Knowledge and Human Interest*. London: Heinemann Educational Books.

Habermas, J. (1973) 'A postscript to knowledge and human interests', *Philosophy and the Social Sciences*, 3 (2): 157–89.

Habermas, J. (1974a) *Theory and Practice*. London: Heinemann Educational Books.

Habermas, J. (1974b) 'Rationalism divided in two: a reply to Albert', in A. Giddens (ed.), *Positivism and Sociology*. London: Heinemann Educational Books.

Habermas, J. (1977) 'A review of Gadamer's truth and method', in F.R. Dallmayr and T.A. McCarthy (eds), *Understanding Social Inquiry*. Notre Dame, IN: University Press.

Habermas, J. (1987) *The Theory of Communicative Action Volume 2; Lifeworld and System: A Critique of Functionalist Reason*. London: Heinemann.

Halfpenny, P. (1982) *Positivism and Sociology: Explaining Social Life*. London: Allen and Unwin.

Halfpenny, P. (1994) 'Causality', in W. Outhwaite and T. Bottomore (eds), *The Blackwell Dictionary of Twentieth Century Thought*. Oxford: Blackwell.

Hammer, M. and Champy, J. (1993) *Reengineering the Corporation: A Manifesto for Business Revolution*. New York: Harper Business.

Hammersley, M. (1991) 'A note on Campbell's distinction between internal and external validity', *Quality and Quantity*, 25.

Hammersley, M. (1992) *What's Wrong with Ethnography?* London: Routledge.

Hammersley, M. (1995) *The Politics of Social Research*. London: Sage.

Hammersley, M. and Atkinson, P. (1995) *Ethnography: Principles in Practice* (2nd edn). London: Routledge.

Handy, C.B. (1989) *The Age of Unreason*. London: Business Books.

Hansen, K.P. (1996) 'The mentality of management: self images of American top executives', in S.R. Clegg and G. Palmer, *The Politics of Management Knowledge*. London: Sage. pp. 36–45.

Hanson, N.R. (1958) *Patterns of Discovery*. Cambridge: Cambridge University Press.

Harding, S. (1987) 'Is there a feminist method?', in S. Harding, *Feminist Methodology*. Bloomington: Indiana University Press.

Hartley, J. (1994) 'Case studies in organisational research', in C. Cassell and G. Symon, *Qualitative methods in organisational research*. London: Sage. pp. 208–29.

Harvey, D. (1989) *The Condition of Postmodernity: An Enquiry into the Origin of Social Change*. Oxford: Basil Blackwell.

Harvey, L. (1990) *Critical Social Research*. London: Unwin Hyman.

Harvey, L. and Myers, M. (1995) 'Scholarship and practice: the contribution of ethnographic research methods to bridging the gap', *Information Technology and People*, 8 (3): 24–39.

Hassard, J. (1991) 'Multiple paradigms and organizational analysis: a case study', *Organization Studies*, 12 (2): 275–99.

Hassard, J. (1993) 'Postmodernism and organizational analysis', in J. Hassard and J. Parker (eds), *Postmodernism and Organizations*. London: Sage. pp. 1–23.

Hassard, J. and Parker, M. (eds) (1993) *Postmodernism and Organizations*. London: Sage.

Heisenberg, W. (1958) *Physics and Philosophy*. New York: Harper Brothers.

Held, D. (1989) *An Introduction to Critical Theory*. Cambridge: Polity Press.

Hempel, C.G. (1965) *Aspects of Scientific Explanation*. New York: Free Press.

Hesse, M.B. (1980) *Revolutions and Reconstructions in the Philosophy of Science*. Brighton: Harvester.

Hindess, B. (1977) *Philosophy and Methodology in Social Science*. Hassocks: Harvester.

Hirschheim, R. (1985) 'Information systems epistemology: an historical perspective', in E.E. Mumford, R. Hirschheim, G. Fitzgerald and A.T. Wood-Harper (eds), *Research Methods in Information Systems*. Amsterdam: Elsevier.

Hirschheim, R. and Klein, R. (1989) 'Four paradigms of information systems development', *Communications of the AMC*, 32 (10): 1199–216.

Hirschman, E. (1986) 'Humanistic inquiry in marketing research: philosophy, method and criteria', *Journal of Marketing Research*, 23: 237–49.

Hogan, R. and Sinclair, R. (1996) 'Intellectual, ideological and political obstacles to the advancement of organizations science', *The Journal of Applied Behavioural Science*, 32: 434–40.

Holland, R. (1999) 'Reflexivity', *Human Relations*, 52 (4): 463–83.

Hollis, M. and Lukes, S. (1982) *Rationality and Relativism*. Oxford: Blackwell.

Hopper, T. and Powell, A. (1985) 'Making sense of reason into organizational and social aspects of management accounting: a review of its underlying assumptions', *Journal of Management Studies*, 22 (5): 429–65.

Horkheimer, M. (1972) *Critical Theory*. New York: Continuum.

Horkheimer, M. (1989) 'The state of contemporary social philosophy and the tasks of the Institute for Social Research', in S.E Bronner and D.M. Keller (eds), *Critical Theory and Society*. London: Routledge.

Horkheimer, M. and Adorno, T. (1947) *The Dialectics of Enlightenment*. London: Verso.

Horowitz, R. (1986) 'Remaining an outsider: membership as a threat to research rapport', *Urban Life*, 14: 409–30.

Hume, D. (1739–40/1965) *A Treatise of Human Nature*. Oxford: Clarendon Press.

Hume, D. (1748–1975) *An Enquiry Concerning Human Understanding*. Oxford: Clarendon Press.

Institute for Workers Control Committee of Enquiry into the Motor Industry (1977) 'A workers enquiry into the motor industry', *Capital and Class*, 2: 102–18.

Jackall, R. (1988) *Moral Mazes: The World of Corporate Managers*. Oxford: Oxford University Press.

James, W. (1897) (reprinted 1956) *The Will to Believe*. New York: Dover.

James, W. (1909) (reprinted 1970) *The Meaning of Truth*. Chicago: University of Michigan.

Jeffcutt, P. (1993) 'From interpretation to representation', in J. Hassard and M. Parker (eds), *Postmodernism and Organizations*. London: Sage.

Jeffcutt, P. (1994) 'The interpretation of organization: A contemporary analysis and critique', *Journal of Management Studies*, 31: 225–50.

Jencks, C. (1984) *The Language of Post-Modern Architecture*. London: Academy Editions.

Jermier, J. (1998) 'Introduction: critical perspectives on organisational control', *Administrative Science Quarterly*, 43 (2): 235–56.

Johnson, H.T. (1978) 'Management accounting in an early multidivisional organisation: General Motors in the 1920s', *Harvard Business Review*, 490–517.

Johnson, P. and Gill, J. (1993) *Organization Behaviour and Management Control*. London: Paul Chapman.

Kahn, P. and Lourenco, O. (1999) 'Reinstating Modernity in social science research – or – the status of bullwinkle in a postmodern era', *Human Development*, 42 (2): 92–108.

Kamoche, K. (1991) 'Human resource management: a multiparadigmatic analysis', *Personnel Review*, 20 (4): 3–13.

Kaplan, R.S. (1984) 'The Evolution of Management Accounting', *Accounting Review*, 59: 390–418.

Keat, R. and Urry, J. (1982) *Social Theory as Science*. London: Routledge and Kegan Paul.

Kellner, D. (1988) 'Postmodernism as social theory: Some challenges and problems', *Theory, Culture and Society*, 5: 239–69.

Kemmis, S. and McTaggart, R. (1988) *The Action Research Reader*. Victoria, Australia: Deakin University Press.

Kidder, L. and Judd, C. (1986) *Research Methods in Social Relations*. New York: Holt Rinehart and Winston.

Kilduff, M. (1993) 'Deconstructing organizations', *Academy of Management Review*, 18: 13–31.

Kilduff, M. and Mehra, A. (1997) 'Postmodernism and organisational research', *Academy of Management Review*, 22 (2): 453–81.

Kincheloe, J.L. and McLaren, P.L. (1998) 'Rethinking critical theory and qualitative research', in N.K. Denzin and Y.S. Lincoln, *The Landscape of Qualitative Research*. Thousand Oaks, CA: Sage. pp. 260–99.

Kirk, J. and Miller, M. (1986) *Reliability and Validity in Qualitative Research*. London: Sage.

Knights, D. (1992) 'Changing spaces: the disruptive impact of a new epistemological location for the study of management', *Academy of Management Review*, 17 (3): 514–35.

Knights, D. and McCabe, D. (1998) 'When life is but a dream: obliterating politics through business process reengineering', *Human Relations*, 51 (6): 761–98.

Knights, D. and Morgan, G. (1991) 'Corporate Strategy, Organizations and Subjectivity: A Critique', *Organisation Studies*, 12 (2): 251–73.

Knorr-Cetina, K. (1984) 'The fabrication of facts: towards a micro-sociology of scientific knowledge', in N. Stehr and V. Meja (eds), *Society and Knowledge: Contemporary Perspectives in the Sociology of Knowledge*. London: Transaction Books.

Kolakowski, L. (1969) 'Karl Marx and the classical definition of truth', in L. Kolakowski (ed.), *Marxism and Beyond*. London: Pall Mall Press.

Kolakowski, L. (1972) *Positivist Philosophy*. London: Heinemann.

Kondo, D. (1990) *Crafting Selves: Power, Gender and Discourses of Identity in a Japanese Workplace*. Chicago: University of Chicago Press.

Kuhn, T. (1957) *The Copernican Revolution*. Cambridge, MA: Harvard University Press.

Kuhn, T. (1970a) *The Structure of Scientific Revolutions* (2nd edn). Chicago: Chicago University Press.

Kuhn, T. (1970b) 'Reflections on my critics', in I. Lakatos and A. Musgrave (eds), *Criticism and the Growth of Knowledge*. Cambridge: Cambridge University Press.

Kuhn, T. (1977) *The Essential Tension*. Chicago: Chicago University Books.

Kuhn, T. (1987) 'What are scientific revolutions?', in L. Kruger, L.J. Daston and M. Heidelberger (eds), *The Probabilistic Revolution*. Cambridge, MA: Massachusetts Institute of Technology Press.

Kunda, G. (1992) *Engineering Culture: Control and Commitment in a High-Tech Corporation*. Philadelphia: Temple University Press.

Lacan, J. (1977) 'The agency of the letter in the unconscious or reason since Freud', in *Ecrits: A Selection* (translated by Alan Sheridan). London: Tavistock.

Lacity, M. and Janson, M.A. (1994) 'Understanding qualitative data: a framework of text analysis methods', *Journal of Management Information Systems*, 11: 137–59.

Laing, R.D. (1967) *The Politics of Experience and the Birds of Paradise*. Harmondsworth: Penguin.

Lakatos, I. (1970) 'Falsification and the methodology of scientific research programmes', in I. Lakatos and A. Musgrave (eds), *Criticism and the Growth of Knowledge*. Cambridge: Cambridge University Press.

Lakoff, G. and Johnson, M. (1980) *Metaphors by Which we Live*. Chicago: Chicago University Press.

LaNuez, D. and Jermier, J.M. (1992) 'Sabotage by managers and technocrats', in J.M. Jermier and W.R. Nord, *Resistance and Power in Organizations*. London: Macmillan.

Lash, S. and Urry, J. (1987) *The End of Organized Capitalism*. Cambridge: Polity Press.

Lather, P. (1991) *Getting Smart: Feminist Research and Pedagogy with/in the Postmodern*. New York: Routledge.

Latour, B. (1987) *Science in Action*. Milton Keynes: Open University Press.

Latour, B. (1988) 'The politics of explanation: an alternative', in S. Woolgar (ed.), *Knowledge and Reflexivity: New Frontiers in the Sociology of Knowledge*. London: Sage.

Latour, B. (1990) 'Postmodern? no simply amodern! steps toward an anthropology of science', *Studies in History and Philosophy of Science*, 21: 145–71.

Laughlin, R. (1987) 'Accounting systems in organisational contexts: a case for critical theory', *Accounting Organisations and Society*, 12 (5): 472–502.

Law, J. and Lodge, P. (1984) *Science for Social Scientists*. London: Macmillan.

Lawrence, T.B. and Philips, N. (1998) 'Commentary: separating play and critique: postmodern and critical perspectives on TQM/BPR', *Journal of Management Inquiry*, 7 (2): 154–60.

Lawson, T. (1994) 'The nature of Post Keynesianism and its links to other traditions: a realist perspective', *Journal of Post Keynesian Economics*, 16 (4): 503–38.

Layder, D. (1994) *Understanding Social Theory*. London: Sage.

Lazarsfeld, P.F. (1958) 'Evidence and interference in social research', *Daedalus*, 87 (4): 99–130.

Legge, K. (1995) *Human Resource Management: Rhetorics and Realities*. London: Macmillan.

Lessnoff, M. (1974) *The Structure of Social Science: A Philosophical Introduction*. London: Allen and Unwin.

Lincoln, Y. and Guba, E. (1985) *Naturalistic Inquiry*. London: Sage.

Linstead, S. (1985) 'Breaking the purity rule: industrial sabotage and the symbolic process', *Personnel Review*, 14 (3): 12–19.

Linstead, S. (1993a) 'Deconstruction in the study of organisations', in J. Hassard and M. Parker (eds), *Postmodernism and Organizations*. London: Sage. pp. 49–70.

Linstead, S. (1993b) 'From postmodern anthropology to deconstructive ethnography', *Human Relations*, 46 (1): 97–120.

Locke, J. (1690/1988) *Essay Concerning Human Understanding*. Oxford: Clarendon Press.

Luthans, F., Paul, R. and Taylor, L. (1985) 'An experimental analysis of the impact of contingent reinforcement on retail salespersons' performance behaviours: a replicated field experiment', *Journal of Organisational Behaviour Management*. 25–35.

Lyotard, J.-F. (1984) *The Postmodern Condition: A Report on Knowledge*. Manchester: Manchester University Press.

Lyotard, J.-F. (1988) *The Differend: Phrases in Dispute*. Minneapolis: University of Minnesota Press.

MacIntyre, A. (1981) *After Virtue: A Study of Moral Theory*. London: Duckworth.

Magee, B. (1985) *Popper* (3rd edn). London: Fontana.

Magee, B. (1987) *The Great Philosophers: An Introduction to Western Philosophy*. Oxford: Oxford University Press.

Manicas, P. (1987) *A History and Philosophy of the Social Sciences*. Oxford: Blackwell.

Mannheim, K. (1952) *Essays on the Sociology of Knowledge*. London: Routledge and Kegan Paul.

Mannheim, K. (1960) *Ideology and Utopia*. London: Routledge and Kegan Paul.

Manning, P. (1995) 'The challenges of postmodernism', in J. Van Maanen, *Representation in Ethnography*. Thousand Oaks, CA: Sage.

Marcus, G. and Fisher, M. (1986) *Anthropology as Cultural Critique*. Chicago: University of Chicago Press.

Margolis, J. (1986) *Pragmatism without Foundations*. Oxford: Blackwell.

Marsden, R. (1993) 'The politics of organizational analysis', *Organization Studies*, 14 (1): 93–124.

Marsh, C. (1979) 'Problems with surveys: method or epistemology', *Sociology*, 13 (2): 293–305.

Marshall, C. and Rossman, G. (1989) *Designing Qualitative Research*. London: Sage.

Martin, J. (1990a) 'Deconstructing organizational taboos: the suppression of gender conflict in organizations', *Organization Science*, 1: 339–59.

Martin, J. (1990b) 'Breaking up mono-method monopolies in organisational analysis', in J. Hassard and D. Pym, *The Theory and Philosophy of Organisations*. London: Routledge.

Martinko, M.J., White, J.D. and Hassell, B. (1989) 'An operant analysis of prompting in a sales environment', *Journal of Organisational Behaviour Management*, 10 (1): 93–107.

Marx, K. (1975) *Collected Works: Volume 5*. Harmondsworth: Pelican.

Masterman, M. (1970) 'The nature of a paradigm', in I. Lakatos and A. Musgrave (eds), *Criticism and the Growth of Knowledge*. Cambridge: Cambridge University Press.

McAuley, J. and Duberley, J. (1995) 'Management in scientific establishments – how scientists construct this reality', ESRC grant reference R000221639.

McCarthy, T.A. (1978) *The Critical Theory of Jurgen Habermas*. Cambridge: Polity Press.

McLennan, G. (1995) *Pluralism*. Buckingham: Open University Press.

Mehan, H. and Wood, H. (1975) *The Reality of Ethnomethodology*. London: Wiley.

Melucci, A. (1996) *Challenging Codes: Collective Action for the Information Age*. Cambridge: Cambridge University Press.

Merton, R.K. (1938–70) *Science, Technology and Society in Seventeenth Century England*. New York: Harper and Row.

Meyer, J. (1986) 'Social environments and organisational accounting', *Accounting Organisations and Society*, 11 (4): 345–56.

Mill, J.S. (1874) *A System of Logic*. London: Longman Green.

Miller, D. and Friesen, P. (1984) *Organisations – A Quantum View*. Englewood Cliffs, NJ: Prentice Hall.

Miller, H. and King, C.S. (1998) 'Practical theory', *American Review of Public Administration*, 281: 43–60.

Mingers, J. (1992) 'Technical, practical and critical OR – past, present and future?', in M. Alvesson and H. Willmott (eds), *Critical Management Studies*. London: Sage.

Mink, O.G. (1992) 'Creating new paradigms for organizational change', *International Journal of Quality and Reliability Management*, 9 (3): 21–35.

Mintzberg, H. (1973) *The Nature of Managerial Work*. New York: Harper and Row.

Mitroff, I. (1980) 'Reality as a scientific strategy', *Academy of Management Review*, 5 (4): 513–15.

Mitroff, I. and Pondy, L. (1978) 'Afterthoughts on the leadership conference', in M. McCall and M. Lombardo, *Leadership: Where Else Can We Go?* Durham: Duke University Press.

Montagna, P. (1997) 'Modernism vs postmodernism in management accounting', *Critical Perspectives on Accounting*, 8: 125–45.

Moon, J.D. (1983) 'Political ethics and critical theory', in D. Sabia and J. Wallulis, *Changing Social Science: Critical Theory and Other Critical Perspectives*. Albany: State University of New York Press.

Morgan, G. (1980) 'Paradigms, metaphors, and puzzle solving in organization theory', *Administrative Science Quarterly*, 25 (4): 605–22.

Morgan, G. (ed.) (1983a) *Beyond Method: Strategies for Social Research*. London: Sage.

Morgan, G. (1983b) 'More on metaphor: why we cannot control tropes in administrative science', *Administrative Science Quarterly*, 28 (4): 601–7.

Morgan, G. (1986) *Images of Organization*. London: Sage.

Morgan, G. (1993) *Imaginization*. London: Sage.

Morgan, G. (1996) 'An afterword: is there anything more to be said about metaphor?', in D. Grant and C. Oswick (eds) *Metaphors and Organizations*. London: Sage. pp. 227–40.

Morrow, R. and Brown, D. (1994) *Critical Theory and Methodology*. London: Sage.

Moser, C.A. and Kalton, G. (1971) *Survey Methods in Social Investigation*. Aldershot: Gower.

Mulkay, M. (1979) *Science and the Sociology of Science*. London: Allen and Unwin.

Mulkay, M. and Gilbert, G. (1986) 'Replication and mere replication', *Philosophy of the Social Sciences*, 16 (1): 21–37.

Murphy, R. (1994) 'The sociological construction of science without nature', *Sociology*, 28 (4): 957–74.

Neurath, O. (1944) *Foundations of the Social Sciences*. Chicago: University of Chicago Press.

Newsweek (1994) 'A Postmodern President', January 17: 19–21.

Newton, T. (1996) 'Postmodernism and action', *Organization*, 3 (1): 7–29.

Nord, W.R. and Jermier, J.M. (1992) 'Critical social science for managers? promising and perverse possibilities', in M. Alvesson and H. Willmott, *Critical Management Studies*. London: Sage. pp. 202–22.

Norris, C. (1996) *Reclaiming Truth: Contribution to a Critique of Cultural Relativism*. London: Lawrence and Wishart.

Olson, H. (1995) 'Quantitative versus Qualitative Research: The Wrong Question'. http://www.ualberta.ca/dept/slis/cais/olson.htm

Orpen, C. (1979) 'The effects of job enrichment on employee satisfaction, motivation, involvement and performance: a field experiment', *Human Relations*, 32 (3): 189–217.

Ortony, A. (ed.) (1979) *Metaphor and Thought*. Cambridge: Cambridge University Press.

Oswick, C. and Grant, D. (1996) *Organization Development: Metaphorical Explorations*. London: Pitman.

Ouchi, W. (1981) *Theory Z*. Reading, MA: Addison-Wesley.

Park, P. (1999) 'People, knowledge and change in participatory research', *Management Learning*, 30 (2): 141–57.

Parker, M. (1992) 'Post-modern organizations or postmodern organization theory', *Organization Studies*, 13: 1–17.

Parker, M. (1993) 'Life after Jean-Francois', in J. Hassard and M. Parker (eds), *Postmodernism and Organizations*. London: Sage.

Parker, M. (1995) 'Critique in the name of what? Postmodernism and critical approaches to organization', *Organisation Studies*, 14 (4): 553–64.

Parker, M. and McHugh, G. (1991) 'Five texts in search of an author: a response to John Hassard's "Multiple paradigms and organizational analysis"', *Organization Studies*, 12 (3): 451–6.

Payne, S.L. (1996) 'Qualitative research and reflexive faculty change potentials', *Journal of Organisational Change Management*, 9 (2): 20–31.

Peirce, C.S. (1931–58) *The Collected Works of Charles Sanders Peirce*. Cambridge, MA: Harvard University Press.

Pennings, J. (1973) 'Measures of organisational structure: a methodological note', *American Journal of Sociology*, 79 (3): 686–704.

Pfeffer, J. (1993) 'Barriers to the advance of organisational science: paradigm development as a dependent variable', *Academy of Management Review*, 14 (4): 599–620.

Pfeffer, J. (1995) 'Mortality, reproducibility and the persistence of styles of theory', *Organisation Science*, 6 (6): 681–93.

Phillips, D. (1973) *Abandoning Method: Sociological Studies in Methodology*. San Francisco: Jossey Bass.

Pinder, C.C. and Bourgeois, V.W. (1982) 'Controlling tropes in administrative science', *Administrative Science Quarterly*, 7 (4): 641–52.

Podsakoff, P.M. and Dalton, D.R. (1987) 'Research methodology in organization studies', *Journal of Management*, 13 (2): 419–44.

Poincare, H. (1952) *Science and Hypothesis*. New York: Dover.

Pollner, M. (1991) 'Left of ethnomethodology; the rise and decline of radical reflexivity', *American Sociological Review*, 56: 370–80.

Pollner, M. and Emerson, R.M. (1983) 'The dynamics of inclusion and distance in fieldwork relations', in R.M. Emerson (ed.), *Contemporary Field Research*. Boston: Little, Brown.

Popper, K. (1959) *The Logic of Scientific Discovery*. London: Hutchinson.

Popper, K. (1961) *The Poverty of Historicism*. London: Routledge and Kegan Paul.

Popper, K. (1962) *The Open Society and Its Enemies: Volume II*. London: Routledge and Kegan Paul.

Popper, K. (1967) *Conjectures and Refutations*. London: Routledge and Kegan Paul.

Popper, K. (1976) *Unended Quest: An Intellectual Biography*. London: Fontana.

Power, M. and Laughlin, R. (1992) 'Critical theory and accounting', in M. Alvesson and H. Willmott (eds), *Critical Management Studies*. London: Sage.

Prasad, P. and Caproni, P. (1997) 'Critical theory in the management classroom: engaging power, ideology and praxis', *Journal of Management Education*, 21 (3): 284–91.

Pugh, D. (1983) 'Studying Organisational structure and process', in G. Morgan (ed.), *Beyond Method*. London: Sage.

Pugh, D. and Hickson, D. (1976) *Organisational Structure in its Context, The Aston Programme I*. Farnborough: Saxon House.

Pugh, D. and Hinings, C. (1976) *Organisational Structure: Extensions and Replications, The Aston Programme II*. Farnborough: Saxon House.

Pusey, M. (1987) *Jurgen Habermas*. Chichester: Ellis Harwood and Tavistock.

Putnam, H. (1981) *Reason, Truth, History*. Cambridge: Cambridge University Press.

Putnam, L., Bantz, C., Deetz, S., Mumby, D. and Van Maanen, J. (1993) 'Ethnography versus critical theory: debating organisational research', *Journal of Management Inquiry*, 2 (3): 221–35.

Pym, D. (1993) 'Post paradigm inquiry', in J. Hassard and D. Pym, *The Theory and Philosophy of Organisations*. London: Routledge. pp. 233–42.

Quantz, R.A. (1992) 'On critical ethnography (with some postmodern considerations)', in M.D. LeCompte, W.L. Millroy and J. Preissle, *The Handbook of Qualitative Research in Education*. New York: Academic Press. pp. 447–505.

Quine, W.V.O. (1969) 'Epistemology naturalized', in W.V.O. Quine, *Ontological Relativity and Other Essays*. New York: Columbia University Press.

Rabinow, P. (1986) 'Representations are Social Facts: Modernity and Postmodernity in Anthropology', in J. Clifford and G. Marcus (eds), *Writing Culture: The Poetics and Politics of Ethnography*. Berkley: University of California Press.

Ramsay, H. (1996) 'Managing sceptically: a critique of organisational fashion', in S.R. Clegg and G. Palmer, *The Politics of Management Knowledge*. London: Sage. pp. 155–72.

Reason, P. (1998) 'Three approaches to participative inquiry', in N.K. Denzin and Y.S. Lincoln, *Strategies of Qualitative Inquiry*. Thousand Oaks, CA: Sage. pp. 261–91.

Reason, P. and Rowan, J. (1981) *Human Inquiry: A Sourcebook of New Paradigm*. London: John Wiley.

Reed, M. (1985) *Redirections in Organizational Analysis*. London: Sage.

Reed, M. (1990) 'From Paradigms to images: The paradigm warrior turns post-modernist guru', *Personnel Review*, 19 (3): 35–40.

Reed, M. (1997) 'In praise of duality and dualism: rethinking agency and structure in organisational analysis', *Organisation Studies*, 18 (1): 21–42.

Reed, M.I. (1992) *The Sociology of Organisations: Themes, Perspectives and Prospects*. Hemel Hempstead: Harvester Wheatsheaf.

Reeves, T.K. and Harper, D. (1981) *Surveys at Work: A Practitioner's Guide*. London: McGraw-Hill.

Reichenbach, H. (1963) *The Rise of Scientific Philosophy*. Berkeley: University of California Press.

Remmling, G.W. (1973) 'Existence and thought', in G.W. Remmling (ed.), *Towards the Sociology of Knowledge*. London: Routledge and Kegan Paul.

Rescher, N. (1977) *Methodological Pragmatism: A Systems Theoretic Approach to the Theory of Knowledge*. Oxford: Blackwell.

Richardson, L. (1998) 'Writing: A method of inquiry', in N.K. Denzin and Y.S Lincoln (eds), *Collecting and Interpreting Qualitative Materials*. Thousand Oaks, CA: Sage.

Robertson, R. (1992) *Globalization*. London: Sage.

Robson, C. (1993) *Real World Research: A Resource for Social Scientists and Practitioner-Researchers*. Oxford: Blackwell.

Roethlisberger, F. and Dickson, W. (1939) *Management and the Worker*. Cambridge, MA: Harvard Business School Press.

Rojek, C. (1995) *Decentring Leisure*. London: Sage.

Roman, L.G. (1992) 'The political significance of other ways of narrating ethnography: A feminist materialist approach', in M.D. LeCompte, W.L. Millroy and J. Preissle, *The Handbook of Qualitative Research in Education*. New York: Academic Press. pp. 555–94.

Rorty, R. (1979) *Philosophy and the Mirror of Nature*. Princeton, NJ: Princeton University Press.

Rorty, R. (1982) *Consequences of Pragmatism (Essays: 1972–80)*. Minneapolis: University of Minnesota Press.

Rorty, R. (1998) *Achieving our Country: Leftist Thought in Twentieth Century America*. Cambridge: Harvard University Press.

Rosaldo, R. (1986) 'From the door of his tent: the fieldworker and the inquisitor', in J. Clifford and G. Marcus (eds), *Writing Culture: the Poetics and Politics of Ethnography*. Berkeley: University of California Press.

Rosen, M. (1987) 'Critical administrative scholarship, praxis and the academic workplace', *Journal of Management*, 13: 573–86.

Rosen, M. (1991) 'Coming to terms with the field: understanding and doing organizational ethnography', *Journal of Management Studies*, 28: 1–24.

Rosenau, P.M. (1992) *Postmodernism and the Social Sciences: Insights, Inroads and Intrusions*. Princeton, NJ: Princeton University.

Rouse, J. (1987) *Knowledge and Power*. Ithaca: Cornell University Press.

Russell, B. (1912) *The Problems of Philosophy*. Oxford: Oxford University Press.

Russell, B. (1946–79) *History of Western Philosophy*. London: Allen and Unwin.

Salaman, G. (1981) *Class and the Corporation*. Glasgow: Fontana.

Sandywell, B. (1996) *Reflexivity and the Crisis of Western Reason: Logological Investigations Volume 1*. London: Routledge.

Saussure, F. (1966) *Course in General Linguistics*. New York: McGraw-Hill.

Sayer, A. (1981) 'Abstraction: a realist interpretation', *Radical Philosophy*, 28: 6–15.

Sayer, A. (1992) *Method in Social Science: A Realist Approach* (2nd edn). London: Routledge.

Scarborough, H. and Burrell, G. (1996) 'The axeman cometh', in S. Clegg and G. Palmer (eds), *The Politics of Management Knowledge*. London: Sage.

Schiller, C.S. (1907) *Studies in Humanism*. London: Macmillan.

Schlick, M. (1981–82) 'Positivism and realism', in O. Hanflinh (ed.), *Essential Readings in Logical Positivism*. Oxford: Blackwell.

Schoenfeldt, L. (1984) 'Psychometric Properties of Organisational Research Instruments', in T. Bateman and G. Ferris, *Method and Analysis in Organisational Research*. Reston: Reston Publishing.

Schon, D. (1995) 'Theory in action: the new scholarship requires a new epistemology', *Change* (Nov/Dec): 27–35.

Schon, D.A. (1983) *The Reflective Practitioner: How Professionals Think in Action*. London: Temple Smith.

Schoonhoven, C.B. (1981) 'Problems with contingency theory: testing assumptions hidden within the language of contingency theory', *Administrative Science Quarterly*, 26: 349–77.

Schriesheim, C., Powers, K., Scandura, T., Gardiner, C. and Lankall, M. (1993) 'Improving construct measurement in management research: comments and a quantitative approach for assessing the theoretical content adequacy of paper and pencil type survey instruments', *Journal of Management*, 19 (2): 385–417.

Schwab, D. (1980) 'Construct validity in organisational behaviour', in B. Staw and L. Cummings, *Research in Organisational Behaviour*. Greenwich: JAI.

Scriven, M. (1969) 'Logical positivism and the behavioural sciences', in P. Atchinstein and F. Barker (eds), *The Legacy of Logical Positivism*. Baltimore: John Hopkins Press.

Shalin, D.N. (1986) 'Pragmatism and social interaction', *American Sociological Review*, 51 (1): 9–29.

Shapin, S. (1984) 'Talking History: Reflections on DA', *Isis*, 18: 533–50.

Sharfman, M. and Dean, J. (1991) 'Conceptualizing and measuring the organisational environment: a multidimensional approach', *Journal of Management*, 17 (4): 681–700.

Sharrock, W. and Anderson, B. (1986) *The Ethnomethodologists*. London: Tavistock.

Shotter, J. (1975) *Images of Man in Psychological Research*. London: Methuen.

Shweder, R. (1984) 'Anthropology's romantic rebellion against the Enlightenment, or there's more to thinking than reason and evidence', in R. Shweder and R. Levine (eds), *Culture Theory: Essays on Mind, Self and Emotion.* Cambridge: Cambridge University Press.

Siegel, H. (1987) *Relativism Refuted: A Critique of Contemporary Epistemological Relativism.* Dortrecht: Reidel.

Silverman, D. (1993) *Interpreting Qualitative Data.* London: Sage.

Simons, J. (1995) *Foucault and the Political.* London: Routledge.

Simons, R. and Thompson, B. (1998) 'Strategic determinants: the context of managerial decision making', *Journal of Managerial Psychology,* 13 (1/2): 7–21.

Slife, B. and Williams, R. (1995) *What's Behind the Research? Discovering Hidden Assumptions in the Behavioural Sciences.* New York: Sage.

Smith, H.W. (1975) *Strategies of Social Research: The Methodological Imagination.* London: Prentice-Hall.

Smith, J.K. (1984) 'The problem of criteria for judging interpretative inquiry', *Educational Evaluation and Policy Analysis,* 6 (4): 379–91.

Smith, J.K. (1989) *The Nature of Social and Educational Inquiry: Empiricism versus Interpretation.* Norwood: Ablex.

Sotorin, P. and Tyrell, S. (1998) 'Wondering about critical management studies: A review of and commentary on selected texts', *Management Communication Quarterly,* 12 (2): 303–36.

Steier, F. (1991) *Research and Reflexivity.* London: Sage.

Taylor, C. (1993) 'Engaged agency and background', in C.B. Guignin (ed.), *The Cambridge Companion to Heidegger.* Cambridge: Cambridge University Press.

Tester, K. (1994) *The Flaneur.* London: Routledge.

Thompson, P. (1993) 'Postmodernism: fatal distraction', in J. Hassard and M. Parker (eds), *Postmodernism and Organizations.* London: Sage. pp. 183–203.

Tiles, M. (1987) 'A science of Mars or a science of Venus', *Philosophy,* 62 (241): 293–306.

Tinker, A.M. (1986) 'Metaphor or reification: are radical humanists really libertarian anarchists?', *Journal of Management Studies,* 23 (4): 65–190.

Tinker, T. and Lowe, T. (1982) 'The management science of the management sciences', *Human Relations,* 35 (4): 331–47.

Tinker, A.M. (1991) 'The Accountant as partisan', *Accounting, Organizations and Society,* 16 (3): 297–310.

Townley, B. (1994) *Reframing Human Resource Management: Power Ethics and the Subject at Work.* London: Sage.

Trigg, R. (1980) *Reality at Risk: A Defence of Realism in Philosophy and the Sciences.* Brighton: Harvester.

Tsoukas, H. (1989) 'The validity of ideographic research explanations', *Academy of Management Review,* 14: 551–61.

Tsoukas, H. (1991) 'The missing link: a transformational view of metaphors in organizational science', *Academy of Management Review,* 16 (3): 566–85.

Tsoukas, H. (1992) 'Postmodernism: Reflexive Rationalism and Organizational Studies: A Reply to Martin Parker', *Organization Studies,* 13 (4): 643–9.

Tsoukas, H. (1993) 'Analogical reasoning and knowledge generation in organization theory', *Organization Studies,* 14 (3): 323–46.

Turner, B.S. (1987) *Medical Power and Social Knowledge.* London: Sage.

Unger, R. (1987) *Politics: A Work in Constructive Social Theory: Its Situation and its Task.* Cambridge: Cambridge University Press.

Van den Bulte, C. and Moenart, R.K. (1998) 'The effects of R&D team co-location on communication patterns among R&D, marketing and manufacturing', *Management Science,* 44 (11): S1–S18.

Van Maanen, J. (1988) *Tales of the Field: On Writing Ethnography.* Chicago: Chicago University Press.

Van Maanen, J. (1995a) 'An end to innocence: the ethnography of ethnography', in J. Van Maanen, *Representation in Ethnography.* London: Sage.

Van Maanen, J. (1995b) 'Style as theory', *Organisation Science*, 6 (1): 133–43.

Vattimo, G. (1992) *The Transparent Society.* Cambridge: Polity Press.

Wakefield, N. (1990) *Postmodernism: Twilight of the Real.* London: Pluto.

Ward, E.A. (1997) 'Autonomous work groups: a field study of correlates of satisfaction', *Psychology Report*, 80 (1): 60–2.

Watson, T. (1994) *In Search of Management.* London: Routledge.

Weber, M. (1949) *The Methodology of the Social Sciences.* New York: Free Press.

Weber, M. (1968) *Economy and Society.* New York: Bedminster Press.

Weiskopf, R. and Willmott, H. (1996) 'Turning the given into a question: a critical discussion of Chia's organisational analysis as deconstructive practice', *European Journal of Radical Organisation Theory*, 3 (2): 1–10.

Whitley, R.D. (1984a) 'The Fragmented state of management studies: reasons and consequences', *Journal of Management Studies*, 21 (3): 331–48.

Whitley, R.D. (1984b) 'The scientific status of management research as a practically oriented social science', *Journal of Management Studies*, 21 (4): 369–90.

Whittington, R. (1989) *Corporate Strategies in Recession and Recovery: Social Structure and Strategic Choice.* London: Unwin Hyman.

Whittington, R. (1992) 'Putting Giddens into action: social systems and managerial agency', *Journal of Management Studies*, 29 (6): 693–712.

Willmott, H. (1992) 'Beyond paradigmatic closure in organisational enquiry', in J. Hassard and D. Pym, *The Theory and Philosophy of Organisations.* London: Routledge.

Willmott, H. (1993) 'Strength is ignorance; slavery is freedom: managing culture in modern organisations', *Journal of Management Studies*, 80 (4): 515–52.

Willmott, H. (1997) 'Rethinking management and managerial work: capitalism, control and subjectivity', *Human Relations*, 50 (11): 1329–59.

Willmott, H.C. (1995) 'What has been happening in organization theory and does it matter?', *Personnel Review*, 24 (9): 33–53.

Wittgenstein, L. (1922) *Tractatus Logico-Philosophocus.* London: Routledge and Kegan Paul.

Wittgenstein, L. (1958) *Philosophical Investigations.* Oxford: Basil Blackwell.

Woolgar, S. (1988a) *Science: the Very Idea.* Sussex: Ellis Horwood.

Woolgar, S. (ed.) (1988b) *Knowledge and Reflexivity: New Frontiers in the Sociology of Knowledge.* London: Sage.

Yamey, B.S. (1977) 'Some topics in the history of financial accounting in England, 1500–1900', in W. Baxter and S. Davidson (eds), *Studies in Accounting.* London: Institute of Chartered Accountants, England and Wales.

Yearley, S. (1988) *Science, Technology and Social Change.* London: Unwin and Hyman.

Zald, M. (1996) 'More fragmentation? unfinished business in linking the social sciences and the humanities', *Administrative Science Quarterly*, 41: 251–61.

Zolo, D. (1990) 'Reflexive epistemology and social complexity: the philosophical legacy of Otto Neurath', *Philosophy of the Social Sciences*, 20 (2): 149–69.

Index

Abbott, A., 43
absolute truth, 159, 161–3
abstract knowledge, 33, 166–7, 171
abstract reasoning, 18
academic conventions, 45
accounting, 76, 89, 136, 172–3
action inquiry, 137
action research, 138–9
Administrative Science Quarterly, 44
Adorno, Theodor, 116–17
aesthetic judgements, 74
'affluent worker' studies, 52
agenda setting, 173
agnosticism, 17
Alvesson, M., 83, 94, 125–6, 128, 130, 133, 147, 151
analysis of analysis, 179
Anderson, B., 36
anomalies in science, 71–2
Arbib, M.A., 144–5, 161
argon, 97
Argyris, C., 138
Aristotle and Aristotelian thought, 16, 69–71
Armstrong, P., 172–3
Aronson, E., 46
Ashmore, M., 184
assumptions
  about data, 58
  shared, 68
  see also taken-for-granted assumptions
Aston studies, 41–2, 53, 55–6, 61
astronomy, 69–73, 163
Atkinson, P., 34, 58
Augustine, St, 53
authoritarianism, 157–8
Ayer, Alfred, 22, 25

Bacon, Francis, 14, 16–17, 26
Bantz, C., 141
Barnes, B., 170–71
Baudelaire, Charles Pierre, 112
Baudrillard, J., 94, 98, 110, 151
Baudrillardian ethnography, 106
Bauman, Z., 95, 112
Beck, U., 149, 185
behaviour, explanations of, 25–6, 33–4, 40, 165–6
Behling, O., 61
belief, 2–3
  revisability of, 160
Berg, P.O., 100
Berger, P.L., 98
Berlin, Isaiah, 13
Bernstein, R.J., 75, 113–14, 148–9
Best, S., 93, 114–15
Bharadwaj, A., 60
Bhaskar, Roy, 10, 148–71 *passim*, 175–6
bias in research, 50–51, 57

Blau, P.M., 42, 44
Bloor, D., 7
Boje, D., 107
Bourdieu, P., 171, 179, 189
Bourgeois, V.W., 90
Brahe, Tycho, 73, 152
Braverman, H., 129
Broad, C.D., 89
Broadbent, J., 136, 142
Brown, D., 123, 131–2, 134, 139, 147
Brown, S., 44
Bryman, A., 53, 61
bureaucracy, 95
Burrell, Gibson, 63, 76–81, 84–6, 89, 109, 150, 183
business process re-engineering, 56, 127

Calhoun, C., 125, 147
Callinicos, A., 22–3
Campbell, D.T., 45, 47–8
Caproni, P., 125
Carlsmith, J.M., 46
Carnap, Rudolf, 22
Carneades, 157
carrier groups for knowledge, 171–3, 175
Carter, P., 81, 108
'Cartesian anxiety', 114
Cartesian dualism, 14–15, 17, 30, 65, 181
catalytic validity, 141
causal mechanisms, 18–21, 26–8, 154–6, 165, 169–70, 175
causal relationships, 39–47
  conditions for, 19
  contingent or invariable, 32
  established from cross-sectional analyses, 47–8
Chia, R., 83, 86, 98–100
Child, J., 56, 130
choice *versus* determinism, 55
Churchill, Winston, 61
circularity in epistemology, 3–4, 33, 77, 85, 177, 192
Clark, T., 172
classification of scholars, vi, 10
Clegg, S., 41, 52, 61
closed and open systems, 163–5
Cobley, P., 96
'Cogito ergo sum', 14
Collier, A., 166–7, 176
Collins, D., 76
common referent of theories, 152–3, 156, 160, 183
communication
  distortion of, 122, 126, 128, 144, 146, 186
  see also interpersonal communication;
    polysemous communication
communicative action, theory of, 135
communism in scientific truth, 6